GLOBAL EDUCATION

SUNY SERIES,
THEORY, RESEARCH, AND PRACTICE
IN SOCIAL EDUCATION

PETER MARTORELLA, EDITOR

GLOBAL EDUCATION

A Study of School Change

Barbara Benham Tye
and
Kenneth A. Tye

State University of New York Press

Published by
State University of New York Press, Albany

For information, address State University of New York
Press, State University Plaza, Albany, N.Y. 12246

Production by Diane Ganeles
Marketing by Dana E. Yanulavich

Library of Congress Cataloging-in-Publication Data

Tye, Barbara Benham, 1942–
      Global education : a study of school change / Barbara Benham Tye
and Kenneth Tye.
            p.   cm. – (SUNY series, theory, research, and practice in
social education)
      Includes bibliographical references (p.) and index.
      ISBN 0-7914-1041-2 (alk. paper) . – ISBN 0-7914-1042-0 (pbk. :
alk. paper)
            1. International education–California–Orange County–Curricula.
I. Tye, Kenneth A. II. Title. III. Series.
LC1090.T97   1992
375'.0082'0979496–dc20

                                                                                              91-19045
                                                                                                  CIP

10 9 8 7 6 5 4 3 2 1

Lovingly dedicated to Helen Devitt Jones,
who understood the importance of wider horizons,
and who made the project described in this book
possible.

CONTENTS

Foreword   xi

Acknowledgments   xiii

Introduction   xv

Chapter 1.   Setting the Stage   1

   The Importance of a Global Perspective
   Understanding the Change Process
   Strategy and Implementation: The CHI Story

Chapter 2.   Research as Reflection on Practice   31

   Seeking New Knowledge
   The Search for Grounded Theory
   Supplementary Data

Chapter 3.   Global Education as a Social Movement   51

   Conditions Which Produce the Movement
   Membership in the Movement
   Sociopolitical Context of the Movement
   Structural Properties of the Movement
   Institutional Responses

Chapter 4. Meaning and Activity   85

Defining Global Education
Activity Reveals and Creates Meaning
Engagement and Resistance

Chapter 5. Competing Demands and the
            Use of Time in Schools   109

Barriers to Participation
Demands Come from Every Direction
The District Ethos
Teachers' Defense Mechanisms
Contemplating the Larger Picture

Chapter 6. The Uniqueness of the Single School   131

Perceptions of Involvement: A Typology
The Culture of the School: Three Case Studies

Chapter 7. The Pivotal Role of the Principal   157

Principal Leadership Today: Key Theories
Goal Orientation of Principals
District Ethos and the Principalship
Two Case Studies

Chapter 8. The Interventionists   193

Three Interconnected Functions
What It Takes to Do the Job
Intervention as an Evolutionary Process
The Inner Life of the Interventionist

Chapter 9.   What *Does* It Take To Globalize the
                   Curriculum of a School?   227

        What We Believe We Know

        What We Hypothesize: Recommendations for
            Further Exploration

Appendices   253

Index   269

FOREWORD

As the world continues to grow smaller and more interdependent, there is a greater need for global education. Our economic, political, social, and environmental systems have become interconnected to such a degree that we must develop a world awareness. This means understanding the interconnectedness of world systems as well as different values and points of view.

By promoting global education, we are strengthening our ability to compete economically with the rest of the world. In an increasingly knowledge-based economy, in which almost one in every four dollars made by Americans is tied to world trade, a good education fostering global thinking is more important than ever before. What we earn depends on what we learn. Global education can teach students to understand these changes and enable Americans to become more competitive internationally.

As the first state to mandate the teaching of global studies, Arkansas has demonstrated to the rest of the nation how important it is to educate our children globally. I am especially proud of the project in Elaine, Arkansas, which has shown teachers how to open the world to our students without ever leaving rural Arkansas.

With the publication of *Global Education: A Study of School Change,* efforts to promote global education will be strengthened and expanded across the country. By including high schools, junior highs, and elementary schools, this project cuts across grades and involves students and teachers at several different levels. Such a broad approach is important if we are to integrate global studies into the curriculum for all children.

Global Education: A Study of School Change is a timely book and a much needed contribution to educational reform. As educators continue to integrate global studies into the curriculum, I hope this project will serve as a model.

Bill Clinton
Governor
State of Arkansas

ACKNOWLEDGMENTS

This project could not have proceeded as successfully as it did without the dedicated work of the CHI staff: staff associates Ida Urso, Joy Phillipsen, and Kathy O'Neil; office managers Linda Short and Leslie Adcock; librarian Janine Chapman; and student workers Paul Whitlock, Encarnita Arambulo Adea, Rhadhika Iyengar, Connie Doti Ryan, Ye Dzen-Min, Stacy Walkon and Bea Molfetta.

We are also grateful for the support of Chapman College and for the active involvement of several members of the Chapman faculty, including professors Roberta Lessor, Art Blaser, Don Will, Bill Boaz, and James Miller. Professor Terry Cannings, of Pepperdine University, helped us with our telecommunications projects.

The Helen Jones Foundation, the Danforth Foundation, and the InterScope Foundation provided the funding without which the project would not have been possible.

The Center for Human Interdependence Board of Trustees helped with public relations and fundraising: Rafer Johnson, Phil Miller, Mike Farrell, Dr. Gloria Haithman, Vivian Hall, Roy Werner, Judge Lester Van Tatenhove, Janet Reece, and Bill Melvin.

Ian Livingstone, Lyn Richards, and the staff of the New Zealand Council for Educational Research made us welcome in February and March of 1990, and gave us office space and collegial support while we were writing the first draft of this book.

Many global educators across the nation influenced our thinking and helped us along the way: George Otero, Steve Lamy, Jane Boston, Robert Hanvey, Lee and Charlotte Anderson, Jim Becker, Bob Freeman, Judith Torney-Purta, Betty Reardon, Tom Collins, Jan Drum, Ron Herring, David King, Larry Condon, John Goodlad, Willard Kneip, Andrew Smith, Gary Howard, Paul Mulloy, Dennis Lubeck, Cheryl Pagan, Jan Tucker, Toni Fuss-Kirkwood, Robert

Woyach, and people at the Center for Teaching International Relations (CTIR) at the University of Denver, the Bay Area Global Education Project in the San Francisco Area, the Mershon Center at Ohio State University, the Stanley Foundation in Muscatine, Iowa, and the Western International Studies Consortium in the greater Los Angeles-Orange County area.

Last but definitely not least, we extend our heartfelt thanks to the school people who participated in this effort to introduce global perspectives into the curricula of their schools. Because we promised confidentiality, we cannot give names—of individuals, of schools, or of districts—but you know who you are: you are the ones who accepted the challenge, worked with us, and made a difference—are still making a difference—in the lives of the children and young people in your classes.

INTRODUCTION

Much has been written and said about global education in recent years. Even more has been written and said about the dynamics of educational change. Seldom are these two bodies of scholarly discourse brought together. Even more rarely are they joined in a way that synthesized the best of the two. *Global Education: A Study of School Change* is such a book. Moreover, it is very well written.

Barbara and Kenneth Tye, together with the highly competent staff associates of the Center for Human Interdependence, working with a cadre of talented and dedicated teachers and school administrators, have produced an analysis of the challenge of globalizing education that is unique and very valuable in several ways. I want to single out four features of the book that, to my way of thinking, are particularly significant.

To begin, the book and the research in which it rests is firmly grounded in a well-articulated conception of global education. They note that global education is a social movement within contemporary American education. While many of us have argued this, the notion is rarely explicated in a systematic manner. The Tyes do so. A very substantial chapter is devoted to an analysis of the conditions that give rise to the movement, to the character of the movement's membership and structural properties as well as the sociopolitical context in which it operates. All in all, this is a novel and most welcome addition to the global education literature.

Their analysis of global education as a social movement greatly helps to resolve much of the ambiguity that resides in the term "global education" and which quite naturally frustrates many people. Global education is a relatively new entry into the lexicon of American education and so people naturally call for a definition.

Asking for a definition of global education is much easier than providing one, at least one that both asker and giver find satisfactory. The reason for this is not to be found in the intellectual inferiority or the muddleheadedness of the people who are involved in the global education movement. It may be true that we do suffer these defects of mind, but even if this be the case, it is not these deficiencies that explain the trouble we experience in responding to the inquiry: What is global education? The source of the trouble lies not in ourselves but rather in that which we seek to define. As a term, "global education" is grammatically equivalent to history education, environmental education, economic education, mathematics education, science education, and so on. Herein lies a major problem because while the terms are grammatically equivalent, semantically global education is very different from other terms. History education, economic education, science education, and so forth can be defined by identifying and describing the peculiar characteristics of the particular discipline or the specific content and subject matter on which these various domains of education are focused. Because of grammatical congruence, one is led to expect that global education can also be defined in the same way. Hence, one naturally asks: What is the content, discipline, or subject matter that is peculiar to global education and differentiates it from other domains of education? The answer to this question is: There is none. Global education is not a domain of education that can be defined in terms of a particular body of content, subject matter, or discipline as we can do in the case of history education, science education, geography education, math education, and so on.

In the past we have sometimes tried to make global education into a content-bounded domain of schooling by saying global or international education is equivalent to the study of things foreign and international. Thus, students were said to be involved in global education when they were learning about another culture, country, or geographical region of the world; or when they were studying foreign policy, international relations, or world problems.

The trouble with this conception is not that it is wrong. It is simply a narrow and incomplete notion of global education. A student need not be studying things foreign or international, as we have conventionally thought of these terms, in order to be involved in a global education. There are ways in which a student can be studying his or her own community and be as much involved in global education as when he or she is studying a community in another part of the world. Similarly, there are ways of studying the American Revolution in a U.S. history class that involves students in global education as much as they are when they study the Arab-Israeli conflict in a world problems or international relations course.

The term, global education, is the name (or one of several names) of a reform movement within contemporary American education that seeks to alter schools, universities, and non-formal educative institutions in ways that provide children and adults with the basic intellectual competencies needed to deal effectively and responsibly with a twin reality of American life. That reality, as the Tyes emphasize, is the fact that the United States is becoming an increasingly globalized society embedded in a world that as a whole is becoming increasingly interconnected and interdependent as a consequence of the growth of worldwide ecological, economic, political, cultural, and technological systems.

The intellectual competencies required of Americans to function effectively and responsibly in their roles as citizens, workers, consumers, leaders, and human beings demand in turn a curriculum firmly grounded in a global perspective. This reference points to a second highly valuable feature of the Tyes' book. They have succeeded in illuminating through a rich array of specific examples the essential elements of curriculum based in a global perspective. These elements turn out to be few in number and can be briefly summarized as follows:

It is a curriculum that engages students of all ages and in all subject matters in the study of humankind as a singular entity interconnected across space and time.

It is a curriculum that engages students of all ages and in all subject matters in the study of the earth as humankind's ecological and cosmic home.

It is a curriculum that engages students of all ages and in all subject matters in the study of the global social structure as one level of human social organization.

It is a curriculum that engages students of all ages and in all subject matters in the study of themselves as members of the human species, as inhabitants of planet earth, and as participants in the global social order.

Can such a curriculum be created? The answer the Tyes give to this question constitutes the third outstanding feature of their analysis. They note that schools are Janus-faced institutions. On the one hand each school is like every other school in many important respects because all schools are embedded in a "deep structure" that is society-wide in scope. On the other hand, each school has its own unique "personality" or character. The deep structure of schooling cannot change independently of a significant and prior change in the society as a whole. Yet features comprising the unique personality of particular schools can and do change rapidly either inadvertently or through conscious intervention. For those who seek to develop curriculum grounded in a global perspective, their portrayal of schools and their analysis of the dynamics of school change is a mixture of good news and bad news. But on the whole, the conclusions that logically flow from the Tyes' insightful analysis of the dynamics of change in schooling is optimistic.

If the Tyes' argument about the deep structure of schools is correct and schooling does in fact mirror society in the sense that the sources or engines of change within schools are located outside of the educational system in the larger society, then social change within the society generates opportunities for educational change. There is little question that one of the basic social changes current-ly underway in American society augurs well for global education, at least in the long run. This change is the rapid globalization of American society. This is evidenced in virtually every domain of social life. Demographically, the population of the U.S. is becoming increasingly cosmopolitan with the rapid growth of Asian and His-panic Americans. Always a race of races as Walt Whitman said, the U.S. is becoming even more so. The American people are a world nation or a universal nation with ethnic, familiar, and cultural ties to peoples in every other part of the globe.

There are multiple indicators of the globalization of the Amer-ican economy. The proportion of GNP derived from international trade is increasing substantially. A growing fraction of the revenues of American business firms come from their investments in other nations. The number of Americans that work for foreign-owned businesses within the U.S. is growing. Joint ventures between Amer-ican and foreign firms are an ubiquitous feature of business organi-zations. Commerce and investment in the Pacific basin are rivaling the importance of the nation's historical economic ties with Europe and the larger Atlantic basin have become increasingly dependent on foreign borrowing in financing both the private and public sector of the economy.

Just as American economic life is becoming increasingly globalized, so are American politics and government becoming more internationalized. State and city governments are increasingly involved in the making and implementation of international economic policy. Many state governors and their staffs spend virtually as much time abroad promoting the interests of their constituents in the global economy as do federal officials. Many Washington lobbyists are in the employ of foreign firms and governments and conversely many lobbyists in the world's other capital cities work to promote American interests abroad. An increasing number of Americans volunteer their time and energy to work in nongovernmental international organizations and global social movements. Participation in international conferences by both public officials and private citizens is rapidly expanding.

To no one's surprise as American demography, economics, and politics become more globalized, so do many facets of American culture. Popular culture is clearly one of these. Today as in the past many elements of American popular culture are exported to the rest of the world as is evidenced by the continuing worldwide popularity of American movies, television shows, professional sports, fast foods, soft drinks, and music. But the converse is also true. American popular culture is being increasingly shaped by the rest of the world. Movies and television shows once designed primarily with an American audience in mind are being influenced in matters of plot and casting by an eye to the European, Asian, and African, and Latin American audiences. Sports once alien to the U.S. are rapidly finding a niche in American schools, universities, and professional areas. Fast foods and soft drinks American families consume are no longer monopolized by hot dogs, hamburgers, and cokes. Popular music is no longer dominated by Anglo-American rock but includes a "world music" hybrid incorporating Caribbean reggae, North African Flamenco, African rap, and Asian heavy metal.

What is true of popular culture is equally true of many more specialized aspects of American culture as well. Take the example of American business culture. Here a dramatic explosion of a global consciousness is very evident. The term "global" and its derivatives such as "globalization" and "globalized" are very prominent phrases

in the *lingua franchia* of industry, commerce, and finance. "Yesterday globalization was a word. Today it is a reality." "There's a distinction between being international and being global, and we have built
it." "Global manufacturing is an intricate game, and we are its masters." These are but a few of hundreds of examples of a global consciousness found in advertising and texts of business publications
such as *Business Work, Fortune,* and *The Wall Street Journal.*

The globalization of American demography, economics, politics, and culture are all aspects of changes in the deep structure of
schools that bode well for the globalization of curriculum over the
long run. But of course social change in the society does not translate in a conflict-free or automatic way into educational change. For
one thing, the globalization of American society does not sit well
with all sections of the society, and thus as the Tyes point out, its
implications for education are resisted by some segments of the
society such as some members of the religious and political right.

Moreover, changes in the deep structure of schools only open
up opportunities for curriculum changes. For real change to take
place, these opportunities must be taken advantage of through
thoughtful strategies of planned change. Herein lies the fourth feature of the Tyes' book that I want to highlight. They tell us what
they think must be consistently done to take advantage of the
opportunities to globalize schools that are being generally created
by the globalization of the society. What they tell us is not a set of
off the top of the head observations, but rather a set of careful
observations grounded in an explicit theoretical framework tempered by several years of careful ethnographic observations.

What seems to emerge from these observations is that schools
are clearly the single smallest unit of change and very likely they
are also the single largest unit as well. This means that strategies of
globalizing curriculum that rely solely upon in-service or pre-ser-
vice education of individual isolated teachers without explicit attention to the social structure and culture of the particular schools in
which the individual teachers work cannot be entirely effective. On
the other hand, this means that strategies that rely on mandating
change from above or beyond the school level will also be less than
entirely effective. Effective strategies must treat a school on the
whole as the basic unit of change, actively involving teachers collectively along with the school's principal in the design and implementation of efforts to globalize the curriculum. If this is correct, then

many more of us must try to do what the Tyes have done so well—link the content of global education reform to the dynamics of school change.

Lee F. Anderson

1

SETTING THE STAGE

What does it take to bring a global perspective to the curriculum of a school? Without sacrificing the many other necessary components of our K-12 curriculum, how can American teachers begin to infuse that curriculum with a vision that looks outward to the world, and brings the world into each classroom? What forces at work in our schools, communities, and nation today tend to encourage global awareness, and what forces act as barriers to such a change? These questions are the theme of this book.

But why? First, why should the American public school curriculum move in this direction at all? And second, why is it important to understand the forces that help or hinder the process of change?

To answer the first of these questions, we must take a short look back into our history. As we do, we will see that in fact our curriculum *has been* moving in this direction all along. We must also take a clear look at the present—at the ways in which the economic, environmental, social, cultural, and technological systems of the world make global awareness a critical basic skill for all of us, but especially for our children as they grow up to become the first generation of the twenty-first century.

The Importance of a Global Perspective

A Story of Widening Horizons

The history of American education is a story of curriculum expansion. New knowledge and skills were added to the curriculum as the young nation became more complex. This process, by which the schools adjust to accommodate the changing needs of society, continues today; it is the nature of the relationship between any culture and its educational system.

A short three hundred years ago, schooling in the New World colonies consisted primarily of the introductory basics: reading and writing and, in some colonies, religion. By the late seventeen hundreds, the curriculum had expanded to include subjects such as spelling, classics, Latin, arithmetic, and some science—but still, only a small percentage of American children attended school at all. Life in the busy port cities—Boston, New York, Philadelphia, Charleston—was closely tied to the coming and going of sailing ships from all over the world, but for most Americans, living on isolated farms in the wilderness or moving westward with the frontier, horizons were very limited indeed.

The three great formative forces of the nineteenth century—industrialization, urbanization, and immigration—placed new demands on the emerging educational system. The common-schools movement created a mechanism for the assimilation of many immigrant cultures. Industrialization would eventually provide an entirely new set of images for thinking about schooling (manufacturing, standardization of parts, separation of tasks and, inevitably, quality control processes). And as the rapid growth of the factory system drew young people from the farms as well as from other nations, the explosive growth of the cities made a different kind of school necessary. The one- or two-room schoolhouse still common in rural areas expanded, in the cities, into large urban schools in which children proceeded through the curriculum with their age-mates. Secondary schools began to appear, although for some time they served relatively few students. Most male children prepared to do what their fathers had done before them, and for that, apprenticeship was sufficient. Girls were expected to become homemakers.

By and large, life in the nineteenth-century United States was still lived within a fairly narrow radius. While there was still some westward movement, made easier by the railroads, most Americans did not venture far from home. The seeds for traditions of local control had been planted, and a localite (some would say *isolationist*) mentality became the norm. While the study of some geography and world history was included in the secondary school curriculum, the history taught tended to be primarily classical and the geography must have seemed remote and unreal to the students of that time. The world was a vast place, and different cultures were exotic and far away.

Twentieth-century technology changed all that forever. The automobile profoundly altered the nature of communities: No longer was it necessary to live fairly close to where one worked. Suburbs were created and roads were built, roads leading away from home. Air travel, too, made the world much smaller. People could think of taking a job in another city or state. Families, spread more widely apart than before, could keep in touch by telephone. We were a little more aware of world events: when we went to the movies we also saw newsreels. Perhaps it was the voice of Ed Herlihy narrating the Universal MovieTone News that gave many Americans their first real sense of life in other parts of the globe. Radio broadcasts from Europe and Asia kept us abreast of developments in the wars with Germany and Japan; not many years later, television brought the Viet Nam war into every American living room.

It's a Different World Today

In just a few generations, then, the world has grown dramatically smaller. While a trip into town on market day was a big event for a youngster in 1840, many American children today take travel to other countries in stride. When the New York stock market crashed in 1929, the nation came apart at the seams; when it wobbled in 1989, people waited to see what would happen on the stock exchanges in Tokyo, Bonn, and London. In 1970 one could still make a meaningful comparison between American-made and foreign-made automobiles; ten years later such a distinction had become impossible. In 1790 the American farmer on his small Ohio homestead was nearly self-sufficient; by 1970 American farms were producing wheat for the world, and American farmers listened carefully to radio and TV reports of crop conditions in other countries.

Economic Systems

In the closing years of the twentieth century, local and national economies are inextricably tied to what has clearly become a global economy (Reich, 1991). For example, all by itself, the California gross state product (GSP) in 1989 was the eighth-largest in the world, and most of its power is due to international trade: two of every three California jobs are in some way connected to the world market (although admittedly the men and women who hold these

jobs aren't always aware of these connections). Multinational corporations, with diversified operations in a wide variety of markets and
both production and sales in nations throughout the world, owe no
allegiance to any particular government. Increasingly, international
economics cut across the political boundaries which used to separate the peoples of the world: in 1990, tariff barriers between Australia and New Zealand were abandoned, and by 1992 this will also
be the case in Western Europe. It will be interesting to see how
quickly other world regions—Africa, South America, Eastern
Europe—follow suit, as it seems they inevitably must, sooner or later.

Environmental Systems

The ecological systems of the planet are closely linked, as
well. Thanks to modern communications networks, people around
the world quickly become aware of industrial disasters such as
those at Three Mile Island (U.S.A.), Chernobyl (U.S.S.R.), and
Bhopal (India), and of their environmental consequences. Awareness about other environmental problems that cut across national
boundaries (acid rain, destruction of the stratospheric ozone layer,
ocean pollution, the disposal of nuclear and other waste products)
is becoming more widespread. None of these issues is remote; many
Americans are experiencing them directly at the local level. For
example, entire stands of trees in the Rockies and New England
show withering damage from acid rain; increases in skin cancer are
already being noted by doctors; the fishing industry has suffered a
series of pollution-related crises; myriad health problems are found
in people who—knowingly or not—live near toxic waste dump sites.
Similar problems are being felt in communities worldwide.

Political Systems

During the final months of 1989, the whole world watched in
amazement as television showed us all the fall of the Stalinist
regimes in Poland, Hungary, Czechoslovakia, Bulgaria, East Germany, and Romania; as well as the beginnings of enormous political
change in the Soviet Union itself. Hailing an end to the Cold War,
Congress began debating proposals for significant reductions in
military spending. Such changes would affect peoples' lives both
within and beyond our own country. As this book goes to press, we

can only speculate about what the future holds for Eastern Europe, but one thing is clear to us all: our future is tied to political developments in other nations as never before.

Cultural Systems

The end of the twentieth century finds more people on the move around the world than has ever been the case in the past. Some of this mobility is deliberately chosen (as when a person takes a vacation which involves travelling to another part of the country or another part of the world), and some of it is job-related (working for a company's branch office in Singapore; being on duty at a U.S. Army base in Germany). But much of the movement in the world today is the result of conditions—economic, political, social, environmental—which make it impossible for people to remain in the places where they were born. Extreme poverty, wars and other political upheavals, natural disasters such as drought or earthquake, the systematic persecution of certain ethnic or religious groups—these are examples of reasons why people willingly or reluctantly leave home to seek a safer, better life somewhere else. All of this mobility, whatever the cause, is creating a world in which people of different cultural backgrounds are much more likely to come into contact with one another than was the case in the past. Contact leads to friction in some cases, but over the long haul it also lays a foundation for greater understanding, tolerance, and cooperation.

Technological Systems

Changes in technology have been at the heart of many of the examples mentioned thus far. Perhaps more than any other factor, improvements in transportation and communication are what has made the world seem to shrink so quickly. A hundred and fifty years ago, Americans traveled by horse-drawn carriage, train, and sailing ship, and news traveled by telegraph. Today, we fly to our destinations in a matter of hours and send people into outer space. And information, aided by orbiting satellite relay, travels instantaneously by telephone, television, computer, or fax machine.

Other technologies dominate our lives also: for example, we can hardly imagine living without our central heating/air conditioning or our many labor-saving devices. And technology is international: not a day goes by that each one of us doesn't constantly make use of products manufactured in other countries.

Reprise: Why Is Global Awareness Important?

We have taken some time to reflect upon the ways in which our educational system has adjusted to the changing needs of our society over the past three hundred years, and we have seen that in general our nation's welfare *has* become more and more closely tied to the welfare of other nations and indeed, to that of the entire planet and its five interconnected systems: economic, environmental, political, cultural, and technological. Schooling is changing too, as it is bound to do, however slowly. Global education is both an inevitable and a necessary curricular reform, then: inevitable because our society as a whole is moving toward global awareness; and necessary because our children and young people *need* to understand the world in which they live if they are to live in it happily and well.

A *Working Definition of* Global Education

At this point, it is probably a good idea to stop for a moment and provide a working definition of *global education*. While there are many definitions currently in use by global educators (open-endedness seems to be a healthy characteristic of the field), the definition which evolved during the course of the project described in this book is as follows: Global education involves

1. the study of problems and issues that cut across national boundaries, and the interconnectedness of the systems involved—economic, environmental, cultural, political, and technological;

2. the cultivation of cross-cultural understanding, which includes development of the skill of perspective-taking—that is, being able to see life from someone else's point of view. Global perspectives are important at every grade level, in every curricular subject area, and for all children and adults.

Already we can see a good deal of work in global education being done throughout the United States (K.Tye, 1990). Powerful groups such as the National Governors' Association in its report, *America in Transition: The International Frontier (1989)* and the Study Commission on Global Education in *The United States Prepares for Its Future: Global Perspectives in Education (1987)*, have spoken out in favor of a global perspective in the curriculum of our nation's schools. Another sign of movement in this direction is the recent return of support for the study of foreign languages, not only at the high school and college levels but in the lower grades as well.

We predict that global awareness will become the first new basic skill of the twenty-first century, as computer literacy has so rapidly become a basic skill in the final decades of the twentieth century.

Understanding the Change Process

At the beginning of this chapter, we posed two questions. The first (Why should global awareness education be incorporated into American schooling?) has been addressed; let us now turn to the second: Why is it important that we try to understand the forces which help or hinder the process of change?

Actually, the answer to this question is fairly simple and straightforward: it is important for school people and others interested in education to understand the change process *in order to make it work for us*. We all have visions about how our schools could be improved, and we all are aware of the day-to-day difficulties of bringing our visions a bit closer to reality. In making the effort to do so, we also make assumptions—about schools, about the nature of change (and of resistance to change), and about how best to go about achieving our goals.

Since this book is as much about school change as it is about global education, it is important that we clarify *our* assumptions and beliefs about how and why changes occur in schools, so that the reader understands our reasons for planning and carrying out activity in the network, our rationale for choosing how to study that activity, and what resulted from it.

Living With a Paradox

To begin with, we believe that one of the persistent paradoxes of the educational enterprise is that each individual school is unique, and yet at the same time is also very much like other schools. This paradox can be accounted for through the recognition that a deep structure, determined by the basic values and assumptions widely shared throughout a society, shapes the educational system of that society in its most fundamental aspects (B. Tye, 1987).

The nature of the deep structure of schooling is such that *it cannot change independently of a significant and prior change in the society as a whole.* Indeed, when we talk about the deep structure of schooling, we refer to society's overall worldview. For example, a major shift in societal perception about what schools are for has occurred in the twentieth century: we now expect schools to solve innumerable social problems, some of which didn't even exist in earlier times and others of which were considered, by most Americans, to be the proper responsibility of other social institutions (church, family).

We tend to take many aspects of the deep structure of schooling for granted: a classroom means a space approximately thirty feet by thirty feet, with four walls, windows, rows of individual desks, blackboards, etc. Curriculum consists of separate subjects, taught in little or no relationship to each other. The school day is divided into six or eight approximately equal periods of time. The teacher is in charge. The principal evaluates the teacher. And so on, and so on. Sarason (1982) refers to these as the regularities of schooling. There are other regularities which have to do with the norms of the teaching profession, the role of parents and community members, and the hierarchical nature of the educational bureaucracy. These are the characteristics of schooling now, at the close of the twentieth century, which are *assumed to be right* and thus are seldom seriously questioned. This is the deep structure of schooling.

The deep structure is pervasive. Each school does not have its own deep structure; the deep structure of American schooling (or of the schooling of any other country) is *nationwide.* The deep structure changes very seldom, and only when the society at large is already leading the way.

On the other hand, though built upon the foundation of the deep structure, each school has its own unique personality. It has its own history, community traditions and mores, and internal factors such as teacher-administrator relationships, number and intensity of problems, and classroom climates. Despite the fact that in many ways schools are the same, when you walk into a *particular* school you can sense its individuality. Spend a week there and you may—if you ask the right questions—know enough about the place to identify the primary components of that school's unique personality.

You may generalize when speaking about elements of the deep structure, but you must be careful when discussing schools on the level of their unique personalities. Assumptions carried with us into a school setting may not hold up, or they may blind us to the realities of a particular school. For example, a school housed in an old, somewhat run-down, inner-city building may be, despite scarce resources and other problems, a happy place inside: leadership could make the difference, morale could be high, teaching could be superb. Likewise, a beautiful new school in the suburbs could feel quite flat and lifeless inside. You must spend time in a school, even live there, before you can understand its unique personality.

Unlike aspects of the deep structure, aspects of the unique personality of a school *may* change, sometimes quite rapidly. The most obvious source of change would be the assignment of a new principal, but there are many others: declining enrollment, changing community demographics, staff turnover, loss of funding, special recognition.

Changes in a school's personality may also be brought about intentionally, as part of a school improvement effort. Improving staff interaction, building mechanisms for shared decision-making, clarifying school goals, and solving specific school problems are all examples of worthwhile activities which may help to make an individual school a happier and more productive place.

In summary, then, it has been suggested that the deep structure of schooling is inseparable from a society's fundamental assumptions about its nature and role. The deep structure tends to resist any attempts to change it, *unless such attempts are in tune with changes also occurring in the society as a whole.* On the other hand, the unique personality of a school is both receptive to change efforts that are planned and responsive to changes that are unplanned. It is always in the process of adjustment as it assimilates these planned and unplanned changes and, like an organism (and it *is* a social organism), struggles to maintain its equilibrium.

This systemic view of educational change leads one to a set of assumptions that guide action. For the global education project reported upon in this book, those assumptions had to do with (1) this being an optimal *time* to begin the globalization of school curricula, (2) the desirability of focusing globalization efforts at the *single-school* level, (3) the necessity of defining a *new role for the superordinate levels* of the educational system, and (4) the importance of creating a *linkage structure* between individual schools and new knowledge about the world in which we all live.

Timing

Earlier in this chapter, it was pointed out that there is a growing recognition of our global interdependence in society as a whole. Further, it was suggested that there is emerging support for efforts to globalize the curriculum of our schools. Such support is far from unanimous. Neither is it clear how such globalization should be carried out. It is precisely at such a time that *thoughtful exploration* should occur. By thoughtful exploration, we mean trying out ideas that seem to have some basis in fact; and, most importantly, we mean keeping track of what is done, how it worked, and what problems arose during attempted implementations. We mean activity and reflection combined.

Too frequently in education, we see attempts to bring about new programs which are high in activity and lacking in reflection. Because of this, they often fail and it is the innovation itself which is blamed. No consideration is given to deep structure conditions or unique personality characteristics of the school. It is hoped that this will not happen to global education.

The Single-School Focus

Because many of the unique personality variables of the single school can be manipulated, it seems wise to focus improvement efforts here. While the facilitating behaviors of superordinate agencies (district, state) and individual classroom teachers are important, what is most critical is to get concerted action at the local school site.

Much of what passes as school improvement work today focuses upon the classroom teacher as the unit of change. Workshops and courses are given on a variety of teaching contents and pedagogical techniques, and countless teachers attend. In some states, minimum amounts of such work are required for periodic recertification. Teacher A may be improving his knowledge of set theory, teacher B may be learning how to create simulation experiences for students, teacher C may be working on her counseling credential. Much of this in-service study may be outstanding; but, in terms of improving the school, it may make no difference at all.

Not only do teachers tend to have individual in-service goals, but they are isolated, one from another, in many other ways. They spend most of the day alone in their own classrooms. Departments are separated in different parts of the school building. When faculties do come together for staff meetings, they tend to deal only with administrative matters. By focusing in-service activity on the school as a whole rather than on the individual teacher, some of this isolation may be overcome.

The Superordinate Level

If our assumptions about deep structure and the unique personality of the school are correct, and if the assumptions about the need to focus improvement efforts at the school level have merit, then there are corresponding assumptions about the role of the superordinate system which also must be clarified. Currently, we assume a hierarchical decision-making system in education. State officials are preoccupied with mandating structures, curricula, and all manner of things for schools and teachers to implement. In order to assure compliance, there are a variety of guidelines, state-adopted materials, and, most important, tests for both teachers and students to take. This is all done in the name of accountability to taxpayers. In the final analysis, and after more than a decade of this top-down mentality, it is quite clear that schooling is no better off than it was before. In fact, by a number of indicators, it is worse off: too many students are not finishing school; many who are still in attendance are turned off; the educational needs of our growing minority populations are not being met; the morale of the teaching force is at its lowest ebb ever; and on and on (Carnegie Foundation, 1990).

In reality, what this top-down, accountability mentality is doing is avoiding the real problems faced by our schools. It is as if we believe that we can change things by simply saying that they are changed. Further, it is unrealistic to assume that mandating change will cause it to occur. Weick (1976) has pointed out that education is not a rational bureaucracy like other large organizations in our society. Rather it is a "loosely coupled" system, with more or less autonomous units operating up and down the hierarchy. Orders from the top to "align" curricula or create certain structures may not only be ignored by subordinate levels, but they can also cause people to spend inordinate amounts of time in unproductive and subversive activity. What a waste of energy and talent!

What *is* needed is a shift in our thinking which leads us to focus our improvement efforts at the level of the single school and its personality. We need to keep in mind the deep structure of schooling. We also need to have the superordinate levels of the system play *facilitating* roles rather than directing ones. Until that happens, our efforts to create lasting change in our schools will probably continue to founder.

Linkage

Focusing upon the single school as the unit of change is probably not enough to bring about significant improvement in schooling even if the superordinate system plays a facilitating role rather than a directing one. Schools and the people in them must have access to new knowledge. It is here that external agencies have a role to play. Freed from bureaucratic constraints, such agencies can bring practitioners from schools together with university educators and others who have the knowledge which the school people need in order to carry out the changes they have decided upon.

It is conceivable that various forms of intermediate agencies—county offices, regional centers, etc.—could serve as linkages if they are *not* set up as arms of the state education agency enforcing accountability by local schools. It is also possible that local school districts could join together to form linkage agencies around given goals or topics. The critical issue is not who establishes or sponsors such entities as much as it is the function they serve. Linkage and service on one hand cannot be confused with administration and accountability on the other.

Tucker (1991) points out that the key issue in global education collaborations (for that matter, in any collaboration) is that they should be mutually rewarding. Too often, the reward systems for practitioners and university educators are so different that the two groups have a difficult time working together. Academics get promotions, in part, from research. Practitioners gain from getting things done. When linkages are made, a good deal of attention must be given to the matter of mutual reward.

Reprise: Why Is It Important to Understand the
Process of Educational Change?

This book is addressed primarily to practitioners—people whose work days are spent in schools. *They* are the ones who need to understand the change process, for it is they who are truly in a position to make use of it. Although classroom teachers do not always conceive of their role in this way, part of their job can—and should—be to join forces with the other adults in the building (administrators, nonteaching professionals, support staff) to make their school an ever more pleasant place to be, for adults and students alike. In doing so, it is helpful to understand the relationship between the deep structure of schooling and the unique personality of individual schools, because then it is possible to be clear about which goals are attainable and which are not, probably because the deep structure would not support them.

In dealing with this question, too, we made clear the four basic assumptions about change which undergirded the work to be described in the next section of this chapter. First, since the optimum *time* to affect a change may well be when society is in a transition period (Pareto, 1935; Mann, 1957; K. Tye, 1968) the time to introduce global education is now, while our society is adjusting to new conditions of world interdependence. Second, the most significant and permanent changes are made at the level of the *single school,* and require concerted action by those most directly involved at the school site itself. Third, focusing our change efforts at the single-school level will necessitate some *redefinition of roles* for people who work at district, county, and state levels. These people will need to view themselves as support staff for those working in schools; their role must be facilitating rather than directive. And finally, successful change efforts will probably require that an outside agency become involved in providing practioners with *linkages* to the new knowledge that they need. Existing norms of teacher isolation and autonomy are part of the deep structure of schooling, and only intervention by appropriate "outsiders" is likely to be powerful enough to create a space within which teachers and administrators can work together on projects or problems which they themselves have chosen.

Strategy and Implementation: The CHI Story

The Center for Human Interdependence (CHI) was formed in 1984 as an organization devoted to helping classroom teachers in southern California to do a better job of infusing global studies into their teaching. The first project undertaken by CHI was the development of a resource directory listing all of the sources of free or inexpensive globally oriented teaching aids (print materials, guest speakers, etc) available in the greater Los Angeles area. This directory proved to be quite a success, and many school districts in Los Angeles County bought copies for each of their school libraries.

During the course of its first year, CHI became officially affiliated with Chapman College in Orange, California. Space next door to the education department was remodeled, and CHI moved in late in the summer of 1985. The staff at that point consisted of two full-time and two part-time professionals, a full-time office manager, and two part-time student workers. Later in the project, a part-time librarian was added.

The second CHI project is the one being presented in this book. Made possible by a major grant from the Helen Devitt Jones Foundation, the second project was designed to involve a number of schools in a collaborative effort to infuse the schools' curricula with global perspectives. The project was to last four years, from September 1985 to June of 1989, and it combined the authors' interest in international studies and global perspectives with their considerable experience in the area of educational change. The remainder of this chapter will be devoted to a description of how this project was designed and carried out.

Forming the Network

An important part of designing the original project proposal for our funding agency involved thinking through how many schools we would realistically be able to work with, and what characteristics the schools should have. Our goal was to see global education spread *throughout* each participating school. This meant that we were committed to working with *all* the teachers in each school. The magnitude of such an undertaking was clear, and it seemed best to limit our group of schools to around fifteen: five "triples" in five different school districts. (A triple would be a high school, one of its feeder junior highs, and one of *its* feeder elementary schools). The triples configuration, we hypothesized, would maximize the chances of communication by teachers across grade levels since, given the time and opportunity, teachers generally *are* interested in talking to their colleagues who have had—or will have—the same students. Triples also would allow us to follow some students from one level to the next, if we chose to do that.

Several other considerations were also important. For example, we hoped to involve a group of schools that would be fairly typical of schools in southern California in terms of size, location, and ethnicity. Also, it was important to us that the teachers at each participating school feel enough interest in the project, as a group, to justify our presence in their building. Principal support, and support from the district level, would be necessary as well. For example, we made it a condition of involvement that each participating school be allocated ten to fifteen extra days of release time per year by its district. These days were to be used for CHI activities and nothing else.

The next step involved contacting district superintendents who had a known track record of supporting innovative program development. We explained what we were prepared to offer, and if they were interested, they arranged for us to meet with a group of principals whom they felt would also be interested. Of ten superintendents approached, only one, who was under considerable political stress at the time, declined to have his district become involved. The other nine endorsed the idea of the project, including the release-time requirement and the idea of using the triples configuration, and before long we found ourselves meeting with groups of principals, three from each district.

After explaining the importance of global education, we described the kinds of resources which we were able to make available to their teachers. It was made clear that our presence in their building, should their teachers choose to become involved, would be very low key. Our goal—to diffuse a global outlook throughout the school—was made equally clear, but we emphasized that *how* this would happen would be left largely up to the teachers themselves: we did not intend to tell anyone *what* to do.

Two of the nine districts were already involved with global education through other institutional affiliations, and the principals in these two districts decided not to complicate matters by becoming involved with what might be viewed as a competing organization. The three principals in another district felt that their teachers were already too overwhelmed with various projects and district requirements, and decided not to permit us to present the project to their teachers. (Interestingly enough, that district office then put us in touch with a *second* set of principals, and this time we got a much more positive response).

At about this time, we had to face the fact that we probably wouldn't be able to form a nice, neat network of triples, as we had originally envisioned. Not wanting to force any principal or faculty to join the project ("No arm-twisting" became a CHI motto), we backed off immediately when a principal seemed reluctant or unenthusiastic. So while in every case superintendents had matched us with a *trio* of principals—elementary, intermediate, and high school—in all but one case we ended up with one or two schools instead of three. This was acceptable, since positive attitudes were more important to us than triples; we really wanted to work with people who wanted to work with us.

During the spring and fall of 1985 we presented the project to the faculties of nine schools. (At a tenth school, we were asked by the principal to defer our first meeting with the faculty until he could do some preparatory groundwork, and at the eleventh we were asked to meet with the department chairs instead of with the entire faculty). During these presentations we explained why we felt so strongly about the importance of global education, and described the kinds of resources we would be able to offer. Not wanting to create preconceived ideas which might be hard to shake later on, we were deliberately vague about providing a definition of global education, and carefully avoided spelling out in any detail what a lesson containing a "global perspective" might actually look like in the classroom. It was made clear that participation would be a matter of personal choice; that there would be no pressure and no hidden strings. We talked about bringing them teaching materials, arranging for guest speakers, planning workshops on topics of their choice, and about the release days promised by their superintendent, which they could use as they saw fit. All they had to do was to decide what their global project would be, and tell us how we could help them to do it.

For some teachers this deliberate ambiguity on our part was unsettling at first. They kept asking us to tell them what they should be doing in order to do global education "right." As time went on, however, they began to see the possibilities for themselves. For other teachers, the vagueness seemed to come as a welcome challenge. They felt it as liberating that resources were being offered in support of work of their own choice, with no final reports or compliance issues attached. (The themes of voluntary membership, receptivity and the timing of personal decisions to join, and deepening understanding of global education will be dealt with in chapters 3, 4, and 8).

At those first faculty meetings, we concluded by assuring the teachers that the project would not come to their school unless they wanted it; the final decision was to rest with them. Then we asked them to fill out and turn in a brief interest inventory, designed to give us (1) a sense of the *potential* for teacher interest and involvement at that school, and (2) data about the level of global knowledge already present within that faculty. We were pleased with the positive response: all of the eleven schools chose to join the project. By Christmas of 1985, we had our network in place. Although we had only one true triple, we had what we considered to be a healthy balance of levels (four elementary, one K–8, three intermediate, and three high schools), and we had schools that were more or less typical in size. We had no rural schools, but we did have one inner-city school and several that were urban, while the rest were suburban. We had a good cross-section of school types by ethnicity: one school was ninety-nine percent Hispanic, one was ninety-five percent white, and the rest were the much more typical heterogeneous mixture now common in southern California: Hispanic, Asian, and white. These general categories mask the remarkable diversity which is part of the day-to-day reality of schools in Orange County and, indeed, in many other parts of California and the nation: the linguistic diversity typical of gateway communities of recent immigrants and refugees. The city of Anaheim is a good example: during the years of the CHI project, one could find fifty-six different native languages being spoken in the schools.

The CHI Philosophy

Elements of the CHI philosophy have already been mentioned, but these bear repeating because it is important that the assumptions we brought to our work with the eleven CHI network schools be completely clear. First, as outsiders who wanted to work with the teachers in those schools, we knew that our attitude would be very important. We wanted to work collaboratively, and to approach the teachers with what Dennis Goulet (1971) terms "active respect"—a determination to provide the help which the *teachers* ask for, rather than what *we* think they need. As McDonald (1989) puts it, "Outsiders who have the right attitude play a role that is interpretive and catalytic, and they play it with patience. They help find answers but never provide them; they help shape outcomes but never determine them. Their efforts are powerful only insofar as they spur efforts by the true insiders—efforts that are necessarily tortuous and messy." In practice, this meant among other things that we would try always to work with the interests articulated by the teachers, rather than bringing them things they hadn't asked for. As a result, for example, we delayed many purchases for the CHI curriculum materials library until the teachers began to let us know what kinds of materials they needed. Likewise, we planned day-long "theme workshops" around topics specifically requested by participating teachers.

Second, while our presence in the school would deliberately be low key and nondirective and there would be no pressure to work with CHI, we *would* make an effort to continually reach out to welcome everyone's involvement. We realized that if we were to reach our goal of diffusing global perspectives throughout a school, we could not afford to have the project come to be seen as belonging to only a certain few teachers. In our experience, this often happens with innovations, and it is deadly to attempts to achieve schoolwide change. Some of the uninvolved teachers feel left out and would *like* to be in, while others use the perception of clique ownership as a justification for their own nonparticipation. In either case, exclusivity can create tremendous barriers to the success of a project.

Third, we didn't expect that the project would evolve in the same way at all the schools. We had no intention of imposing a single vision of what global education should look like, and every intention of nurturing whatever variety of interpretations would emerge. This was consistent with our belief in the single school site as the most effective locus of change, and it meant that, throughout the four years of the project, we devoted a great deal of time to discussing the schools, one at a time, always seeking the key to what would work best at each site.

Getting Started: Year 1

Within a few days after each initial faculty meeting, CHI staff members had analyzed the interest inventories filled out by the teachers and identified the various topics in which the teachers at each school seemed most actively interested. Armed with this information, they returned to each school for a second meeting (this time, attendance was optional, so the number of teachers who showed up could be taken as additional data revealing the depth of genuine interest in the project). Keeping the agenda purposely brief, the CHI staff members engaged those teachers who came to the meeting in a dialogue about the topics selected at their school. More often than not, it was possible to collapse a number of topics into more general categories, or themes, around which some global education projects might form at that school.

When this process had taken place at almost all of the schools, a matrix was constructed showing how often each theme had been identified across all of the schools. By far the most popular theme, selected at every school, was cross-cultural awareness, and this was hardly surprising given the ethnic diversity of the students in CHI network schools. Global economics, global communication, environmental issues, and the arms race were chosen by teachers at about half of the schools, and world hunger, human rights, technology and development, and migration issues weren't far behind. This matrix was used as a tool to help us plan a series of day-long theme workshops for the remainder of that first year. Later in the project, we came to know the teachers well enough that we could ascertain the kinds of workshops they wanted during informal conversations with them.

Our first theme workshops were very successful. Two to four teachers from each school attended, which gave us a manageable group of twenty-five to thirty at each workshop. (In keeping with our philosophy of trying to involve the entire school, as a general rule we encouraged the principals to send *different* teachers to each workshop, but this didn't always work out, since there were some teachers who were very anxious to attend them *all*.) The teachers enjoyed getting away from school for a day to learn something new, and we soon learned that talking with each other and with teachers from the other network schools was equally important to them. The Chapman College campus is a pleasant environment, and we were able to involve a number of the Chapman faculty as guest speakers for some of the workshops, when their expertise coincided with the teachers' interests. The themes of the workshops during that first year included: cross-cultural awareness; local-global environment issues; the global economy; and folklore-folk art.

Since the interest inventories had not been anonymous (although some teachers had chosen not to sign theirs), CHI staff were able to prepare special packets of materials for those teachers who had indicated specific immediate interests. These were delivered to the teachers in question shortly after the meeting at which the school's global themes had been chosen, in an effort to demonstrate that we could "deliver the goods" when teachers told us of their interests or made special requests. As year 1 progressed, CHI staff developed procedures for delivering materials to the schools and picking them up again a few weeks later. They would usually take a variety of materials—books, videotapes, lesson plans, simulations and role plays—and spend several hours in the teachers' lounge, delivering what had been requested, displaying the rest for teachers to look through, and generally getting to know—and be known by—the teachers at each of the eleven schools.

To disseminate information throughout the network of schools, we started a newsletter during year 1. Intended primarily for the teachers in the eleven schools, it included features on global awareness activities planned or under way at each school, an editorial column on some aspect of global education, a calendar of events in the Los Angeles-Orange County area that had some relevance to global perspectives or that provided relevant opportunities for teachers, news about CHI workshops and other activities, and information about new acquisitions in the CHI curriculum materials library. Despite the purely local focus of the newsletter, during years 2, 3, and 4 requests to be put on our mailing list came in from nearly every state and several foreign countries. Clearly, it served a much wider networking function than we had originally planned.

A minigrant program, which we started in year 1, did as much over the four years as any other CHI activity to encourage teachers to incorporate some global material into their teaching. Small grants, from two hundred to six hundred dollars, were made available for teachers to work on curriculum, developing lesson plans and units containing global perspectives; to acquire the supplies or equipment they would need in order to teach their new lessons; to buy some release time to visit global education programs in other schools; or to attend some event which would better prepare them to teach with a global perspective. The grant application forms were as simple as we could make them: on a single page, we asked for a brief description of the planned grant project, a statement of purpose, an estimated budget, a timetable for completion, and a list of teachers involved. As long as the project would clearly make a contribution to the enhancement of global awareness at the school, it was funded. No progress reports or final reports were required; but the teachers almost always gave us a copy of their final product—if it was a teaching unit or a lesson plan—to put in the CHI curriculum materials library.

Not all of our year 1 activities succeeded. Special films and guest speakers scheduled for 3:30–5:00 P.M. on the third Thursday of every month failed to draw more than a handful of teachers. Informal conversations at the various schools revealed that although there was considerable interest in these "third Thursday" events, teachers simply felt pulled in too many directions and did not have the time to attend. (The theme of competing demands became a major force in our work, and is discussed in detail in chapter 5).

Toward the end of year 1, one of our intermediate schools decided to withdraw from the project. The principal told us that his teachers felt that their district wanted them to attend to other things, and also that some of them felt that global education wasn't what their students needed most (the school was located in a relatively poor area). We opened discussions with a different school district, and by the beginning of year 2 we had replaced this school with another, even poorer, school. This replacement school turned out to be one of our most successful, even though it got started with us a year later than the other ten.

"Waiting for the Hook"

Sad but true, teachers in American schools almost *never* encounter a project which genuinely involves them in decision-making and makes no demands other than those they choose for themselves. When CHI staff members appeared at each school for the first faculty meeting in September, 1986 (year 2), just to remind the teachers about what CHI had to offer, many were amazed. *"You're back!"* they said. *"You didn't disappear during the summer!"* So many innovative programs just sort of fade away, and teachers can become cynical about the reliability of new projects in general. At the beginning of year 2, we found more teachers starting to take part in CHI activities. "Well," they told us, "we were waiting for the hook last year. CHI just seemed too good to be true. But you did exactly what you told us you would do, and now we're ready to get involved." The challenge of trust-building is probably the number-one concern of external support people in projects such as this one; this theme will be dealt with in more depth in chapter 3.

Throughout the project, but especially during years 1 and 2, CHI staff members spent a great deal of time in the schools simply hanging around and getting acquainted. This type of activity, which may *seem* somewhat aimless on the surface, is in reality quite purposeful. It gives the project consultants an opportunity to learn the culture of the school; to find out what resources for global education already exist within the school (e.g., which teachers have traveled abroad recently, and how can these teachers' experiences be incorporated into learning activities for students?); and to demonstrate good faith by quickly providing teachers with requested materials, by being around to talk about how a first attempt at a global lesson went, or by occasionally cutting some corners to facilitate a planning meeting or the visit of a guest speaker.

When some aspect of global awareness was included in an assembly, a parent night, or some other special event, CHI staff members were always there. Without being obtrusive, their presence conveyed support for the teachers' efforts to infuse global perspectives into all aspects of school life.

Years 2, 3, and 4

Theme workshops, newsletters, minigrants projects and individual teacher trials of new material continued throughout years 2, 3, and 4, and many other activities were added for those who were interested. For example, a number of schools purchased modems and, with help from CHI, established telecommunications links with schools in other countries. The physical education teachers at the four intermediate schools and the one K–8 school got together with CHI staff and planned an International Sports Day for 250 seventh graders. Held each year in late May on the Chapman College athletic field, the day-long event brought 50 students from each of the five schools together to play eight noncompetitive games from other countries. On a smaller scale, this event is still being held each May at several of the schools.

CHI purchased additional release time during years 2 and 3 for twenty-five teachers to participate in a project entitled "Orange County in the World." Dr. Art Blaser, a Chapman College political science professor who had been involved in development of the successful prototype, "Columbus in the World," at Ohio State University in the 1970s, served as the trainer-facilitator for the teachers. The group met at CHI every six weeks for a full day of planning and of progress reports. In between, they involved their classes in the systematic exploration of some aspect of their community's connections to other parts of the world. For example, at the high school level an English class visited a number of ethnic restaurants and grocery stores, a science class investigated environmental issues connecting Anaheim to the world, and a world cultures class did research on the many multinational corporations located in Orange County.

Several junior high school class groups studied the different ethnic groups living in their communities; one class did a project on the many ethnic newspapers to be found in the county; and another honed their interviewing and data-gathering skills by conducting a survey of the travel habits of people living in their school's geographic attendance area. At the elementary level, two classes of sixth graders studied TV commercials for cultural bias; a group of second and third graders explored the connections between the clothes they wear and those worn in other parts of the world; and two classes of first graders charted the ethnic heritage of every child in the two classes, and followed up by asking some parents and grandparents to visit and share the stories, music, customs, and sometimes the food of their native lands.

Specific needs were identified by teachers as the project continued, and in most cases CHI was able to help with these. For example, during year 2 a group of teachers of English as a second language (ESL) began to notice that good ESL materials containing a global perspective were very hard to find. The following summer, ten of them met at CHI for a week and produced their own globally oriented lessons, games, and other materials which they could use the next year in their classes.

At one high school, a group of teachers who had attended a CHI theme workshop on conflict resolution decided to try to do something about the interethnic tensions on their campus. First they surveyed their colleagues to find out if other teachers thought that prejudice was a problem at the school. Then they designed a short, ten-item questionnaire for students, and with the cooperation of the entire faculty they administered their questionnaire to the whole student body. CHI helped to process and tabulate the responses, and CHI staff members were present when the group presented its findings to a full meeting of the faculty. Both the data and the subsequent discussion revealed that the students perceived more of a problem than the teaching staff were willing to acknowledge. Nevertheless, some plans were made for follow-up activities which would involve students from the various ethnic groups in dialogue sessions. Communication, it was hoped, would help lead to some constructive suggestions for solving—or at least reducing—the problem.

As teacher involvement increased, it became difficult to keep track of all of the global-perspectives activities that were going on at each of the eleven schools. Individual teachers would try something out and wouldn't necessarily tell us about it. Our policy of being supportive but nondirective helped them to stand on their own. No teacher *depended* on CHI, but every teacher knew it was there, if and when needed, to provide certain kinds of resources and help. The CHI staff felt strongly that this type of a relationship would be most likely to encourage independent teacher growth leading to continuation of global perspectives teaching beyond the four years of the project.

Working with Administrators

Well aware of the importance of the principal to the success of any change in the way things are typically done in a school, CHI staff made special efforts to keep in close touch with all eleven principals. Frequent informal contact—at the school or by phone— was maintained. Most of the principals made a point of touching base with project staff members whenever they were in their building, but when this didn't happen, the CHI consultant would usually make a courtesy call to the principal's office before leaving.

A special publication, *Principal's Notes*, was developed as another means of keeping communication lines open between the project office and school administrators. Once a year, CHI scheduled a special half-day lunch or dinner meeting just for the school principals and key people at each district office, including the superintendents. A keynote speaker would give a talk on some aspect of global education of interest to the group, each of the eleven principals would report on the global awareness activities under way at his or her school, CHI staff members would report on upcoming events, and there would be plenty of time for informal conversation.

During the course of the project, principal turnover occurred at six of the eleven CHI network schools, and at a seventh, severe illness made a substitute principal necessary for much of year 4. In all cases, CHI had to devise special strategies for acquainting the new administrator with the project philosophy and the activities in progress at his or her new school. Principal turnover is a real problem for innovative programs and cannot be brushed aside lightly. Many school districts have a policy of moving principals around every five to seven years, regardless of what may be happening in their schools, and the incoming administrator may or may not feel an interest in or commitment to the existing progams of his or her predecessor. Chapter 7 will present our findings regarding the impact of principal behavior on such efforts for change as the CHI project.

Networking: Local, State, and National

Networking became increasingly important to CHI in years 2, 3, and 4. First, in order to do a good job of connecting teachers in our eleven schools to the sources of new knowledge and materials they needed, we had to know a good deal about what was available for them in the greater Los Angeles–Orange County area. CHI was a charter member of WISC, the Western International Studies Consortium, a group of five Los Angeles area organizations involved with global education.* Through WISC, CHI learned of many individual teachers and groups of teachers in other school districts who were introducing global perspectives into their teaching. Often, such teachers were invited to present their work at CHI

---

*The other four WISC organizations, besides CHI, are the Immaculate Heart College Center, the USC Center for Public Education in International Affairs, the Area Studies Centers at UCLA, and the Constitutional Rights Foundation.

theme workshops. It was important for the CHI project teachers to know that they were not alone in their efforts to help their students become globally knowledgable.

CHI also arranged for some of its teachers to present their own work at state conferences such as the California Council for the Social Studies. This was a special event for these teachers, some of whom had never made presentations at professional conferences before. The audience response to these presentations was very good, and the teachers felt proud of their new professional identity as global educators.

Project staff seized every possible opportunity to connect CHI teachers with each other and with teachers in other schools—and even in other parts of the country. We also participated, as an organization, in networking with other global education organizations nationwide. It quickly became apparent that many different approaches are being tried: appropriately, there are many different ways of getting to the same general goal—increased global awareness on the part of the American people.

Public Relations

All too often, innovative educational programs are held up for public scrutiny far too soon, while teachers are still struggling to master the new materials or methods. For this reason primarily, and also in keeping with its philosophy of being low-key and unobtrusive, CHI did not aggressively seek media attention. Consequently, only a handful of activities in the four years received newspaper coverage although many deserved it. This policy of quietly going about the business of providing learning experiences and resources for teachers may also account for the complete absence of conflict between CHI and individuals or groups who are uncomfortable with the idea of global education. Such can certainly be found in Orange County—or anywhere; in fact they have been vocally and visibly opposed to global education projects in other parts of the country in recent years. But CHI encountered no opposition during its four years of work in the eleven Orange County, California, schools.

Learning from Experience

The CHI story would be incomplete if it omitted the research component, which was just as important to the project as implementation. In order to be able to contribute something substantial to the literatures of both global education and educational change, we studied what we were doing as we did it, right from the first visit to a superintendent. Our basic research question opened this chapter, and now we have come full circle: What *does* it take to bring a global perspective to the curriculum of a school?

The research component will be explained more fully in chapter 2, but it can be briefly summarized here as follows: The study employed qualitative field-study methodologies in an effort to develop what Glaser and Strauss (1967) call "grounded theory." Further, while we were not limited to one theoretical perspective, we were heavily influenced by Herbert Blumer (1969) and other symbolic interactionists. Simply put, this means that we were mostly interested in the *meanings* which people gave to their experiences with global education through their exposure to CHI activities and resources.

Each CHI staff member kept careful field notes of every visit to any of the eleven participating schools. As these accumulated, they were grouped into observational notes (what actually happened), theoretical notes (what it might mean), and methodological notes (what CHI should try next, do differently next time, etc.). Periodically, staff members prepared "memos" which pulled together a person's thinking about an emerging pattern or concept.

We met frequently as a team to discuss and reflect upon our findings. Often a memo served as the starting point for discussion. The usual outcome of such a meeting was the raising of further questions which became the foci of subsequent observations and/or interviews. The process was one of data gathering; coding, reduction and display; discussion and reflection; hypothesis generation; further data gathering, and so on.

Data *feedback*, in this process, became an integral part of our implementation strategy, because we kept coming back to the school sites to check our emerging hypotheses with the people there. Sometimes the patterns we thought we were seeing, or what we assumed were the reasons for certain teacher or administrator behavior, were strongly verified by many others at the school site. At other times our interpretations turned out to be incorrect, in the sense that they were not shared by the people most closely involved.

During the closing months of year 4, we also collected some *quantitative* data: we interviewed all principals and a random sample of teachers (both those who had become involved with CHI and those who had chosen not to do so) at each school, and we asked every faculty member at every school to fill out a fifteen-item questionnaire; again, we wanted their responses whether or not they had participated in the project, so we administered this questionnaire at a faculty meeting toward the end of the year. These data were organized and analyzed during the summer of 1989, and early in the fall, one of the CHI staff members visited each faculty one more time, to thank them for their participation and to share some of the response patterns from the questionnaire.

In one sense, this is the end of the "CHI story." But it isn't, really, for several reasons. First, because many of the teachers who began to incorporate some global perspectives into their teaching during the four years when CHI was around will continue to do so. Second, because the world itself has changed so much since the CHI project started in 1985, many more teachers are now beginning to acknowledge the importance of global awareness and to do something about it. And third, the story continues because this book will enable others to think about what global education could be in their own schools and perhaps act upon those thoughts with some awareness of how to make the change process work *for* them.

Conclusion

In setting the stage for the remainder of this book, three important things have been set forth in this chapter. First, a rationale for the importance of global education was developed. This included an historical perspective as well as a quick look at some of the contemporary events affecting people across national boundaries and worldwide (see also Anderson, 1991). Second, we set forth our assumptions about the process of educational change. These assumptions shaped and guided our project, and they are the result of many years' work in schools by both of us.

Finally, we've described the four-year project itself: what we actually *did* in the project schools. Some readers will be interested primarily in this story, which will be further developed in chapters 4 through 8. Others will be more interested in reading about what we learned and the conclusions we reached, but these readers, too, need to know what the project looked like as a day-to-day part of the lives of the teachers in the eleven participating schools.

Chapter 2 will present the research methodology of the project, and chapter 3 takes a more sociological look at the significance of global education, applying findings from the study to the conceptual framework of social movements. Chapters 4 through 7 are devoted to presentation of findings, grouped into four major categories, and chapter 8 takes a step often left out of research reports: CHI staff reflect upon their own work as interventionists and share what they learned about change—and resistance to change—in the course of this project. Finally, chapter 9 will present findings, hypotheses, and recommendations for further study.

We do not pretend that the hypotheses we present in this book will hold true for all American public schools. Each reader must reflect upon our findings and determine what is true and useful in his or her setting. It is our hope and our belief, however, that much of what we have to say will ring true for educators in general; and that our findings will help others in their own efforts to introduce global education—or other innovative programs—into the life of their school.

References

Anderson, L., "A Rationale for Global Education," in K. Tye, ed. *Global Education: From Thought to Action* (Alexandria, Va: Association for Supervision and Curriculum Development, 1991).

Blumer, H., *Symbolic Interaction: Perspective and Method* (Englewood Cliffs, N.J.: Prentice-Hall, Inc., 1969).

Carnegie Foundation for the Advancement of Teaching, *The Condition of Teaching: A State by State Analysis, 1990* (Princeton University Press, 1990).

Educating Americans for Tomorrow's World: State Initiatives in International Education, National Governor's Association (Washington, D.C., 1987).

Glaser, N. and A. Strauss, *The Search for Grounded Theory* (Chicago: Aldine Publishing Co., 1967).

Goulet, D., "An Ethical Model for the Study of Values," *Harvard Education Review,* 41(May 1971): p. 47.

Mann, F. C., "Studying and Creating Change: A Means to Understanding Social Organization," in *Research in Industrial Relations, A Criti-*

cal Appraisal, C. M. Arensburg et al., eds. (New York: Harper and Brothers, 1957): p. 162.

McDonald, J. P., "When Outsiders Try to Change Schools from the Inside," *Phi Delta Kappan* (November 1989).

America in Transition: The International Frontier. 1988–1989 Chairman's Agenda Report, National Governor's Association (Washington, D.C.).

Pareto, Vilfredo, "On the Equilibrium of Social Systems," in *The Mind and Society,* A. Livingston, ed., A. Bongiorno and A. Livingston, trans. (New York: Harcourt, Brace & Co., 1935).

Reich, R. B., *The Work of Nations: Preparing Ourselves For 21st Century Capilalism* (New York: Knopf, 1991).

Sarason, S., *The Culture of the School and the Problem of Change* (Boston: Allyn and Bacon, 1982).

Study Commission on Global Education. *The United States Prepares For Its Future: Global Perspectives in Education* (New York: The American Forum, 1987).

Tucker, J., "Global Education Partnerships between Schools and Universities," in K. Tye, ed., *Global Education: From Thought to Action* (Alexandria, Va: Association for Supervision and Curriculum Development, 1991).

Tye, B., "The Deep Structure of Schooling," *Phi Delta Kappan* (December 1987).

Tye, K., "Creating Disequilibrium," in *The Principal and the Challenge of Change,* Institute for the Development of Educational Activities (IDEA) monograph (Los Angeles: IDEA, Inc., 1968), pp.15–38.

——, ed., *Global Education: School-Based Strategies* (Orange, Cal.: Interdependence Press, 1990).

Weick, K. E., "Educational Organizations as Loosely Coupled Systems," *Administrative Science Quarterly* 21(1) (1976), pp. 1–19.

2

RESEARCH AS REFLECTION ON PRACTICE

Seeking New Knowledge

Global education as a curriculum movement is relatively new, and consequently research in the field is still relatively thin. What has been done can be grouped into four general categories, as follows:

1. developmental studies of students

2. studies evaluating curriculum materials

3. action research involving the teachers themselves

4. studies of changes in schools when global education is introduced into the curriculum. (Tye and Tye, 1983.)

Developmental studies of students constitute the strongest body of work thus far, thanks to the efforts of Judith Torney-Purta and other developmental psychologists who are interested in questions of when and how children are able to conceptualize attachments to entities beyond their own immediate experience. The formation of one's identity as a member of a large and, to a child, somewhat abstract cultural or political group ("I am a Navaho," "I am Canadian," etc.), and the eventual ability of young people to see themselves also as members of a *world* community are of interest to these researchers.

Some of the work that has been done in this area suggests that American youngsters between the ages of about eight and twelve years are particularly open to knowledge about other cultures and worldviews, and can internalize this knowledge with a reasonable degree of tolerance (Hess and Torney, 1967; Torney,

31

1969). By junior high age, however, *in*tolerance of differences begins to intensify, and by high school many American students become extremely ethnocentric. The important question for global educators, of course, would be whether exposure to a more globally oriented curriculum in the fourth, fifth, and sixth grades would mean less ethnocentrism, prejudice, and intolerance in later years. Such longitudinal studies are expensive, and as yet none have been initiated. This is a fertile area for investigation which will make a valuable contribution to our understanding of early adolescent development.

Some work has been done to evaluate the effectiveness of global education curriculum materials, but to date these studies have not been extremely strong, and much more could be done in this area (Benham and Tye, 1979). What we *can* say with a fair degree of certainty, based on our own work with the project behind this book, is that teachers report high levels of student interest in materials and lessons containing a global perspective. However, while interest levels and even sheer enjoyment of global lessons are important, there are other ways to evaluate effectiveness, and this work needs to be done.

A third type of research that holds great promise for the global education field is smaller, "action research" studies involving the teachers themselves as either the primary investigators, or as co-investigators with global educators from intermediate agencies such as district or county offices or institutions of higher education. In point of fact, much of this kind of work may already be going on, but it remains unidentified—particularly when teachers do it themselves. First of all, while teachers often do small-scale evaluation projects within their own classrooms, they do these as *practitioners*, seeking more effective ways to teach. They do not *think* of themselves as researchers, though the steps they follow may be perfectly acceptable research practice.

Secondly, the adult culture of most schools doesn't particularly encourage substantive professional discussion of research. A teacher involved in action research would probably not talk about it much in the teachers' lounge. Consequently, the work does not become widely known, either within or beyond the school. And finally, teachers do not usually have the time to write up the results of their classroom studies for publication, even if it would occur to them to do so. Competing demands intervene and besides, as a general rule, classroom teachers have not been socialized to think of themselves as capable of making that type of a contribution to the profession. It is far more likely that the teacher who has concluded a small-scale action-research project would cycle the findings back into his or her daily classroom life without making them known to anyone else.

The role of the intermediate agency in providing teachers with links to new knowledge is discussed in chapter 3. But ideally, knowledge flows not just from the field to the teacher but also from the teachers to the field. District, county, and state consultants, district and school site administrators, and university people working collaboratively with classroom teachers can help the teachers find a professional, public voice of their own. Teachers can be encouraged to design and carry out action resarch projects and then helped to present their findings at appropriate professional conferences and in professional journals. Also, beginning teachers need to acquire this orientation—that they will have important knowledge to contribute—during their preservice training. A critical outcome would be that the research questions would more likely be addressed to matters of genuine relevance to practitioners, not merely to what administrators, consultants, or policymakers think is needed.

Global educators in intermediate agencies of all kinds need to be alert to opportunities both to encourage classroom-based and school-based action research and to see that teachers have chances to report to the appropriate audiences about their work. Since global education is considered important for children of all ages as well as relevant in all subject areas, there is plenty of scope for the generation of many interesting research questions.

The fourth and final category in which more global education research is needed is that of the change process. Very little has been done to document, in a systematic way, what schools and the teachers in them go through when they decide to make global/international studies a part of their mission in the education of children. In any project, of course, there will be a history: participants will have stories to tell, of what worked, and what didn't. But as a rule these will not be seen as data which could lead to insights about how to manage successful and lasting change in a school.

The CHI project was deliberately designed to make a contribution in this fourth area, partly because staff members brought considerable prior experience with educational change to their work at CHI, and partly because it is an area in which much more needs to be learned. It is also an area in which findings can be applied to *any* innovative effort, not just to global education.

Preliminary Thoughts about a Research Component

Having decided in general terms *what* we wanted to investigate, we had to decide how to proceed. Two familiar approaches were immediately rejected as being too simplistic for our purposes: first, a chronicle of "what worked" and problems encountered at the various schools—leading to the all-too-common list of "steps to successful change"—would be interesting but superficial, not really of much lasting significance to the field. Second, given the kind of project we planned (the reader may wish to refer back to the CHI philosophy summarized in chapter 1), a traditional experimental design would, clearly, be inappropriate. We were not interested in prediction and control, nor did we set out to prove any hypotheses. Rather, we hoped as a result of our work to *generate* the hypotheses—to frame the questions—that could provide a basis for further work by others.

Generalizability of findings, in the strict experimental sense, also did not matter. We didn't want people to *assume* that our findings would necessarily be true of all American elementary and secondary schools. Obviously, with a sample size of just eleven, this would be impossible anyway. But we *do* hope that people who read this book will find much that rings true for the schools in which they work and decide for themselves what, of our findings, they can use.

A better way for us to come to grips with questions of educational change, we felt, might be to amass a significant amount of descriptive data about practice and then begin to examine these data for patterns, relationships, and exceptions. Such examination could be inductive or deductive, or both; and could make use of a priori concepts or not. Rather than ending up with a "how to do it" list, we might gain some real understanding of the complex phenomenon of schooling.

A qualitative methodology, yielding "thick" descriptive data and supplemented with some survey data toward the end of the project, seemed best suited to our needs. During the summer and fall of 1985, we reviewed the literature on qualitative research in education and the other social sciences. We also turned for help to Dr. Roberta Lessor, a colleague in the sociology department at Chapman College, who steered us toward the conceptual framework we would ultimately choose: symbolic interaction theory.

Symbolic Interaction Theory

George Herbert Mead is generally considered to be the father of symbolic interaction theory, but it was Herbert Blumer, a student of Mead's, who developed its basic premises into a fully articulated framework. Symbolic interaction differs from the other basic families of theories (in particular, structural-functionalism and conflict theory) in that it focuses primarily on individuals (rather than on groups) as they interact within the context of daily life. As we shall see, it is a very flexible orientation, one which acknowledges that peoples' interpretations of events and things are never static and predictable, but are constantly changing.

The focus of this theoretical orientation on the interaction of people within their daily contexts, as they interpret their experiences and attach meaning to them, was well suited to the CHI study, with its emphasis on the internal dynamics of eleven individual schools and the people working in them. This framework should not be seen as exclusively phenomenological, however:

> Symbolic interactionists study people interacting and developing common meanings or joint interpretations of events. They view people as being in the active process of creating structures as well as being constrained by them, which is what makes symbolic interaction so useful in studying organizations and organizational development. Individuals interact with institutions as well as with each other; this is the more macro or structural side of symbolic interaction. (Lessor, 1987.)

In recent years, symbolic interaction theory has been used as a framework to study hospitals, corporations, people in certain occupations (such as airline flight attendants), and many other social structures. It is certainly appropriate to use in a study of schools.

Every conceptual framework—even those most open to modification, such as symbolic interaction—rests on certain basic assumptions. Blumer (1969) identified the basic assumptions, or what he termed the "root images" of symbolic interaction as follows:

1. human beings act toward things on the basis of the meanings those things have for them;

2. these meanings are derived from the social interactions
   that a person has with other people;

3. these meanings are continually modified through an interpretative process.

It is easy to exemplify these "root images" in terms of the CHI study,
and in so doing to clarify Blumer's terminology. First, *human beings
act toward things on the basis of the meanings those things have
for them.* When we made our initial offer to provide resources for
infusing global perspectives into the curriculum, we got a wide range
of responses from the teachers at each school. At South High
School, one said "This is too controversial, it'll never be accepted in
this community and *I wouldn't touch it with a ten-foot pole.*" But
another at the very same school said, "This is just what our students
need—it could be the key to de-fusing some of the tension between
the ethnic groups on our campus." While to the first teacher the
term *global education* was fraught with danger, for the second it
meant something potentially positive and constructive. The latter
teacher got involved with CHI; the former teacher did not.

Second, *these meanings are derived from the social interactions that a person has with other people.* Further conversations
with the two teachers mentioned above revealed that the first
teacher had been deeply involved with another, somewhat similar
innovative project some years before but had been "burned" by a
negative community reaction. In fact, she had almost lost her job as
a result. The experience had left her cautious and unwilling to risk
any changes in her established curriculum. The second teacher, on
the other hand, who was studying for his counselor's credential and
had a good deal of contact with students outside of the classroom,
was less worried about community reaction and more concerned
about what he perceived to be the needs of the students and the
social climate of the campus.

Third, *these meanings are continually modified through an
interpretative process.* As the years went by and CHI continued to
work with teachers at South High School, no negative community
reactions occurred. The first teacher never did participate in CHI
activities, but by year 4 she was ready to admit that her perception

of global education had changed. She had seen some of her colleagues supplementing their regular lessons with learning activities incorporating global perspectives and getting good results. She was aware that some of the teachers at South High were working on curriculum projects supported by small grants from CHI. And she knew of several of her fellow teachers who had enjoyed attending CHI theme workshops. No longer did this teacher view global education as dangerous.

Methodology

The naturalistic methodology which follows logically from Blumer's theoretical framework resembles anthropological fieldwork to a certain extent. Observation and conversation form the primary behaviors of the researcher at the site, and these are recorded in detailed field notes, written shortly after each encounter.

Conversations may be formal, as in a structured interview, but are more often informal. Early in the project, conversations between CHI staff and teachers in the eleven schools usually revolved around getting acquainted, establishing trust, and clarifying how global education might actually look in practice. By years 3 and 4, many teachers were initiating more substantive conversations: comparing perceptions about how a global lesson had "gone over" with the students, and how it might be improved; or sharing ideas for new lessons, units, projects or activities, for example. What was working, what wasn't working, and what was either helping or hindering the global education projects at each school was a very important focus of many conversations, both formal and informal. What did it mean at Mesa Junior High that *no one* from the English department was participating? Why was the principal at North High School behaving so unpredictably? What was it about Buena Vista School that made it such a pleasant place to work?

Observations led to more conversations, also. Researchers had to verify their perceptions of who were the informal opinion leaders on each faculty, for example. They had to understand the dynamics of faculty meetings, at which times the relationship between teachers and administrators might be most evident, or hidden agendas might surface. And they had to know how the principal's support for CHI's efforts was affected by his or her relationships with the superordinate system. One thing led to another as the CHI staff worked to understand each school and its progress (or lack of it) toward a global perspective.

This kind of field work requires not only that the researcher ask questions but also that he or she share perceptions with the people at the site. In other words, communication about things and events must flow both ways: "This is how I see it; how do *you* see it?" As time goes on, the researcher will also become more adept at what is known in global education terminology as "perspective-taking"—being able to see things or events through someone else's eyes, and to comprehend reasonably accurately the meanings which the other person attaches to those things or events (Malinowski, 1922). This ability to understand and empathize must, however, stop short of what anthropologists call "going native"—the point at which the researcher loses his or her critical perspective altogether (Schatzman and Strauss, 1973, p. 53).

Symbolic interaction theory was compatible with the CHI philosophy primarily, as we have just indicated, because of its emphasis on the lived world of certain people (teachers and school support personnel) in certain contexts (schools), and at both a personal and an institutional level. The naturalistic and qualitative methodology which extends logically out of symbolic interaction theory was well suited to CHI's nondirective implementation strategy, too: not only did we have no particular program to impose, but—from a research standpoint—we weren't out to prove anything, either. Both strands of the project, therefore, required the same kinds of behavior from CHI staff members: being helpful to teachers (in ways defined by the teachers themselves), coupled with alert observation and lots and lots of conversations.

Our choice of symbolic interaction and of a qualitative methodology does not imply a general rejection of positivist experimental approaches. We have both been involved with traditional methodologies in the past and recognize their many advantages. Indeed, we have watched with interest as the lines between "quantitative" and "qualitative" research have become increasingly blurred, and tend to agree with Miles and Huberman that

> it is getting harder to find any methodologists solidly encamped in one epistemology or the other. More and more "quantitative" methodologists, operating from a logical positivist stance, are using naturalistic and phenomenological approaches to complement

tests, surveys, and structured interviews. On the other side, an increasing number of ethnographers and qualitative researchers are using predesigned conceptual frameworks and prestructured instrumentation, especially when dealing with more than one institution or community.... The paradigms for conducting social research have shifted beneath our feet, and most people now see the world with more ecumenical eyes. (Miles and Huberman, 1984.)

There were two other reasons why symbolic interaction was compatible with the CHI project. First, it is a theory which is by its very nature open-ended, and it requires of its adherents that *they* remain open-minded. Researchers who feel drawn to this theoretical position and its naturalistic methodology must have a high tolerance for the ambiguity and general messiness of human life. They must be willing to be surprised—or even disappointed—by their findings, and *willing to let go* of hypotheses that don't hold up under continued exploration.

An example from the CHI files will show how this can (and must) happen. By the end of year 2, the project staff was thoroughly frustrated by its experience at North High School, and in a number of discussions the hypothesis that North was, in fact, a "sick" school had begun to emerge. Evidence of dysfunctional—even pathological—structures and behaviors were documented, and because it seemed impossible to make any headway at all at that school, during year 3 the project staff decided to discontinue special efforts at North High, confining work there solely to responding to any requests which might be initiated by teachers. Our expectation was that we wouldn't hear much from North High School that year.

Not only was that expectation wrong, but by the beginning of year 4 it had become obvious that the entire hypothesis about North High being a pathological environment was completely erroneous. A new hypothesis, one increasingly supported by new evidence (as well as by a fresh look at the old evidence) was proposed: it had been the impact of one man—the principal—which had made the school seem dysfunctional. This was made dramatically clear when the first principal retired at the end of year 3 and a second principal entered the picture at the beginning of year 4. Under a different kind of leadership, the school became a different place. The potential for global education was released (potential which we discovered had existed all along at North High) and more progress was made in year 4 than in the first three years together. The North High story will be told in greater detail in chapter 7, but this quick overview serves to make a point: Even an hypothesis that seems to be well-supported can turn out to be wrong, and qualitative researchers must never be so devoted to their emerging themes that they become blinded to this possibility.

Last but not least, symbolic interaction was compatible with the CHI philosophy because, while it discourages the a priori imposition of preconceived theories or hypotheses, it *does* allow for the testing of insights from other theoretical sources. In other words, if a pattern is emerging which leads the researcher to think of a construct developed by someone else but which seems to fit well with the emerging pattern, this construct might be used as another lens through which to view the data. For example, at Mesa Junior High certain teachers took ownership of the CHI project almost from the very first day, while others held back. So obvious did this pattern become that the CHI staff was reminded of Ron Havelock's (1971) classic work identifying the typical behaviors of "early adopters" of an innovation. Application of Havelock's framework to the Mesa Junior High setting proved helpful up to a point, but it failed to account for all aspects of that school's internal dynamics. The point is, the use of symbolic interaction methodology permitted the use of different lenses when that seemed appropriate, but only *after* our own theories about the early adopters at Mesa began to take shape. As Glaser and Strauss put it,

> Our approach, allowing substantive concepts and hypotheses to emerge first, on their own, enables the analyst to ascertain which, if any, existing formal theory may help him generate his substantive theories. He can then be more faithful to his data, rather than forcing it to fit a theory. He can be more objective and less theoretically biased. Of course, this also means that he cannot merely apply Parsonian or Mertonian categories at the start, but must wait to see whether they are linked to the emergent substantive theory concerning the issue in focus. (Glaser and Strauss, 1967.)

The Search for Grounded Theory

While CHI staff members spent a great deal of time in each of the eleven participating schools over the four-year duration of the project, this research is not considered to be an ethnographic study. We tend to agree with Rist (1980) and others that the term *ethnography* has been much abused by education researchers in recent years. We doubt if the term can be rightfully used at all in a study involving more than two or possibly three sites. Indeed, even a study of *one* school may not be an ethnography if certain criteria of duration, frequency, and type of involvement are not met. CHI staff did not actually live in the schools, so to speak, spending their days there as full-time participant-observers. A term used in Miles and Huberman's helpful 1984 work, *Qualitative Data Analysis,* "repeated-visits field study," comes much closer to describing the data-gathering component of CHI's research methodology.

The Research Process

Step 1: Observation and Data Collection

Visits to school sites could be as brief as a few minutes—just to deliver materials to a teacher, for example—or as long as several days, if some special activity, such as an international fair, was happening. Most often the visits lasted from one to three hours. As described in chapter 1, on one level the purpose of these visits was to provide resources and opportunities for teachers to incorporate global perspectives into their teaching. Bringing a guest speaker into a classroom; dropping off (or picking up) a requested book, videotape, game, or other teaching materials; stopping by to observe a lesson or to sit in on a planning meeting—these are examples of the implementation activities of CHI staff.

From the perspective of research, the same people who were delivering services had also to observe, note, and reflect upon what was happening at each school, both while they were there and when they were not. After every site visit, regardless of its purpose or duration, the CHI staff member would return to his or her office and make a thorough written record of the key interactions which had just taken place at that school, recording the important things about "people, events, issues, conversations, and the settings in which these were observed" (Lessor, 1982, p. 355). This might also—in fact, it often did—include information revealed during the visit about things that had happened in the interval since the researcher's last visit, whether that visit had been two weeks ago or the day before. The written field notes for each school were typed up verbatim by a student worker and inserted into the loose-leaf binder for that school. The eleven binders got very full very quickly, and by year 4 there were several binders for each school.

Field notes were not simply stream-of-consciousness accounts, nor did they resemble diaries. Guidelines from Lofland (1971) were kept in mind during the recording process. Consequently, observers made it a point to notice (and make note of) whichever of the following seemed significant:

1. Practices: what were people doing?

2. Meanings: what did people make of what was happening?

3. Natural history: what preceded this event; was it part of a larger whole?

4. Encounters: What was the specific type of interaction (for example, "checking in with the principal")?

5. Roles: what formal and informal roles are people playing? What triggers a transition from one role to another? etc.

6. Relationships: what is the range of available relationships within the setting, and do these shift or change in response to events?

At the direction of Roberta Lessor, our consultant-colleague from Chapman's sociology department, the CHI staff members also made an effort to capture their own impressions of and reactions to events occurring at each school. This, in effect, introduced yet a *third* dimension to CHI's work. Not only was it an intervention agent (providing resources to teachers as they attempted to change the curriculum and their delivery of that curriculum) *and* a research agent (studying the change process as it evolved), but it was *also studying itself* as it did both of those things. (Chapter 8 takes a look at CHI's four years in the eleven schools from this perspective.)

Step 2: Coding the Field Notes

CHI staff members went through a training period during which they were taught how to code the field notes according to a system suggested by Schatzman and Strauss (1973). Taking up a volume of field notes covering a period of several months, the researcher reads through the material from beginning to end, as if reading a novel. While reading, one makes quick marginal notes of three kinds: observational notes (empirical data: simply what happened, free of interpretation), theoretical notes (reactions, interpretations, speculations—the beginnings of hypotheses), or methodological notes (reminders or critical comments on the data-gathering process itself). The three kinds of notes can be distinguished from each other by prefacing each note with an ON, TN, or MN or, for the more visually oriented, three different colors of ink could be used.

Coding the field notes is an early form of analysis which leads to the identification of categories. That is, one begins to see that certain marginal notes "hang together"—the data to which they are attached are connected in some way. For example, the category or theme "competing demands" was an early one that showed up whenever teachers explained why something else prevented their becoming involved with the global education project. This would be a theoretical note (TN), because it did not simply relate what happened, but proposed a phenomenon, competing demands, which might explain *why* it was happening.

Coding is a way of reducing the enormous quantity of material in the field notes to manageable proportions. Miles and Huberman refer to it as data reduction:

> The process of selecting, focusing, simplifying, abstracting, and transforming the "raw" data that appear in written-up field notes...is not something separate from analysis. It is part of analysis. The researcher's choice of which data chunks to code, which to pull out, which patterns summarize a number of chunks, what the evolving story is, are all analytic choices. Data reduction is a form of analysis that sharpens, sorts, focuses, discards, and organizes data in such a way that "final" conclusions can be drawn and verified. (Miles and Huberman, 1984.)

As a reliability check, at periodic intervals each member of the project staff read the same uncoded set of field notes and then a staff meeting would be devoted to a comparison of how each person had coded that set of notes. It was found that, as might be expected, everyone had identified the most obvious and/or powerful patterns. In some cases, more subtle patterns had also been picked up by more than one staff member. This led to the next step, theoretical sampling.

Step 3: Theoretical Sampling

The patterns which begin to emerge in the coding process, if they seem potentially significant or promising, must be verified: the researcher must return to the field and ask questions about the patterns, to see if they hold up. Care must be taken to check perceptions with a wide variety of people, and not just with those who are most likely to agree with the researcher's interpretation. To take a specific example, suppose that when the field notes are read and coded, a number of researchers notice that at one school the principal *always* makes a point of coming out to spend a few minutes with CHI project staff whenever they are in his building. None of the other ten principals seem to behave in quite this way. The staff speculates together about what the behavior means: does it indicate anxiety and a need to keep an eye on the "outsiders?" Or does it suggest that the principal is truly intrigued with the notion of global education, and wants to demonstrate his interest and support? Are there other possible interpretations?

We don't rush right back out to follow up on that one thing, but over the next few weeks whenever a CHI project person is at that school, questions about that particular aspect of the principal's behavior will be raised, if and when they fit into the natural flow of conversation. Not only will a number of teachers and other staff be asked, but when the time feels right the question may well be put directly to the principal himself.

The CHI staff found the term *theoretical sampling* a bit cumbersome, and preferred to think of this aspect of their activity as "checking perceptions" or "verifying the emerging patterns." Whatever it is called, it really constitutes additional data-gathering and is a vital part of the process, because "the meanings emerging from the data have to be *tested* for their plausibility, their sturdiness, their 'confirmability'—that is, their *validity*" (Miles and Huberman, 1984).

Eventually the field worker who is carefully seeking verification of a perceived pattern or a preliminary hypothesis will reach the point at which the same explanations and interpretations are coming up over and over again. He or she will notice that nothing new has been suggested around that topic for some time. Although with this methodology we never think in terms of a conclusion being absolutely final, this *is* the point at which one accepts the pattern or category as being "saturated." It is time to pursue a new pattern or hypothesis.

Step 4: Developing Memos

At staff meetings every Friday, much time was devoted to strategy—discussion of progress being made at each of the schools and concerning what our next steps should be at each site. That was the *implementation* strand of the project. Beginning in year 2 and gradually increasing in years 3 and 4, more time was spent on discussion of the patterns which were becoming increasingly noticeable in the field notes—and which shaped much of our subsequent interaction with teachers—as we attempted to verify those patterns. This was the *research* strand of the project.

More often than not, these staff discussions of emergent patterns (we began to call them *themes*) were prompted by memos prepared for the purpose by one or another of the staff members. These memos could be as short as a few sentences or as long as two pages. Sometimes, a memo would not be in narrative form at all, but would be a diagram, chart, or figure. In a sense, they were like extended theoretical notes because they took one idea or pattern and speculated about its implications and/or its significance. In some cases, connections would be made to other patterns, and a larger configuration would begin to take shape. This was a data "display": an organized assembly of information that permits conclusion-drawing and action-taking (Miles and Huberman, 1984).

Step 5: Drawing Conclusions–Framing Hypotheses

Joint collection, coding, and analysis of data is the underlying operation. The generation of theory...requires that all three operations be done together as much as possible. They should blur and intertwine continually, from the beginning of an investigation to its end. (Glaser and Strauss, 1967.)

As the researcher moves back and forth between data-gathering, data organization and display, analysis, and verification activities, slowly the powerful themes emerge and the weak or discredited ones drop by the wayside. One can feel increasingly certain that the powerful themes, framed now as hypotheses or propositions, are indeed the important educational issues raised by the study. If one has been thorough and meticulous, it is unlikely that anything relevant of importance has been left out; if each emerging pattern (or tentative hypothesis in its early stages) has been truly saturated in the verification process, all possible explanations have been considered and one is left with a set of statements, propositions, questions or hypotheses which may be presented, with confidence, as the *findings* of the study.

Supplementary Data

Early in year 4, it became clear that having some *quantitative* data would help to round out the picture for a number of our strongest emergent themes, as well as provide us with some supplementary information (such as demographic data about teachers) which we needed in order to provide a more complete picture of the context within which the study had been conducted. Accordingly, two decisions were made: (1) Teachers at *every* participating school would be asked to fill out a short, fifteen-item questionnaire. The questionnaire was designed in such a way that responses could be given by all teachers, whether they had been involved with CHI or not; and in order to reach nearly everyone, it was administered during a regular meeting of the full faculty at each school. (A copy of this questionnaire is included as Appendix A.) (2) Formal, structured interviews would be conducted with a random sample of both participants *and* nonparticipants at each school. The principals helped by scheduling these interviews in back-to-back time slots, so that all of the interviews at any given school could be completed in just one or two days. Both the questionnairing and the interviewing were done during the spring 1989 semester, the final semester of CHI's active presence in the participating schools. (A copy of the structured interview agenda is included as Appendix B.)

The Questionnaire

Of the fifteen items in the questionnaire, thirteen were closed—that is, a limited number of possible answers were given and respondents had to select from among them. Of these, several were complex, requiring rank-ordering of several response choices or containing a number of subcomponents. Item 1 asked the respondent to indicate the degree to which he or she had been involved with the globalization effort (five possible answers, from "I was never involved" to "I was very active"). During analysis, the questionnaire packets were grouped according to the response given to this first item, and responses to many of the remaining items (2–13) were cross-tabulated with the response that had been given to item 1. This was done because the CHI staff assumed that the teacher who said "I was very active" would respond differently to other items than would the teacher who said "I was never involved," and we were very interested in finding out what those differences would be.

Items 2–13 were constructed to supplement the themes and patterns which had emerged from analysis of the field notes and been verified through the process of theoretical sampling. For example, item 3 was designed to double-check perceptions around the theme of "competing demands;" it read, "Please check those items below which get in the way of your being involved with the CHI global education project," and ten possible answers were given. Item 5 was also related to the "competing demands" theme: "Please rank order the four items below which have the highest priority at this school"; ten possible answers followed, of which one was "developing a global perspective." Item 6 had two parts; the first part probed the theme of "meanings," and the second part was designed to gather additional data on the *perceived work environment of the school*. Item 12 asked for teachers' views on the behavior of the *principal* vis-à-vis global education efforts at the school.

Items 14 and 15 were open-ended format items, requiring that each respondent write in his or her own answers to the following: (14) "What does the term *global education* mean to you?" and (15) "What could CHI have done to have more of an impact at this school?" Responses to these items were typed up *by school*, and coded according to degree of involvement with CHI and respondent's gender.

The Interview

Some of the things we were interested in knowing did not lend themselves to being asked in a closed format; these were included in the nineteen-question structured interview. As in the questionnaire, however, the items in the interview were related to the themes which seemed to be among the strongest of our find-ings: how the meanings attached to the words *global education* changed for the teachers over the four years; turning points, or when and why people decided to get involved; the role played by the principal in support or nonsupport of the project; the sociopo-litical context, and the issue of opposition to global education; sup-port from the superordinate system; and so forth.

It was felt to be important that we interview people who had chosen not to participate as well as those who had. A CHI staff member met with each principal to go over the staff master list and divide the two groups into two separate lists. It was agreed that from a quarter to a third of the faculty would be interviewed, and of these, half would be from the participants list and half from the nonparticipants list. The principal then selected, at random, the people to be interviewed (usually picking every third or fourth name from each list), notified each teacher of the time and place for his or her interview, and forwarded a master interview schedule to CHI. CHI staff members negotiated who would conduct which interviews at which schools on which days; an effort was made to distribute this task more or less evenly among the staff, and every-one—even the office manager, the librarian, and one of the student workers, took part.

The person conducting the interview took notes on the answers to each of the nineteen questions directly on the interview form; space had been left for these notes. When all of the inter-views at a given school were finished, the responses for that school were typed up, question by question. That is, all of the answers to question 1 were typed up, then all of the answers to question 2, and so forth. This made it relatively easy to compare responses to each item quickly, either within or across schools.

Findings based on the questionnaire and interview data, along with findings based on the grounded-theory methodology described earlier in this chapter, will be reported in the remaining chapters according to thematic clusters.

Conclusion

It has always been our intention to be as clear as possible about how we conducted the research strand of the CHI project. In this chapter, therefore, we have set forth the theoretical frame-work—symbolic interaction—which served as the foundation for this project, and explained why it was compatible with the project philosophy. Next, the actual research methodology was described, step by step. Finally, we discussed the use of supplementary data of a more quantitative kind, specifically, questionnaires and interviews.

At every stage, the CHI team members were conscious of the ultimate goal: to be able to share, with other interested educators, a set of firmly grounded hypotheses about *what it takes to bring a global perspective to the curriculum of a school.* The remainder of this book is devoted to just that goal.

References

Benham, B., and K. Tye, "Global Perspectives: A Humanistic Influence on the Curriculum," evaluation of National Endowment for the Humanities grant ES 27194-72-544, conducted for Global Perspectives in Education, Inc. (June 1979).

Blumer, H., *Symbolic Interaction: Perspective and Method* (Englewood Cliffs, N.J.: Prentice-Hall, Inc., 1969).

Glaser, B. G., and A. Strauss, *The Discovery of Grounded Theory* (Chicago: Aldine Publishing Co., 1967).

Havelock, R. G., *Planning for Innovation through Dissemination and Utilization of Knowledge* (Ann Arbor: Institute for Social Research, Universityof Michigan, 1971).

Hess, R., and J. Torney, *The Development of Political Attitudes in Children* (Chicago: Aldine Publishing Co., 1967).

Kobus, D. K., "The Developing Field of Global Education: A Review of the Literature," *Educational Research Quarterly* 8 (1) (1983):21–28.

Lessor, R., "Unanticipated Longevity in Women's Work: The Career Development of Airline Flight Attendants," unpublished doctoral dissertation (University of California: San Francisco, 1982).

———, unpublished memo: "The Theoretical Orientation of Symbolic Interaction and the Field Work Method of Research Which Flows out of It," May 18, 1987.

Lofland, J., *Analyzing Social Settings: A Guide to Qualitative Observation and Analysis* (Belmont, Cal.: Wadsworth Publishing Co., 1971).

Malinowski, B., *Argonauts of the Western Pacific* (London: Routledge & Sons, 1922).

Miles, M. B., and A. M. Huberman, *Qualitative Data Analysis* (Beverly Hills, Cal.: Sage Publishing Co., 1984).

Rist, R., "Blitzkrieg Ethnography: On the Transformation of a Method into a Movement," *Educational Researcher* 9 (February 1980) pp. 8–10.

Schatzman, L., and A. Strauss, *Field Research: Strategies for Natural Sociology* (Englewood Cliffs, N.J.: Prentice-Hall, Inc., 1973).

Torney, J., "Research on the Development of International Orientations During Childhood and Adolescence," paper presented at the American Political Science Association Conference, 1969.

Torney-Purta, J., "Research and Evaluation in Global Education: the State of the Art and Priorities for the Future," paper presented at the National Conference on Professional Priorities: Shaping the Future of Global Education (Easton, Maryland, May, 1982). Sponsored by Global Perspectives in Education, Inc.

Tye, B., and K. Tye, "Global Education Research: A Partial Agenda for the Future," paper presented at the National Council for the Social Studies, annual conference, 1983.

3

GLOBAL EDUCATION AS A SOCIAL MOVEMENT

A social movement is defined as a "program or set of actions by a significant number of people directed toward some social change" (Gusfield, 1970). Such movements are very much a part of the everyday ebb and flow of American life. The nation began as the result of a revolution which was part of an eighteenth-century worldwide social movement. Along with the French revolution and others, our own struggle for nationhood produced, depending upon your view, independence from tyranny, the establishment of democracy, or the rise of bourgeois nationalism. Abolition, secession, temperance, labor, women's suffrage, populism, civil rights, McCarthyism, and Christian fundamentalism are all examples of social movements which have been or currently are important in shaping thinking and action in the nation. At times, social movements can be in conflict with each other as is now the case with the pro-choice and pro-life movements or which, in the recent past, was true of civil rights and states' rights.

The push for global education resembles a social movement. We will examine this resemblance from five perspectives: (1) the conditions which produce the movement, (2) membership in the movement, (3) the sociopolitical context within which the movement resides, (4) stuctural properties of the movement, and (5) behaviors of the members of the movement. In this examination, data from the CHI study will be used.

Conditions Which Produce the Movement

The changes in world conditions which have caused a need for global education are described in chapter 1. Others have done outstanding jobs of articulating strong rationales for the movement (Anderson, 1991; Kniep, 1987; Hanvey, 1976), and the case for global education is really quite overwhelming. Nevertheless, convincing teachers, administrators, and the lay public of this fact is not such an easy task.

In the early stages of the project, at meetings of network administrators and/or teachers, CHI staff members always presented a brief rationale for the infusion of a global perspective into the curriculum. Frequently, appropriate written materials were handed out which explained such a rationale. An attempt usually was made to include local data as part of that rationale (e.g., considered as a nation, California has the eighth-largest GNP of any country in the world; one-third of all jobs in Orange County are related to international business). Throughout the four-year project, participants were continually made aware of the growing need for a global perspective. As the project matured, it was interesting to hear teachers and administrators also periodically present their rationales.

The impetus for something as challenging to traditional modes of operation, and thus to the deep structure of schooling described in chapter 1, cannot be expected to come from within schools themselves. Just before the CHI project began, there were individual teachers and even a few informal groups of teachers in the eleven network schools who were teaching with what could be called a global perspective. Basically, though, those teachers, at that time, were isolated and out of the mainstream.

After the initial presentation of CHI's rationale, goals, and resources to the faculty of one junior high school, a teacher there said, "We have just been waiting here for you for years." That group perceived that their long-standing interest in global education was somehow legitimated by this outside group (CHI), which, in turn, was authoritative. because it was part of a respected local institution of higher education, Chapman College. While the story of making global education legitimate was never as dramatic in the other schools in the network, it was clear throughout the project that CHI played that role over and over again for interested teachers and administrators. The importance of this legitimating role of an outside agency, such as CHI, for a social movement like global education cannot be underestimated.

As has been described in chapter 2, during the final weeks of the four year project, we administered a questionnaire to teachers at ten of the schools (Buena Vista School had been closed at the end of year 3 due to declining enrollments). The questionnaire took approximately one-half hour to complete and was, for the most part, objective. It was administered at each school during a before-school or after-school faculty meeting. Of the 383 possible respondents at all ten schools, 347 completed the questionnaire for a 90.6 percent response rate (see Appendix A for a copy of the questionnaire).

One question asked teachers to agree or disagree on a six-point Likert scale with the statement, "Global education is important and all students should be exposed to it." Ninety percent agreed with the statement, with approximately half agreeing strongly. Three percent responded "I don't know" and only seven percent disagreed. Clearly, most teachers in this project understood the importance of global education.

We also asked teachers if and why they had become involved with the project. While numbers varied from school to school, approximately half of the teachers in the ten schools indicated that they had been involved. Among those who perceived that they had been *very* active, forty percent said it was because "I felt it was part of an important educational movement." Thirty-six percent responded "I saw it as a professional opportunity" while the remainder divided their responses between "I wanted to meet and share with other teachers," "I sought validation or recognition of work in which I was already involved," and "I received monetary assistance to carry out educational projects" (this referred to the small grant awards which were part of the program).

Eighty-two percent of all of the respondents agreed with the statement "I am more aware now of global issues than I was four years ago." Sixty-eight percent credited this awareness, at least in part, to CHI's presence. Given the media focus during the recent past on issues of ecology, trade, terrorism, changing political systems, and the like, it is no wonder that many teachers are sensitive to the conditions which produce the need for global education. It is our belief that it would be easier now than ever before to interest educators in global education because the need is currently so obvious.

On many occasions, teachers who were involved in CHI activities indicated that global education was important to them because demographics were changing rapidly and ethnic diversity was growing at their schools. Over the four years of the project, the workshop topic most often requested by teachers in the network schools was "cross-cultural awareness." ESL teachers were particularly sensitive to the possibilities that global education held for their work. More will be said about this topic in chapter 4.

While global education advocates might wish to think that everyone who joins the movement does so because he or she values it highly, that may not be the case. There were people who reported that they were attracted to the CHI global education project because they saw it as (l) a vehicle for changing what they perceived to be "traditional" curriculum and/or pedagogy which they thought stood in the way of student learning, or (2) a way to be personally energized because they felt they had "gotten into a rut." Both of these groups of people saw their school situations as negative in one way or another and believed that, perhaps because it was new, global education might bring about improvement.

In summary, then, the conditions which seem to be right for the growth of global education are (l) an increasing awareness of worldwide, systemic interdependence; (2) the promotion of the movement by agencies which are viewed by practitioners as legitimate, and which possess knowledge and resources needed by those practitioners; (3) the existence of a few people in the schools who already believe in the movement; (4) a significant number of people who feel that global education holds promise to develop cross-cultural understanding in school settings, which are becoming more and more ethnically diverse; and/or (5) the presence of at least a few people who are disenchanted with the present system and who see global education as having some possibility of serving as a vehicle for change.

Membership in the Movement

The reader will recall that, once there was agreement from district administrators and principals to proceed, the next step was to explore possible collaboration with the teachers and support staff at each school. Our goal was to bring as many people as possible into membership in the global education movement. We chose a deliberate strategy which included inviting people to participate, providing them with resources and support, and generally treating them with professional respect. We attempted to avoid any form of coercion.

Field notes from the early stages of the project shed light on three important areas of concern regarding membership. These are (l) conditions for engagement, (2) the setting of expectations, and (3) the building of trust. In addition, reflective questionnaire and interview data helped us determine who participated in the project and why.

Conditions for Engagement

In the previous section, we discussed conditions which seemed to be right for the growth of global education. Let us explore that notion a bit further.

The CHI staff met weekly to reflect upon what was happening in each of the eleven network schools. Such reflection led to the planning of further intervention activity. There was not a conscious use of the "conditions for engagement" construct during these discussions, but perhaps there should have been.

Assessing such conditions is similar to constructing an inventory of resources and doing a needs assessment, important activities in the problem-solving process. For example, early in the project at one of the staff meetings, we were examining events at Mesa Junior High. We determined such things as the following:

1. There was an interdisciplinary team in place, taught by three teachers combining five different disciplines. Since interdisciplinary planning and teaching were important to global education, this appeared a good group upon which to focus initially.

2. The core curriculum within the interdisciplinary setting was new and in need of content and focus. Global education materials and ideas were thought able to provide some "glue" to hold it together.

3. Key persons in the team had international experience and a good deal of sensitivity to global issues and the need for global education.

4. The principal, also, was sensitive to global education and was supportive of the interdisciplinary team. In fact, he encouraged work with the team.

At the time, it seemed quite clear that at Mesa Junior High work should begin with this interdisciplinary core team. And so it did. Instructional materials were identified and made available to them.

They attended early workshops held at the college. They received one of the first small grants. Their work was acknowledged in one of the first newsletters. Most of all, attempts were made in every way possible to make these people proud of what they were doing. They had a right to be proud; their work was exemplary. However, some important things had been overlooked, not adequately anticipated. We shall return to this story a bit later.

Setting Expectations

Outsiders such as the CHI staff members who go to school faculties with the intention of soliciting participation in a new project find themselves in a very delicate position. On the one hand, they must be convincing about their own program and ideas. In order to do this, they must present a set of supposed benefits and rewards. On the other hand, they have to be realistic about what they have to offer so that they do not build false expectations, ones they will not be able to meet with the resources they have at their disposal.

At each of the eleven schools, at the beginning of the project, we asked for time to make an overview presentation to the faculty. With the exception of North High School, Mesa Junior High, and Pacifica Junior High, all of these meetings took place in September or October of 1985. At North, we first met with department chairs and then with the faculty in November. At Mesa, we met with a handful of people selected by the principal (the team described in the previous section) and then with the total faculty in January 1986. The principal at Pacifica never let us meet with the entire faculty during year 1. We met only with department chairs.

We were given anywhere from thirty to seventy minutes at these initial meetings and we began with a set agenda which was passed out and which addressed six questions:

Who are we?

What is a global perspective and why is it important to bring a global perspective into education?

What are the objectives of the project?

How will the objectives be accomplished?

What is expected of participating teachers?

What are the next steps?

After briefly identifying ourselves, emphasizing both our Chapman College affiliation *and* our years of experience as practitioners, we gave a very general definition of global education (Hanvey, 1976), and explained why we believe global education to be so important. We attempted to make it clear that we had no set program to impose nor any intention to make specific demands upon their time. We repeated over and over that we wished to help anyone who wished to bring a global perspective into his or her classroom. The group was told of the resources available from CHI: teaching materials, small grants, newsletters, workshops, speakers, and so forth. The meetings were concluded by inviting them to complete a brief survey, which asked them to identify (l) ideas they would like to pursue in their classrooms, (2) kinds of help they might wish from us, (3) things they were doing already which developed global understanding, and (4) resources they knew of which might be available. Responses to these items were collated and subsequently presented at meetings with interested teachers.

Originally, it had been thought that the results of this survey might serve as a kind of agenda for action at each school. They did not, because the questions and responses to them lacked sufficient specifity. It also was too early in the game. People were still trying to understand concepts and expectations. Our instincts were good, however. The survey did accomplish several things. It demonstrated that we meant what we said; we wanted their ideas and we had no hidden agendas. Also, it caused people to begin focusing their attention on the process of globalizing their curricula. It helped us identify topics for network-wide workshops. Finally, since it gave us a measure of what global education meant to them at the beginning of the project, it was a form of baseline data to which we shall return in chapter 4.

Building Trust

"Waiting for the axe to fall" and "waiting for the hook" were expressions given to us by teachers in network schools. There were many statements made by teachers and recorded in field notes which indicated that teachers did not believe us in the beginning when we said that participation was completely voluntary, that we would require nothing special of those who participated, and that we were at their schools solely to offer resources and support (and to study what was happening). It was well into the second year of the project before suspicion of our motives and requirements was really put to rest in the minds of most teachers. The following are selected responses from a reflective interview at the end of the project (1989) to the questions (a) "What was your initial reaction to CHI?" and (b) "How do you feel about CHI *now?*"

1. (a) "Negative...too vague...couldn't believe there weren't too many strings attached.... I didn't believe it."

   (b) "Good...worthwhile program...weren't any strings...you were right in your initial presentation."

2. (a) "Here was another project that would take up my time."

   (b) "Offers wonderful services...heard very good things about the workshops."

3. (a) "That it was going to require too much work and time."

   (b) "It's a wonderful idea...it has given me resources (financial, educational, and emotional) I needed to do my job."

4. (a) "Anxious and curious...no opinion for or against...just wait and see attitude...we have so many programs that come by and want us to buy something or other."

   (b) "Very positive thing...CHI does not push its entirety on anyone...I like the wide range of possibilities offered by CHI and its supplemental approach because no one can just totally throw out the whole curriculum." (This is a reference to "infusion.")

5. (a) "Everyone waited for 'the catch' and wondered how much work it was going to be."

   (b) "Wish I had it at my school now...miss the grants." (She had transferred to a school outside the network.)

As was stated previously, it took a year or more for many people to believe that working with CHI was "safe" in that there would not be a *requirement* of a great deal of extra work on their part. Participation increased significantly from year 2 onward as the trust level grew. Allowing adequate time for trust-building is critical to programs such as the one described here.

Questionnaire and Interview Data

While ninety percent of the faculty members who responded to the end-of-project questionnaire felt that global education was important and that all students should be exponsed to it, only fifty-two percent who responded indicated that they had been involved actively (although everyone, of course, had been at faculty meetings where we presented and had received the project newsletter four times each year). From interviews, we determined that nonparticipation occurred for a variety of reasons. Most people indicated simply that they were too busy with other things. Some saw global education as the job of social studies teachers or, more specifically at the high school level, the world history, world cultures, or world geography teachers. A few said they didn't understand global education or didn't know what to do to implement it. Although few people admitted it in formal interviews, we know there were a small number who were philosophically opposed to global education. Resistance to change and, specifically, to globalizing the curriculum, will be dealt with in chapter 4.

CHI never focused solely upon social studies, and always argued that global education is not a matter of adding a new course to an already overcrowded curriculum. The task was to infuse a global perspective into existing curriculum in all subjects. In fact, at the six secondary schools which worked with CHI, one-third of the teachers in the end-of-project survey who said that they had been actively involved were language arts/reading teachers. Only eighteen percent were social studies teachers, ten percent taught science, and the remainder represented nine other subject areas.

The question arises as to what kinds of people are attracted to this social movement. From our data, we would hypothesize that teachers who have lived overseas, those who began following world news early in life, and those whose parents discussed current events with them while they were growing up would be more apt to become involved with global education.

In the interviews, faculty members were asked, "What characteristics do you believe distinguish those teachers who have been involved with CHI?" Responses were quite varied but there were five categories into which the greatest number fell. The most frequent comments were about personal characteristics (approximately fifteen percent). These included such descriptors as, "creative," "flexible," "enthusiastic," "inquisitive," and "caring." A second category, with almost as many responses, had to do with "openness," specifically with regard to other cultures. Words such as *cosmopolitan* and *awareness* were used. A third category, representing about ten percent of the responses, was also concerned with "openness," but with regard to new ideas and a willingness to try new things. A fourth and smaller group of responses suggested that involved people worked harder and were willing to do more than others. About five percent of the respondents thought that participants had taught a long time and equated that with having extra time to be involved. A few people said they didn't know, a few said the subject area taught made a difference, one said there was no difference between participants and nonparticipants, and two people said that weaker teachers were the ones who became involved, at least initially.

Conventional wisdom often has it that older, more experienced teachers are less apt to participate in something new. In this project, quite the opposite seemed to be true. The more active teachers averaged twelve or more years of experience.

There has been speculation within the global education movement about it being male dominated because, supposedly, men are more apt to be concerned with external affairs while women are more inward-looking. Sixty-four percent of the teachers involved with this program were women as were many of those who provided leadership to the project at their schools.

It is probably safe to say that, nationwide, there are more formal global education projects at the high school level. However, a conscious decision was made to involve primary and middle as well as high schools in the CHI program. In terms of which teachers participated or became members, level of the school did not seem to be a significant variable. Other factors, apparently, were far more important.

There has been some criticism nationally that global education seems to be an elitist curriculum. That is, some individuals perceive it as most often offered to academically oriented, college-bound students. Given the strong relationship between educational aspirations, socioeconomic status, and race and ethnicity, the criticism is often extended to it being a curriculum for schools which serve predominantly white, upper socioeconomic class, college-bound students.

CHI chose to work with schools in a variety of settings. While the composition of the student body of schools, per se, did not seem to determine how many teachers ultimately came to participate, it did make a difference as to what topics interested them. For example, teachers who worked in schools with students of mixed ethnicity were far more interested in multicultural awareness than those who worked in predominantly Anglo schools.

Finally, it should be noted that some individuals are attracted to social movements for psychological reasons, particularly if they have failed to achieve a satisfying status and/or identity with normal membership groups. The prestige and sense of belonging provided by a movement may be more important than the movement's own perceived value (Sherif and Sherif, 1968). There were instances of this in the CHI project. In fact, in at least three cases this was a problem, because people who identified with the program early were seen by the majority of the faculty as being on the fringe, and thus some staff, at least early on, saw global education as also being on the fringe. In one school, the principal actually chastized CHI for giving a small grant to one teacher "because he was not accepted by the other teachers." The particular story of this school is far more complex than this one incident suggests and will be dealt with in more depth in chapter 7 when the role of the principal is discussed. With regard to so-called fringe people, it was our policy to work with everyone who expressed interest. In the long run, this seemed to add to the trust that was extended to the project rather than detract from it.

Sociopolitical Context of the Movement

Lamy (1988, 1990) observes that it is impossible to avoid controversy when teaching international or global issues. He further points out that controversy should be welcomed as an essential part of the learning process. Most thoughtful educators and lay people would agree. Students should be taught to examine the many sides of the complex global issues with which they, their families, their neighbors, their fellow citizens, and humankind are faced. But herein lies a major problem. There are people, perhaps a growing number of them, who do not believe that there are differing, but equally legitimate, positions on issues. They believe that only *their* views are correct, and that the schools should teach those views as truths. They represent their own social movements, which are in conflict with the global education movement.

Lamy has developed a framework which clearly articulates the sociopolitical context within which global education operates today in the United States. That framework discloses four interest communities with contending worldviews which seek to influence and perhaps control global education in U.S. schools.

What Lamy calls the "neomercantilist" or "national interest" view states that global education should prepare U.S. citizens for participation in an anarchic and competitive international system where self-interest rules and where chances for cooperation are limited. It is basically a "system-maintainer" point of view. This has historically been the dominant view in the United States and it has led policymakers to believe in the use of force in the international arena (e.g., Korea, the Dominican Republic, Vietnam, Grenada, Lebanon, Libya, the Persian Gulf, Panama) and to divide the world into friends and foes.

A second view, labeled the "international society-communitarian" view, is a reformist position which recognizes both the need and potential for cooperation in attempting to respond to problems and challenges which are global in scope. This is a more pluralistic view of the international system which places a high value on cooperation, multilateralism, and burden-sharing. In this view, a state's position in the world is, in part, determined by its interests and expertise. This is not a dominant view in our society. However, it is a significant, if not majority, view among educators, particularly global educators.

There are two minority views which Lamy labels "system transformer" views. In the "utopian left," Marxists or neo-Marxists seek to create a more equitable international system through creation of social-democratic systems in which power is decentralized, and in which economic well-being, social justice, and peace are dominant domestic and foreign policy goals. Although the "utopian right," or "ultraconservatives," tend to label all global educators as proponents of this position, the advocates of this position do *not* play a significant role in schools.

The second minority view is quite influential in some communities. Lamy refers to it as the "utopian-right" or ultraconservative" view. Actually, there are two separate views here which, at times, work together. Both are particularly threatened by global education. The first group, mostly comprised of religious fundamentalists, sees global education as a manifestation of secular humanism which threatens their own deeply held religious beliefs. The other group is made up of individuals and subgroups, often interlocking, who see global education as a threat to the promotion and dominance of American values and ideals. It is their view that these values and ideals should be taught in our schools as truths and that, in fact, they should be transported throughout the world.

The current political controversy which surrounds global education is between the international society-communitarian position and the utopian right position. It seems fair to note that, more and more, because of shifts in world economic and political systems, proponents of the dominant neomercantilist position (mainly business people and politicians) are coming to recognize and align themselves with the international position.

In January 1989, CHI gathered together a group of leading global educators and invited them to examine data from the network project. Following that examination, members of the group returned to their respective institutions and wrote chapters for a monograph published by the Association for Supervision and Curriculum Development (1991). As might be expected, Steve Lamy looked at the data from a sociopolitical perspective. He noted, for example, that a few teachers and administrators asked, at various times, about CHI's connection with the Center for Teaching International Relations (CTIR) at the University of Denver. These questions were in reference to a study commissioned by Thomas G. Tancredo, an official of the U.S. Department of Education, that critically reviewed materials produced by CTIR. CHI, in fact, had in its library many of the outstanding global education materials developed by CTIR.

In "Blowing the Whistle on Global Education," Greg Cunningham (1986) published a personal review of CTIR materials. Applying his own political view, a utopian right view, he found the materials biased toward "naive world order values such as peace, social justice, and economic unity." As Lamy points out, Cunningham accused CTIR and, by inference, other global educators of being ideologues guilty of misinterpreting reality and attempting to convert young students to their millenial cause.

Tancredo and Cunningham devoted vast amounts of time and taxpayers' money to publicizing their attacks on CTIR. Caporaso and Mittelman (1988) pointed out that, leaving aside the legality of the federal Department of Education behaving in this way, the report caused havoc in Colorado schools. Conservatives in various communities accused teachers of promoting communism, atheism, and anti-American ideas. Teachers in many school districts expressed fear of taking courses from CTIR, using its materials, or even offering any instruction in international relations (Hursh, 1987).

Mr. Cunningham's report was promoted and widely distributed by a variety of ultraconservative organizations such the Eagle Forum and the National Council for Better Education. The report was circulated among California educators and Lamy, in his analysis of CHI data, noted that a few administrators within the network were concerned with these charges. It is hard to ignore statements, as untrue as they might be, which suggest that global education misrepresents U.S. history, criticizes our government and its constitution, and seeks to denigrate patriotism (Schlafly, 1986).

Lamy's perspectives on the sociopolitical context of global education are helpful in creating an understanding of the objections to the movement. Given these perspectives, however, one wonders how conscientious educators can bring what some people are calling "balance" into the movement. Surely advocates of "balance" can't mean that teachers should not teach students to think critically, that they should teach them to be blindly ethnocentric. People connected with the utopian right do not seem interested in engaging in a discussion about what constitutes "balance," except in their own limited terms. In such a situation, it seems advisable that conscientious global educators should simply get on about their business of helping people to view their world realistically.

Lamy, after reviewing the CHI data, suggested that the project had little political trouble in traditionally conservative Orange County because (1) it did not push a particular worldview and (2) it most often dealt with less controversial issues such as ecology and multicultural relations rather than more controversial ones such as arms control. This was true; and it was also true that CHI had no predetermined curriculum to introduce. Rather, assistance was offered to individuals and groups of teachers who had decided to globalize their curricula. CHI did promote *inter-disciplinary* collaboration in its newsletter and through the criteria which were set for receipt of minigrants.

Two school districts chose to present the project to their boards of education and communities as something other than global education. One designated it "international studies" and the other called it "multicultural education." Apparently, these are less controversial titles than "global education," at least in the minds of some people. To our knowledge, there were never any negative reactions to the project on political grounds in these districts.

In the Buena Vista school district, a board member who belonged to a Christian fundamentalist group expressed concerns about the CHI program in its early stages. The principal of the network school in that district met with the board member frequently. She and the assistant superintendent regularly forwarded written materials to the board member. We submitted to that district, and all others, a list of instructional materials checked out from our library by teachers. There was only one question raised about instructional materials, and the episode turned out to be inconsequential.

There were problems with only two of our many consultants. In one case, the person accurately described the changing world economic situation as one in which American hegemony is declining. This was early in the project and a group of teachers from Pacifica Middle School returned to their site and and branded the consultant (and the project) as un-American. Subsequent events, namely the shifting of ninth graders out of the school and the transfer of many of the more conservative teachers to a local high school, allowed that perception to be overcome. However, the incident very much impeded progress at that school for a long while.

The second consultant who created controversy was contracted to present at South High School. A small group of teachers there had done an outstanding job of surveying racial attitudes within the multiracial student body. The consultant, an expert on immigrant experiences, was employed to address the faculty after the results of the survey were reported by the task group. Everything went quite well until the consultant commented on the role of the CIA in Central America. That one comment, out of context and made to a faculty with many politically conservative members, slowed momentum from our considerable early progress at the school. The incident was particularly unfortunate in that CHI staff and the principal had gotten special permission to have an early release day for the faculty meeting. The incident caused CHI's credibility to be questioned a bit by district administrators. The incident highlights the importance of avoiding the interjection of personal comments into otherwise factual presentations.

In the end-of-project survey, teachers were asked to estimate the number of staff members at their school who were opposed philosophically to global education. Only twenty percent responded that there were none. Four percent said that the number was large, while eight percent felt it was "about half," and forty percent thought it was small. Perhaps the most significant finding was that twenty-eight percent of the teachers chose not to respond. While Lamy is correct that educators tend to hold somewhat more reformist views than the general population, it is also true that teachers are drawn from that population and many hold comparable views.

The reflective interviews conducted at the end of the project substantiated the patterns discussed above. The overwhelming number of teachers who were interviewed did not feel that global education was a political issue at their school. At South High School, the incident with the consultant was mentioned by only three of the fourteen interviewees while the other eleven indicated that they did not see global education as political. At Pacifica Middle School, two of the teachers who were interviewed said that it (global education) "used to be" a political issue at the school but that "those teachers were gone." At one other school, La Puente Elementary School, some teachers who were interviewed indicated that there were a few teachers who felt that global education was "leftist." Those who said this attributed this attitude to the fact that there were a number of Christian fundamentalists on the faculty. They also suggested that some faculty members were unhappy with the growing number of minority children at the school and they equated global education and crosscultural issues.

Social movements, including global education, have a greater chance for development and growth in a society such as ours in which we value freedom of expression and have systems of mass communication. However, a movement can be slowed and even destroyed by its own advocates if it becomes exclusionary or too limited in scope. Unfortunately, there has been a tendency on the part of some global educators to shy away from working with other groups interested in related issues such as third world development, peace, hunger, or the environment. The CHI project sought such collaboration and saw it as advantageous in reaching the goals of global education. Thus, at various times, there were collaborations with Model United Nations, Educators for Social Responsibility, and other groups.

With all that has been said in this chapter, it is clear that global education is a value-oriented movement in that it is part of a larger societal change which involves a new view of how our nation (or any nation) relates to the rest of the world. It is becoming increasingly difficult for one nation to dominate others or enforce its own values. Regional configurations, such as the European Community, seem to be replacing sovereign nation-states as the political and economic pattern of the future. As part of this larger movement, global educators are dedicating themselves to helping others understand and adjust to these new norms in international relations.

As suggested in chapter 1, this move away from a competitive, individualistic view of the world toward a more interdependent, cooperative one is a major change for our society. However, viewed from the perspective of other values we hold— cooperation, democracy, fair play, the golden rule, and the like—it is not. The idea that global education is somehow a left-wing movement is simply wrong. It draws on rich cultural themes deeply imbedded in the fabric of our society. As Boyte (1980) points out, Marxist theory calls for a radical rupture with the past while American society has a tradition of social movement which builds on that which goes before. Global education is one current manifestation of such a social movement.

Structural Properties of the Movement

Many of the structural properties which will be discussed in this section have already been described in chapter 1 or earlier in this chapter. However, here they will be elaborated upon and/or viewed from different perspectives. The properties selected for discussion are: (1) legitimation, (2) knowledge flow, (3) resource generation, (4) team focusing, and (5) professionalization.

Legitimation

For schools interested in globalizing their curriculum, the value of affiliation with an organization such as CHI and an institution of higher education such as Chapman College has been pointed out. However—and particularly given the sociopolitical context discussed previously—it was important to constantly take and create opportunities to legitimate the movement in the eyes of administrators, teachers, board members, parents, and the community in general.

Chapman College is a well established, respected institution of higher education in the Orange County community. It has an attractive campus and is well known for its community service orientation. At one time it was the home of the World Campus Afloat, a nationally recognized program which took college students, on a ship, to visit countries around the world during a "semester at sea." It has a peace studies program, a significant international student population and a junior year abroad program. In addition, it is recognized for its Disciples of Christ affiliation. CHI was a project of the college and, during the first two years of its existence, its offices were actually located on the campus adjacent to the Department of Education. At the end of the second year, CHI moved its offices off campus because the department needed the space for its expanding programs. An attempt was made to hold as many workshops, meetings, and other affairs on the campus as possible so that the college affiliation was as visible as it could be. In addition, wherever possible, consultants were drawn from the Chapman faculty, again in an effort to reinforce the fact that CHI and the college were affiliated.

CHI had a small board of trustees whose members assisted with the establishment of policy and the identification of resources. Individuals who served in this capacity were selected both for their sensitivity to global issues and for their recognition in the community. Such recognition was another form of legitimation.

In chapter 1, it was made clear that district superintendents were contacted initially to ascertain their interest in participating with CHI in a global education project. In some cases, the superintendent remained as the contact person for the district. In other districts, another administrator was designated for this role. In any event, at the end of each year, a report was given to the contact person and the principal(s) of the network school(s) from the district. That report included a listing of all involvements of teachers in CHI activities: workshops, grants, special projects such as sports day, "Orange County in the World," telecommunications. In addition, a list of all materials checked out of the CHI library by district teachers was provided in case there was ever any question from the community about that. At those meetings, principals had the opportunity to discuss activities in their schools and it was also a time to clarify plans for the upcoming year—for example, teacher release time to be provided by the district to the school for participation in CHI activity.

In the spring of each year, there was also a conference and dinner planned for superintendents, district contact persons, and principals. We encouraged principals to invite representative teachers, also, as a way of showing them that the project had some district support (legitimation). CHI board members were also in attendance at those meetings, and in a few instances superintendents invited district trustees. These meetings were held in a local hotel, conference center or other suitably pleasant facility. The program consisted of a presentation by some nationally recognized global education figure, announcements and statements by CHI staff, and reports from principals about activities in their schools.

Whether or not district boards of education gave approval for participation of schools in the global education project was a matter to be decided by district administrators. Some superintendents wanted board approval, others felt that participation was an administrative matter. CHI, as a matter of policy, did not make presentations to boards of education.

Activities directed toward informing and gaining the support of district personnel were important. Upon reflection, it might have been better if more had been done. Certainly, more should have been done with and for principals, separate from their work with teachers at their schools. This will be discussed at some length in chapter 7.

In chapter 1 we mentioned that it is unwise to expose teachers who are trying to do something new to media coverage before they feel comfortable with the new program. However, by the end of year 2 that point had been reached for many teachers, and we began to seek some media coverage for global education activities sponsored by CHI, as another method of legitimating the project. Arranging for such coverage was not an easy task in a large metropolitan area such as Orange County. However, reports of activities such as the International Sports Day appeared in the major local papers and one article about the telecommunications project appeared in a national magazine. There were also stories about network school projects in local newspapers. Coverage of this kind was always noticed by teachers and was very much worth the time invested in trying to get it.

Of some value in terms of legitimation, although to a lesser extent, was CHI's connection to what can loosely be called a "national network" of global educators. CHI was a charter member of the Western International Studies Consortium (WISC) which also included the Center for Public Education in International Affairs (CPEIA) at the University of Southern California, the Outreach Studies Centers Program at the University of California at Los Angeles, the Immaculate Heart Center (IHC), and the Constitutional Rights Foundation (CRF). WISC had its own global education project, partially funded by the Danforth Foundation, and it was one of the original six state-funded global education centers of the California International Studies Project (CISP) which had its management center at Stanford University. While it was sometimes difficult to explain all of those affiliations to network teachers and others, the fact that they existed was often seen as impressive and, thus, in a way, legitimating.

Knowledge Flow

We have mentioned that while the school was seen as the unit upon which to focus change efforts, it was critical to have an outside agency which was responsible for bringing new knowledge to the school.

Materials Visits

A number of knowledge-transfer strategies were employed. The most straightforward involved CHI staff going to the schools both to deliver instructional materials and talk informally with staff members, and to gather data about what was happening there to globalize the curricula. A variety of methods were used to make these visits as effective as possible. Sometimes materials were selected from the CHI library and taken to a school to be displayed. This procedure became more effective after CHI staff had the opportunity to learn what topics individual teachers found interesting. On some days, CHI staff members went to a school in the morning, set up their display in the teachers' lounge, and stayed through lunch hour. At other times, they went after school. In the elementary schools, of course, teachers had no time during the day to interact with CHI staff so it was important to use noontime or time after school. At the secondary schools, teachers could be visited during planning periods. The use of the teachers' lounge was more effective at some schools than at others. Most teachers at North High School, for example, never used the teachers' lounge because it was the place for smokers and because the norm was for departments to pretty much stay to themselves in their own "houses." The point is that informal visits were a good vehicle for bringing global education knowledge to the schools, but they had to be planned according to the norms and procedures of the individual schools. One generalization was developed, however. CHI staff members found it more productive to conduct these visits in pairs. They found the pooling of their observations both in a strategic and a research sense to be of great value.

Newsletter

The CHI newsletter, *Network News,* also was a fairly successful vehicle for transferring global education knowledge to members of the network. It was distributed to all teachers in the eleven schools four times per year except during year four, when there were only three issues. Each issue contained several regular features. There was always a calendar of events which included upcoming CHI activities plus those of other global education or related organizations. This included such things as programs put on by peace groups such as Educators for Social Responsibility and Beyond War, environmental groups such as the Sierra Club or Tree People, United Nations Association activities, activities sponsored by other WISC or CISP organizations and special programs such as World Vision programs and the Peace Child touring group, featuring performances by children from both the United States and the Soviet Union.

Network News also featured stories, most often written by network teachers, about global education activities in the eleven schools. New library acquisitions were described and each issue contained one curriculum outline or classroom lesson plan. There was always an editorial on some relevant topic. Editorials often attempted to give network members some sense of what was happening nationally with regard to global education.

A conscious effort was made to keep the newsletter from becoming too slick. It was done on a Macintosh and then printed.

There were always a few pictures featuring teachers and administrators involved in network activity. By the fourth year of the project (1989), CHI was distributing approximately eight hundred copies of *Network News*. These went to readers *outside of the network* and throughout the nation as well as to each faculty member in the eleven schools. Feedback on *Network News* was quite positive both from network members and from other people. Positive comments were made about both the contents and the simple style.

Workshops

It has been noted that network workshops were planned around topics identified by teachers as those which were of interest to them. The number of participants was limited to between thirty and thirty-five, divided more or less equally between the eleven schools. Principals were responsible for identifying participants, substitute time was provided by districts (a variety of procedures were used for this), and it was suggested that as many different people as possible be selected to attend different workshops. A variety of consultants were utilized: some from Chapman, some from WISC, some from other agencies. The format followed for the 8:00-3:00 workshops usually included a presentation by the consultant, small group discussion-activity with follow-up from the consultant (often involving network teachers as small group leaders/presenters), a nice lunch, and some type of topic-related sharing among participants. Each workshop was evaluated by participants. Evaluations were generally quite positive for these workshops, and the teacher sharing segments were particularly appreciated.

Special Projects

There were some special projects sponsored by CHI. The International Sports Day involved seventh grades from the four middle schools and Buena Vista School (K-8). This was a very successful project. Students and teachers were very pleased with it. It involved many people beyond the physical education teachers and it provided very good public relations for the schools as well as for CHI.

There were telecommunications projects at four schools: Caldwell Elementary, Birmingham and Pacifica Middle Schools, and North High School. These projects met with varying degrees of success. Problems included a lack of technical knowledge on the part of both school personnel and CHI staff members, difficulties with hardware, and the simple press of time. The idea for this project actually came from staff members at Caldwell. The first principal there and two of the upper grade teachers were very much involved with computers. When CHI arrived on the scene in 1985, they were in the process of developing an electronic community bulletin board. Eventually, the separate notion of setting up communication with classrooms in another country took root. Initially, activities included letter exchanges between classrooms at Caldwell and several schools in the Sydney, Australia area. The CHI staff and its technology consultant attempted to encourage the development of an expanded curriculum. For example, it was suggested that students communicate with each other in order to build data banks for planning trips to each others' countries or that they share information about the recent celebrations of the U.S. Constitution bicentennial and Australia's bicentennial as a means of comparing the constitutions and governmental structures of two western democracies. To CHI the computer was only a means to an end. However, the Caldwell teachers did not see it that way. Despite a great deal of publicity given to the project, it never did grow much beyond the pen pal level.

The foreign language department at North High did make connections with an international school in Bogota, Columbia, through CHI, and they were also part of the GEMNET computer network. At this writing, the two middle schools are still attempting to get their projects off the ground. Despite the limited success of this CHI project, it seems quite clear that computer linkages have tremendous potential for increasing student global awareness. It should be noted, too, that it is not an expensive proposition. Most schools these days have computers. A modem is not very costly nor is the necessary bit of telephone time. Other forms of technology (e.g., video, faxing, satellite communication), while they were not used in the CHI project, seem to hold promise as vehicles for globalizing the curriculum, also.

The "Orange County in the World" project, modeled after the "Columbus in the World" project (Alger, 1974), was also a success. Carried out during 1987 and again in 1988, it involved approximately twelve teachers from several schools (all levels) each year. During 1987, it was led by a Chapman faculty member who had worked with the original project at Ohio State. In the second year, three teachers who had been involved in the first year provided the leadership. Teachers had their classes do such things as study the ethnic grocery stores, ethnic newspapers, and multinational corporations in the area. Some of the very youngest children did family tree studies.

Release time was provided for participating teachers and they also received small stipends for working a few Saturdays. The Saturday stipend idea seemed to be quite popular because (1) substitute teachers were becoming quite scarce in some school districts and (2) many teachers do not wish to spend much time away from their classes.

There were other special projects. A group of ESL teachers came together one summer to share and develop new instructional materials with a global perspective. Another small group of ESL teachers from one school with a large Hispanic student population was brought together to develop an American culture unit for newly arrived immigrants. Unfortunately, this project did not really go very far. It was determined through an informal survey of state departments of education, however, that there is a real need for such a unit and for good teaching materials in this area of interest.

During the second, third, and fourth years of the project, once school interests were determined, CHI did provide some consultants directly to schools. George Otero, for example, made presentations on cross-cultural awareness at all network schools except University Elementary. Two visiting Australians went to Caldwell Elementary (where the Australian telecommunications project was); an expert on immigrant experiences presented at both South and Central High Schools, a futurist spoke at North High, and a person who had travelled in then-Soviet-occupied Afghanistan visited classes at South High. In many instances, an attempt was made to utilize each consultant in several schools as well as at some function at Chapman College.

The network, itself, served to promote knowledge flow, albeit probably not as much as it could have. As indicated, teachers shared ideas and experiences at network workshops and during participation in special project meetings (e.g., "Orange County in the World"). Teachers shared ideas in the newsletter. Principals met infrequently and shared. We encouraged cross-school visits but there were only a handful of these. Certainly, the lack of time discussed in chapter 5 had something to do with this, but, on the other hand, CHI could have done more to encourage broader interaction within the network.

Finally, CHI made it a point to use data feedback as an intervention and knowledge flow strategy. That is, data about participants own behavior was collected through observation or through interview and was then fed back to them. This was then discussed both for its correctness and for its implications. The process was carried out individually and in groups, at times at whole-faculty meetings.

Resource Generation

Most of the special resources devoted to the global education project were provided by CHI. School districts did contribute ten to fifteen days of release time per network school per year for teacher attendance at workshops, school visits, planning sessions, and the like. In some cases, district funds were used, in others school budgets were charged. In a few cases, special state funds were available for staff in-service. However, by the end of the project in 1989, most of those state funds had disappeared.

The most important resource provided to network members was the assistance of CHI staff members. For the entire four years, two full-time professional staff people (Ida Urso for the entire time, Joy Phillipsen for the first two years, and Kathy O'Neil for the second two years) plus ourselves as part-time staff (we were also employed full-time in the education department at Chapman College) were available to the teachers in the eleven schools. In addition, there was a half-time librarian for most of the life of the project (Janine Chapman) and there were always one or two graduate students who worked for CHI in a variety of capacities (Paul Whitlock, Encarnita Arambulo, Connie Doti, Bea Molfetta, Stacy Walkon, and Radhika Iyengar). Staff members organized network activities, visited schools with materials and ideas, occasionally made presentations on relevant topics, and constantly gathered data using procedures described in chapter 2.

The CHI library was also a major resource provided for teachers. A basic global education collection was put together in 1985 and added to over the life of the project, based upon the expressed interests of network teachers and upon CHI staff reviews of pertinent materials in the field. A major collection of free and inexpensive materials was developed and some audio-visual materials were also purchased. By 1989, there were well over a thousand items catalogued and available in the CHI library. Network teachers could check such materials out and keep them for two weeks or longer if needed. Other teachers in the area could use materials in the CHI center and anyone could use the duplicating machine there to reproduce single copies of curriculum materials, lesson plans, or even teaching units.

In 1986, CHI developed a directory of free and inexpensive resources in the greater Los Angeles–Orange County area to distribute to network schools and make available at cost to other schools in the area. This directory contained the names and addresses of approximately two hundred organizations and individuals who had materials, would make presentations, and the like. Each entry consisted of name, address, cost (if any), and brief description of material or service. Permission was received from appropriate sources before entries were made.

It already has been pointed out that CHI paid for substitute time for teachers involved in special projects such as "Orange County in the World" and for consultants for network and school-based workshops. The one other critical resource provided by CHI to faculty members was the minigrant program. Over the four-year period, sixty-five grants worth a total of $43,926 were given. The projects which were funded involved 142 teachers and every one of the eleven schools was represented. The number of grants awarded ranged from two at University and La Puente Elementary Schools to ten at Caldwell Elementary. In the first year, CHI staff selected grant recipients. In subsequent years, a panel of judges was selected from the previous year's grantees. Requirements for grant applications were kept quite simple as were those for final reporting (see Appendix D for a copy of the grant application). Descriptions of actual grant projects can be found in chapters 4 and 6.

In the end-of-project reflective questionnaire, teachers were asked to rate CHI activities from outstanding to poor using a five-point scale. Overall, minigrants, library materials, and theme workshops were all rated highly. In those schools where consultants had visited and made presentations, those also received positive responses. At the middle schools, there was quite a favorable response to International Sports Day. That was particularly true at Mesa Junior High where, in addition to the network event, they held their own international sports day for all students. Very few people rated any activity as "poor" or "not very good." Interestingly, only five teachers at (South High School) gave a negative rating to *presentations at school.* The reader will remember that this is where there had been some upset over a consultant's comment about CIA activity in Central America.

The resource question is a serious one for the global education movement. Nationally, many global education projects are facing cutbacks or are even disbanding because extramural funds are no longer available. As of this writing, there does not appear to be much chance of significant funding from government sources, either. The CHI project would not have accomplished what it did without money to invest in people, time, and materials. Part of the answer to the question, "What does it take to globalize the curriculum of a school?" is financial support, but the amount of financial support needed is bound to vary from project to project. Likewise, the resources may already be available and what is required is a resetting of priorities. In that case the question becomes, "Is global education an important enough movement to merit the provision of scarce resources to its growth?" We would answer yes. In fact, we would argue that it is imperative. Nevertheless, one other fact about resources is made clear by the CHI study: money alone is not what is needed. An understanding of how schools do and do not change is even more important.

Team Focusing

Team planning, teaching, and evaluating can be a very productive way of organizing for teaching. Many global education projects around the country have focused upon the development of global education teams at local school sites. Many have been successful, but in some cases team focusing has caused problems (K. Tye, 1990, pp. 134–35). There are two potential problems with teaming which can be avoided if people take appropriate precautions.

First, it cannot be assumed that people can work together simply because they have a common interest, in this case global education. Culturally, Americans are highly individualistic and there is no reason to assume that things should be different in our schools and among our teachers. Teacher isolation has always been the norm in our schools because we have created structures to promote it. Teaching is done, by and large, in separate classrooms by teachers who are alone. Subjects in our secondary schools are separated one from another and sometimes are even located in their own special "houses." Many curriculum innovations in schools have foundered, not because the curriculum was bad itself, but because people were expected to work together, to team, and they just didn't know how. Teaming is a learned skill.

Also, when a particular team in a school is identified as having *ownership* of a particular innovation, other members of a faculty may feel that they need not or should not become involved with it. Earlier in this chapter, the almost exemplary beginning of a global education project at Mesa Junior High was described. It was pointed out that a seventh grade core group was eager and ready to work with CHI to globalize their curriculum. It was also noted that some unexpected problems developed. Those problems had to do with team focusing.

During the second year of the project, CHI staff began to pick up some messages from Mesa that, despite all the good things happening there, not everything was right. Some teachers who were not part of the core indicated that they felt left out and that all resources were going to this group. One CHI staff member who was thought to have a good relationship with the Mesa principal met with him to discuss the problem. Together they designed a small study. A sample of teachers, including active participants and teachers who had not yet participated, was identified. They were interviewed and data were analyzed and given back to the staff at a special, voluntary meeting. What was found was that the project *was* perceived as being channeled by the principal through the core group. The people in the seventh-grade core group—the key teachers referred to earlier—were well liked and respected but there was some resentment and a few people felt shut out. For their part, the core group did acknowledge getting a lot of satisfaction from their involvement, and they saw that it would be helpful if they would reach out to include their colleagues. At a faculty feedback session a pledge was made to encourage broader participation.

Professionalization

We are not sure that it is appropriate to discuss the issue of professionalization as a structural property of global education or, indeed, of education. However, where it is discussed is not the issue. The fact is that this topic is of critical importance to our schools.

Nationally, we have moved so far into neoscientific and pragmatic ways of thinking about our schools and the people who work in them that we have almost lost sight of why we have schools. In chapter 1, in a discussion of the assumptions which undergirded this project, a case was made for viewing the current accountability movement as, at best, meaningless, and, at worst, detrimental to schooling. Later it was pointed out that teachers took some time to trust us because they were so used to being used and/or misled by the superordinate system. Time and again, teachers remarked on how important it was to them that, in the CHI project, they were treated as professionals with all of the respect which that entailed.

Just how far the deprofessionalization of teachers has gone is evidenced by the recent school-based management movement. This movement is hailed as one which will give authority to teachers and parents at the site level. This change of authority is to occur while at the same time state-mandated testing and state-mandated curriculum are kept in place. The incongruity of these conflicting positions seems to escape most people. Further, and more insidious, perhaps, is the accompanying rhetoric about "empowering" teachers. At best this is a form of *malefic generosity*, wherein politicians and members of the superordinate system behave as if it is somehow *their* role to give (and take away) the professionalism of teachers (Benham, 1979). What would seem more appropriate and more productive in the long run is a model more closely akin to that of the medical profession. In a hospital, the administrator's role is to respect the professional expertise of the doctors and to facilitate their work.

Institutional Responses

Culture of the School

Obviously, many factors contribute to the growth in a school of something such as global education. Clear initial expectations, supportive leadership, linkages to knowledge and sufficient resources are all examples of such factors. However, from the experiences gained in the CHI project, it would seem that the major determining factor is what has come to be called the "culture" of the school (Sarason, 1982). That culture is made up of the norms and expectations which ultimately define how people behave.

This is a complex concept which we will deal with in some depth in chapter 6, where the special qualities of the network schools will be considered. At this point, it is adequate to point out that each school did have its own unique culture. For example, in the reflective end-of-project questionnaire, people were asked to respond on a six-point agree/disagree Likert scale to a number of statements about the culture of the school, and the responses from school to school varied considerably. When asked to respond to the statement "Staff members are proud to be working here," the range of agreement was from 100 percent at Caldwell Elementary and Mesa Junior High (at Caldwell, 83 percent *strongly* agreed) to a low of 63 percent at University Elementary (29 percent strongly *disagreed*). Also at Caldwell, 100 percent of the staff agreed with the statement, "Information is shared between teachers from different departments, teams, or grade levels." At South High School, by contrast, 42 percent disagreed with that statement. There were school-to-school differences on other culture items as well; these will be explored later. At this point, it is important to note that such differences must be taken into account because they impinge upon efforts to globalize the curriculum of a school or to otherwise bring about some kind of curriculum change. To ignore such variables is to doom any change effort to failure.

To carry this point just a bit farther, we can examine responses to our end-of-project interviews. We asked the question, "Has anyone discouraged you from participating in CHI activities?" At Caldwell Elementary, everyone who was interviewed said no. At some other schools there were responses such as:

> "I've heard more discouraging remarks from the perpetual cynics, but those remarks aren't directed against CHI, specifically."

> "No, but there are people who don't want to do anything else other than their day-to-day work."

> "Yes.... No principal has ever run this school. The principal is run out if he opposes the old-time teachers who are the powers-that-be on the faculty. They make up over fifty percent of the faculty."

Resistance to Change

In several of the network schools, as is the case in many places where there is an attempt to create new programs, there were teachers who were seen by the more active participants as being resistant to *change*, not just to global education. CHI took the position that it was not that they were resistant, but, rather, that they were in favor of that which was considered traditional and more generally practiced. The view was that resistance is not, per se, a bad thing and that, in fact, people often had good reasons for being skeptical (Eicholz, 1963). It was thought to be CHI's responsibility to find out the reasons for resistance so that specific strategies could be designed to better convince individuals about the merits of global education. This theme of resistance by individuals will be dealt with more fully in the next chapter.

Change Strategies

From the perspective of organization development, educational change strategies can be classified into four general categories (Harvey and Brown, 1988). Probably the most commonly observed strategies are those which can be labelled "political." These have to do with setting policy, always involve the accumulation and use of authority and power, and, almost inevitably, lead to conflict. In schooling today, the most common manifestation of political strategies is the mandating of curriculum, administrative arrangements, use of time, and the like by state authorities. This "accountability press" upon network schools was alluded to earlier. Also as was pointed out earlier, such strategies by themselves do not seem actually to change basic classroom practice, particularly given the "loosely coupled" nature of the educational system (Weick, 1976).

CHI did use political strategies in that superintendents and principals were first enlisted for their support. Also, it did so by positioning itself with a number of legitimatizing groups and networks. However, it was never in a position—nor did it seek—to *tell* people what to do. Many educators have become used to being told what to do and some even rely on being directed, more or less. Responses by teachers to formal and informal interviewing suggested that some felt that there would have been more participation if people *had* been "told what to do" and/or given detailed lesson plans. That was not the dominant view, however.

There are also a lot of *technical* change strategies. These have to do with altering the technology of the field. Most people would think immediately of the introduction of computers and other teaching machines. That is correct, but more common is any form of in-service or staff development wherein people are given new skills with the intent that they will do their jobs better. Much, if not most, of what happened in the CHI project could be called technical. The provision of consultants, workshops, and materials all fell into this category. As is the case with political strategies, these are not enough, by themselves, to create significant change at the school level.

Structural change strategies are the ones to which educators seem to be the most attracted. Perhaps that is because they appear to be easier to carry out. However, as with other kinds of change strategies, without accompanying changes in behavior, they tend not to be very productive. Changing time schedules, reorganizing line and staff relationships, reconfiguring who works with whom, changing grade level patterns (e.g., K–8 to K–5, 6–8), and redistributing resources are kinds of structural changes. The formation of interdisciplinary programs was an example of such a strategy in the CHI project. The reader will recall that such formation was encouraged through the giving of small grants to groups of teachers representing two or more subject areas.

What is called for, in addition to political, technical and/or structural changes is what organization development (OD) people refer to as "behavioral" change. This means that people actually learn to behave in different ways toward each other: administrators to teachers, teachers to teachers, teachers to students, and so on. Such things as clear communication, shared leadership and decision-making, healthy conflict resolution, and thoughtful problem-solving are the targets of behavioral change strategies and OD people, who, after assessing a situation, use either training or data-feedback as their means.

Behavioral training is only effective when leadership in an organization recognizes the need for and desirablility of it. No principals in the network ever suggested that such training was needed or desired although there were schools where it might have been of value. As stated earlier, data-feedback was a strategy used frequently by CHI, and, at times, it was directed at the kinds of behaviors under discussion.

Conclusion

It will be some time before the global education movement reaches all or even most schools in the United States. It is true that the conditions exist in the world that make it desirable and inevitable, but it is also true that the current sociopolitical context of schooling in the United States is not only *not* totally supportive but, in many ways, is hostile to it.

Throughout the CHI project, attention was paid to such important change processes as trust-building, legitimation, the bringing of new knowledge about global education to the school, and the setting of appropriate and reasonable expectations. In addition, culture differences at each school were taken into account, albeit sometimes after the fact. A variety of change strategies were employed with, of course, varying degrees of success. All of this has been described in this chapter.

One thing which is missing in this story so far is a clarification of what global education meant originally or came to mean ultimately to the participants. It is quite all right to suggest that people's behavior should be changed in one way or another. It is unrealistic, however, to expect such change until people have some understanding of what they are changing to and/or from. In chapter 4, we will turn to the issue of meaning: what global education came to *mean* to the faculty members in the eleven CHI network schools and how they behaved in light of their perceptions of those meanings.

References

Alger, C. F., *Your City in the World/The World in Your City: Discover the International Activities and Foreign Policies of People, Groups, and Organizations in Your Community* (Columbus, Ohio: The Mershon Center, Ohio State University, 1974).

Anderson, L., "A Rationale for Global Education," in K. Tye, ed., *Global Education: From Thought to Action* (Alexandria, Va.: ASCD, 1991).

Association for Supervision and Curriculum Development, *Global Education: From Thought to Action,* K. Tye, ed. (Alexandria, Va.: ASCD, 1991).

Benham, B. J., "None so Holy as the Recently Converted: Malefic Generosity and Multi-Cultural Education," *Educational Studies* 9, (2) (Summer 1978):125–31.

Boyte, H. C., *The Backyard Revolution: Understanding the New Citizen Movement* (Philadelphia: Temple University Press, 1980).

Caporaso, J. A., and J. H. Mittelman, "The Assault on Global Education," *PS: Political Science and Politics* (Winter 1988):36–44.

Cunningham, G., "Blowing the Whistle on Global Education," unpublished report U.S. Department of Education, Region VII, 1986.

Eicholz, G. C. "Why Do Teachers Reject Change?" *Theory into Practice 2* (December 1963):264–68.

Gusfield, J. R., *Protest, Reform, and Revolt: A Reader in Social Movements* (New York: John Wiley & Sons, Inc., 1970).

Hanvey, R. G., *An Attainable Global Perspective* (Denver: Center for Teaching International Relations, 1976).

Harvey, D. F., and D. R. Brown, *An Experiential Approach to Organization Development*, 3d ed., (Englewood Cliffs, N.J.: Prentice-Hall, Inc., 1988).

Hursch, H., "CTIR under Fire," *University of Denver Faculty Forum* 1(1) (April 1987).

Kniep, W. M., "Global Education as School Reform," *Educational Leadership* 47(1) (September 1987):43–45.

Lamy, S. L., "Worldviews Analysis of International Issues," in *Contending Perspectives* (Boulder, Col.: Lynne Rienner Publishers, 1988), pp. 1–25.

———, "A Conflict of Images: The Controversy over Global Education in U.S. Schools," in K. Tye, ed., *Global Education: From Thought to Action* (Alexandria, Va.: ASCD, 1991).

Sarason, S., *The Culture of the School and the Problem of Change* (Boston: Allyn and Bacon, Inc., 1982).

Schlafly, P., "What Is Wrong with Global Education?" *St. Louis Democrat* (March 6, 1986).

Sherif, M., and W. C. Sherif, eds., *Attitude, Ego-Divolvement, and Change* (New York: John Wiley & Sons, 1967).

Tye, K., *Global Education: School-Based Strategies* (Orange, Cal.: Interdependence Press, 1990).

Weick, K. E., "Educational Organizations as Loosely Coupled Systems," *Administrative Science Quarterly* 21 (1) (1976): 1–19.

4

MEANING AND ACTIVITY

The reader will remember that the theoretical orientation which undergirds the study described in this volume was identified as symbolic interaction. In chapter 2, the basic assumptions of this orientation were identified and exemplified in terms of the study. These are the assumptions, or "root images," set forth originally by Herbert Blumer (1969):

1. human beings act toward things on the basis of the meanings those things have for them;

2. these meanings are derived from the social interactions that a person has with other people;

3. these meanings are continually modified through an interpretive process.

In this chapter, selected data from the CHI study will be analyzed in light of these assumptions. This analysis will be carried out using three different perspectives: definition, activity, and engagement/ resistance.

Defining Global Education

As has been pointed out, global education is a value-laden construct which means different things to different people, and toward which people respond based upon those various meanings. Over the past twenty years, a great deal of energy has been invested in trying to define global education. Frequently, at gatherings of people interested in the field, this has been a favorite activity. This is understandable because in attendance at such gatherings there usually has been a mixture of social studies educators, international studies scholars, social psychologists, educational policy makers, teacher educators, and so forth. The bringing together of people with such varied perspectives always leads to healthy and thought-provoking discussion. It does not always lead to agreement, particularly with regard to something as volatile as the definition of global education.

In the CHI project, because of a belief that the field is an emerging one and because there was a wish to study the relationship between activity in the schools and the meaning given to global education, a conscious effort was made to avoid the imposition upon participants of a narrow definition of the field.

Not everyone agrees with this position. Duggan and Thorpe (1986), for example, contend that definitions of global education are crucial to its integration into the K–12 curriculum. They base this belief on their own development of two global education case studies and they also cite Fullan (1982), who concurs. Fullan maintains that definitions determine purpose and content, that they affect decisions made by educational policy makers, and that studies of educational change, in general, have shown that both advocates and recipients of any innovation must have a shared understanding of that innovation.

At the beginning of the CHI project, in initial visits to schools, all faculty members were given a handout containing a summary of Robert Hanvey's (1976) definition which suggests five interdisciplinary dimensions of global education:

Perspective consciousness: an awareness of and appreciation for other images of the world, and recognition that others have views of the world that are profoundly different from one's own.

State-of-the-planet awareness: an in-depth understanding of prevailing global issues, events, and conditions.

Cross-cultural awareness: a general understanding of the defining characteristics of world cultures with an emphasis on understanding similarities and differences.

Knowledge of global dynamics: a familiarity with the nature of systems and an introduction to the complex international system in which state and nonstate actors are linked in patterns of interdependence and dependence in a variety of issue areas; consciousness of global change.

Awareness of human choices: a review of strategies for action on issues in local, national, and international settings.

This is a very general definition which did not call for the reshaping of the world and, thus, seemed to allay the fears of some of those people who suspected that the project might have political motives which could be troublesome. Also, it was so general that it did not preclude any of the varied meanings given to global education by participants from the network schools and districts. It was not until the third year of the project that, influenced by experience with the network, a new and more specific definition was developed by CHI and disseminated to network faculties.

> Global education involves (l) the study of problems and issues which cut across national boundaries, and the interconnectedness of cultural, environmental, economic, political, and technological systems, and (2) the cultivation of cross-cultural understanding, which includes development of the skill of "perspective-taking"— that is, being able to see life from someone else's point of view. Global perspectives are important at every grade level, in every curricular subject area, and for all children and adults.

Early in the project, rather than focusing on definition, we moved rather quickly to help people decide upon and carry out *activity* based upon whatever meaning global education had for them. This focus upon activity was consistent with both the theoretical framework and the research plan chosen for the project. At most schools, it was possible to get some idea of what people thought global education meant through the administration of a brief interest survey at the first faculty meeting. It consisted of four questions, and the responses to two of these are relevant to this discussion.

The first question was, "From information you have gathered on your own, and from what the Center for Human Interdependence (CHI) has shared with you, which ideas regarding global education would you like to pursue with your students?" This query came at the end of the meeting at ten of the eleven schools following the presentation of (l) a rationale for global studies, (2) the Hanvey framework, (3) what CHI had to offer, and (4) expectations for those who wished to participate (see chapters 1 and 3). At Pacifica Middle School, the question was asked of department chairs only and at Mesa Junior High the project had been channeled through the seventh-grade core group.

There were 183 responses to the question from approximately one-third of the network faculty members. Each person was allowed to list as many topics as he or she wished. Forty-six different topics were listed, although many were related and it was difficult to know just what individuals had in mind in some instances. By and large, these initial choices of topics were general in nature, reflected subject matter interests and were more varied at the secondary level, and showed an interest across several schools in cross-cultural awareness and understanding. The largest number of responses (27) had to do with the development of such understanding at the local school level and the next largest number (22) referred to studies of cultures in other areas of the world (see Table 4.1). Further analysis of these data is not necessary. The point is, the initial meaning given to the concept of global education varied widely among network faculty members. In fact, it was obvious that many people simply gave back key terms they had picked up from the presentations by CHI staff. Others stated their own interests, global or not. A small number gave the task serious thought and attempted to begin the journey of sorting out meanings.

Only fifty-seven faculty members in initial meetings at seven schools responded to the following request, "Please share some of the ways you are presently helping students develop a better understanding of global issues and concepts." Examples of these respons-

**Table 4.1: Global education topics initially suggested
by network faculty members.**

Topic	Number of responses	Number of schools
Cross cultural understanding	27	7
Culture studies (pen pals, customs, folk dance, clothing, etc.)	22	5
World hunger, food	10	6
Global economics	9	7
War and peace	8	7
Self-esteem	7	2

Table 4.1: Global education topics (cont.).

Topic	Number of responses	Number of schools
Human rights	6	4
Technology	6	4
Handicapped awareness	6	3
Human choice	6	3
Political awareness	5	5
Cooperative learning	5	2
Disease prevention, health	4	3
Teach students that they can make a difference	4	3
Global geography	4	2
Endangered species	3	2
Environment	3	2
Human migration, refugees	3	2
International job market	3	2
Math teaching methods	3	2
Natural resources, energy	3	2
Perspective consciousness	3	2
Population	3	2
Terrorism	3	2
Conflict resolution	2	2
World religions	2	2
Communications systems	2	1
Teaching controversial issues	2	1
Use of telecommunications	2	1
Values clarification	2	1
Advancement of science	1	1
Application within state literature framework	1	1
Application within state science framework	1	1
Futures	1	1
Global poverty	1	1
Human history	1	1
Interrelatedness of time and events	1	1
Japan and Africa	1	1
Materials in Spanish	1	1
Materials for ESL students	1	1
Overcoming ethnocentrism	1	1
Pollution	1	1
Third world development	1	1
United Nations and other international organizations	1	1
World literature	1	1

es are given in Table 4.2. These are representative responses and seem to indicate that at the beginning of this project very few people had an understanding of what global education was and an even smaller number did anything much to globalize their curricula. Many of the responses to this request had to do with cross-cultural understanding at the local school level, some were at the level of being concerned with current events, and a large number had to do with "cultural" understandings—foods, clothing, customs, etc. Except for the response from the MUN teacher, there were no examples of international studies and no one spoke of "problems or issues which cut across national boundaries."

**Table 4.2: Global education activities already in use
by network faculty members.**

Elementary Schools

1. Current events, social studies curriculum, ecology day, international food day, group project work, philharmonic music program, artists from around the world.

2. I do a unit based on "Unlocking your potential" to help students become aware of how to treat others, increase their own effectiveness and set goals.

3. I am always stressing to my students the network of relationships that exist when lecturing or discussing global events and issues. However, I'm sure there is more I can do to make this a part of my students' thinking process, thus my interest in this program.

4. Studying four countries: Japan, Peru, Egypt, France. We compare and contrast the land, social groups, art, and religions of each.

5. Folk tales and literature: story time, cultures and customs, slides.

6. News sharing and discussions.

7. "We all live together" theme.

8. "It's a Small World" unit (children of the world), we take a "trip" around the world, we have passports and suitcases, we eat food from the various countries, we do art projects for each country.

9. I have traveled to and have slides from: a) Mexico, Guatemala, Peru, Bolivia, and Ecuador—emphasis on archeology and anthropology, pre-Columbian Indians; b) Egypt; c) Greece—emphasis on classical history; Europe; e) Japan (have a penpal of thirty years). I have units on Japan and Africa with an emphasis on cross-cultural awareness and I have slides of Easter in Guatemala with an emphasis on assimilation of cultural beliefs.

Secondary Schools

1. We do discuss these ideas (energy, arms race, natural resources, mathematical methods and ecology) in biology and chemistry and more ways of incorporating them into my lesson plans would be helpful.

2. Sometimes we read the paper or watch the news; we have frequent classroom discussions of current events; we relate older cultural phenomena to modern phenomena.

3. Business systems: comparing different economic systems: free enterprise, socialism, communism.

4. Sponsoring a model United Nations (MUN) in which we deal with many different issues from the point of view of many different countries and try to learn to compromise. The MUN Club is planning an intercultural event on campus to benefit famine relief.

5. Through literature, I am trying to get kids to identify the cultural self—to see how culture determines values and perspectives and how different societies affect those people living in them. We look at dominant cultures and their influence on subcultures and vice-versa.

6. Discussion of various cultural attitudes and values; comparison of folklore tales and legends; sharing foods from ethnic backgrounds relating to cultures studied in literature.

7. Whenever appropriate I share experiences my ESL students have had with regular English classes. I try to stress the similarity of all people. I attempt to raise the awareness level of American students. I also hope by my own example to model dignity and respect for all cultures and people.

8. I use a cross-cultural (game) simulation in the Adult Living course. This works well for me. I'm a world traveler: Europe, Africa, South and Central America, Indonesia, Asia, Singapore, Mexico, Canada, Japan, Egypt, Turkey, Israel, Yugoslavia, and Hungary. I include energy conservation I've seen throuot the world that I can share with the Foods classes during our energy unit.

Four years later, in the end-of-project questionnaire, teachers were asked to respond on a six-point agree/disagree scale to the statement, "It is clear to me what global education is." They could also respond, "I don't know" and seven percent chose to do so. Eighty-one percent agreed with the statement, with twenty-eight percent agreeing strongly. Twelve percent disagreed. Most teachers felt that they had some idea of what global education was, despite an annual teacher turnover of about fifteen percent. The reader is reminded that over ninety percent of the teachers in the eleven network schools responded to this questionnaire in 1989, year 4 of the the project.

In the same questionnaire, teachers responded to an open-ended item, "What does the term *global education* mean to you?" It was at the end of the questionnaire and time was short at some schools. Consequently, nearly one-third of the faculty members did not complete this one item. Of the two-thirds who *did,* a small number did mention "learning about problems and issues that cut across national boundaries and about the interconnectedness of systems." Many spoke of interdependence or of understanding the cultures of others. One teacher said it was a Marxist threat and two others suggested that it had to do with one-worldism, but most teachers gave simple, straightforward, and meaningful responses. Here are some examples:

> Relating education to global issues, current events, and worldwide concerns in an interdisciplinary approach.

> Understanding the social and economic interdependence of all the countries with each other. We, the U.S., are no longer the determiner of world policy but a part of it.

> Increasing our awareness of the interconnections between all parts of the world ecologically, culturally, historically, and economically.

> Teaching awareness about universal basic themes.

> We live in a global village—every American must be cognizant of the economic, social, and political interdependence of the world.

> A realization that Americans are a part of a world community and that global issues (poverty, war, etc.) affect all people. An understanding of diverse cultures and languages is essential in creating global awareness.

> An integrated perspective and understanding of major political, economic, and cultural events in any part of the world, or the personal need to understand such events; motivating students to feel this way.

> Making students aware of the interaction among countries and how this interaction affects political and economic decisions in America. It is also an exploration of the social interaction among countries.

We are all affected by what happens in the world. Improved technology makes the world a giant community. We should all be concerned about what happens everywhere.

Global education means bringing an awareness of global problems and situations (cultures, politics, etc.) to my students. Most of my students have no knowledge of world geography.

These responses demonstrate a significant increase in sophistication about the meaning of global education. While each definition was personal to the respondent, most showed an understanding of the systemic nature of today's world and a number also combined systems awareness with the idea of perspective-taking.

It would be great if it could be said that all or even a majority of faculty members responded to this item in this fashion. Unfortunately, that was not the case. There were still a number of "soft" answers (e.g., "awareness of the planet as one world," "integration of the world into everyday classes"). There were still many teachers who saw global education only as the development of cross-cultural awareness at the local school site level. Finally, there was still a handful of people who believed that global education was a subversive plot. The major point is, however, that a significant number were able to clearly articulate an accurate meaning for global education as a result of being involved in various forms of *activity*. Let us look, now, at the effect of that meaning in the schools and classrooms in the network.

Activity Reveals and Creates Meaning

Network-wide activities such as the delivery of instructional materials to the schools, theme workshops, newsletters, minigrants, and so forth were described in chapters 1 and 3. These activities were carried on throughout the four-year life of the project, and for a significant number of participants they contributed to the development of meaning for global education and to subsequent activity (curriculum, instruction, and personal behavior) in their classrooms.

At the beginning of the second year of the project, CHI consciously added a new element to its intervention strategy. While it continued network activity, it began to emphasize school-centered programs and projects. Thus, on early release days or at regular faculty meetings, staff development activities were planned jointly by

CHI staff and school principals and teachers. Both the planning procedures and the actual formats for such events varied from school to school depending upon needs, time available, principal style, and other factors. The content also varied depending upon the perceived needs and wishes of faculty members.

Cross-cultural awareness was, by far, the most popular topic. As has already been indicated, George Otero, codirector of Las Palomas de Taos in New Mexico, was a very popular consultant who visited ten of the eleven network schools. He made two presentations to faculty members at Buena Vista School and the principal there invited principals from two other district schools not in the CHI network to attend. He worked directly with students at North High, Mesa Junior High, and Caldwell Elementary. At Central High he was the keynote speaker at a half-day in-service. Subsequent to the main presentation at Central, Otero, CHI staff members, and selected teachers conducted small group workshops for the entire faculty. The district superintendent attended, adding support. At La Puente Elementary, University Elementary, Birmingham Junior High, Columbus Middle School and Pacifica Middle School, Otero spoke at specially called faculty meetings.

There was a variety of other speakers and topics, including working with refugee students, futures, Afghanistan, and Australia. Some of these were for full faculties, others were for selected classes working on specific projects, and some involved both students and faculty.

Shiman and Conrad (1977) speak of the necessity of moving from global awareness to an understanding of global realities to action on behalf of global concepts. This paradigm closely parallels the learning-curve type model that Havelock (1971) has developed regarding the adoption of educational innovation and is relevant to this discussion of teacher activity in network schools. Awareness and understanding of global education ideas were developed through both network and school-based workshops and other activities. The real test of that understanding of global education came when teachers attempted to implement actual lessons and/or curricula in their own classrooms.

Four types of classroom global education programs were developed in the network schools: (1) infusion programs, (2) special projects initiated by network teachers themselves, (3) special projects initiated by the outside interventionists (CHI), and (4) what we've labeled "alternative programs."

Infusion Programs

The reader will recall that CHI encouraged the infusion of global concepts into the existing curriculum rather than the creation of new and separate global education courses. In fact, this is what tended to occur most often in network schools. When CHI staff visited a school they made themselves available to talk with interested teachers. That discussion almost always focused upon what teachers were doing in their classes at that time or what they planned to do in the near future. That led to exploring ways in which global concepts might be brought into the plan and to the identification of instructional materials which might be of assistance to the teachers. It was the responsibility of the CHI staff person to bring back or have such materials from the CHI library delivered to the teacher.

At first, teachers were not able to be very specific about the kinds of materials they wanted or needed. Early requests were for "anything in Spanish; anything on foods; anything having to do with eighth grade science curriculum—plants, animals, communicable diseases, energy, ecosystems; anything...." Later, as meanings developed, teachers who participated were far more able to articulate what it was that they wanted. The following field note from year 3 exemplifies the point:

> A meeting was scheduled by me [CHI staff member] because of a request from Larry, seventh grade science teacher at Mesa Junior High. Larry recently told me that he was very interested in coordinating his science curriculum with Jim's [another teacher at Mesa] geography curriculum by joining forces on some global themes that might run through both of their courses. Larry had made a similar request in the fall, but now he has specifically expressed an interest in working with Jim. In the fall he had asked for global education science materials with no particular issue focus. At that time I did not know how to fill that kind of a broad request. When I visited Mesa in February of this year, Larry asked for global education materials in specific areas (hunger, the rain forest, and health) and mentioned Jim's name, both of which made me realize that there was a lot of potential in his request in terms of encouraging cross-disciplinary global education projects at the school. While others at the school have been working together in this way for some time already, it

seems that Larry was wanting to join the ranks of those who are already working on global education at Mesa.

Many teachers infused a global perspective into their curricula. Below are some examples of known successful efforts at network schools:

At Buena Vista School, one sixth grade teacher culminated a social studies unit by having an International Awareness Day. Each of the twenty-seven students in the class had to prepare a written and oral report on one country in the world. In the oral report, the student had to locate his or her country on a large world map made by the class. The report had to contain information on such things as the geography of the country (main rivers, mountains, cities, etc.), population, language, customs, music, dress, food, products, animals, and history. Students were encouraged to bring artifacts to share, also. There was a buffet after the reports. Students brought the food, preferably representing the country in their report or, if that was not possible, representing their own ethnicity.

A second–third grade teacher at Caldwell Elementary School developed a two-month unit integrating social studies, science, language arts, art, and even mathematics. The overarching goal was to have students become aware of how clothing connects us to other places and peoples in the world. Students had to find out what fibers are used to make clothing, where different clothing fibers come from, and where clothing is manufactured. The teacher's knowledge of spinning and weaving allowed the children to experience firsthand the process of turning wool fleece into woolen fabric. Another activity had the students designing their own survey form and interviewing local shop owners about the clothing they had for sale from various countries. They did map work, examined closets at home, cooperatively developed reports and bulletin boards, and planned a special Ethnic Dress Day.

An ESL teacher at Birmingham Junior High, using an old issue of *Intercom* (Global Perspectives in Education, 1979) entitled *Data Base*, developed his own discs entitled "Countries and Continents" for his students to access. His point was that the seventh grade ESL students need to have access to computers before they are mainstreamed. At the time the project began, they were not allowed to use computers. The bulletin boards in the computer lab where this took place were covered with maps and materials from the CHI library.

At Pacifica Middle School, which had a diverse ethnic population, two eighth grade U.S. History teachers working together had students do a study of their own family histories as a means of demonstrating the ethnic and cultural diversity in the world and in the school community. A family history display was developed as a culmination to this project. This was a popular idea and a number of teachers at various grade levels used variations on this theme.

An English teacher and a home economics teacher at Central High School collaborated on a three-week unit wherein the English class read short stories from a variety of countries while the home economics class learned to prepare food and studied fashions from those same places. There also were some common activities such as films, presentations, and a luncheon at which many of the foods were sampled.

At North High, the foreign language department set up a telecommunications project with sister schools in Japan, Colombia, and France. One cross-disciplinary activity was particularly interesting. A Spanish teacher went to a home economics class and spoke about Colombian climate, culture, and food. The home economics students wrote out American recipes which were translated into Spanish by the teacher's Spanish class. The recipes were sent to the Colombian school along with a videotape of the entire process and recipes eventually were received from Columbia to share in both classes at North High.

Special Projects Initiated by Network Teachers

While infusion was the main strategy of the CHI project, there were many opportunites to create special projects that were instrumental in developing global awareness among faculty and students alike. We have chosen to briefly describe two classes of these special projects: (1) those which were initiated by faculty members and supported by CHI, and (2) those which teachers developed in response to a CHI initiative. CHI-initiated projects resulted from the "Orange County in the World" program or were projects which came about as a result of individuals or groups submitting proposals for small grants from CHI.

Before describing examples of specific programs intitiated by faculty members in the schools, it should be noted that eight of the schools had some type of international festival involving food, dance, costumes, guest speakers, and various kinds of data gathering. This ranged from a quite sophisticated Multicultural Month at Caldwell Elementary which very much involved the community, to two teachers working alone with their classes at La Puente Elementary. Only South High School and Pacifica Middle School did not create such an occasion. North High had a festival which contained several dimensions, including some activities with an international focus. We shall return to a discussion of international festivals a bit later in this chapter. The following are examples of special projects initiated by network faculty members and supported by CHI:

A fifth grade teacher at University Elementary School was concerned because in his ethnically mixed class he had evidence of the existence of at least three gangs at the school. In response to this problem, he developed a unit on conflict resolution and used a number of the instructional materials from the CHI library which were particularly appropriate. In addition to written materials, he used films, filmstrips and a number of simulations.

Many teachers have traveled internationally, and, in fact, encouraging such travel and connecting it to curriculum development is a good strategy for bringing a global perspective to individual classrooms. There were many units taught by teachers about countries to which they had traveled. One in particular, a fourth grade study in Japanese culture at La Puente Elementary, was of particular note. The teacher shared artifacts with the class, described personal experiences, had students work on developing written reports on various topics using resource materials gathered by her, had them write Haiku poetry, and had them participate in many other learning activities. Parents were involved in the culminating activity for which Japanese food was prepared.

One of the most successful special projects was the "Walk in the Real World" for seventh graders at Mesa Junior High. This school serves upper middle class, predominantly Anglo, suburban students. The day-long walk took students through a variety of ethnic neighborhoods in and around downtown Los Angeles and it also exposed them to poverty and homelessness. The focus was on perspective-taking. Thirty students were selected each year from several different classes. They received a pretrip orientation and were expected to do a written and oral report in the participating class soon after the trip.

Another feature by the seventh grade core team at Mesa was "Anthropology Night." In this program, parents were invited to experience an evening of a region or nation's culture as it would be taught to their children. Students in appropriate traditional dress greeted the parents when they arrived. Slides from teachers' travels were shown and parents were asked to participate in a simulation activity that was used as part of the regular curriculum. Each year, parents were invited to a slightly different cultural experience. This global education feature became quite popular in the community. Eighty parents attended the "African Night" in December, 1987, for example.

A group of four teachers at South High School, concerned about the increased racism among students as the demographics of the school population changed, decided to do a survey of teachers and one of students about the extent of racism on campus. The data were collected and then fed back and discussed in a variety of forums at the school. Interestingly, students perceived a much more serious problem than did teachers. A number of positive things have grown out of this activity, not the least of which is a raised consciousness among students and faculty.

At Central High, one English teacher, working with several other teachers from a variety of subject areas, had the journalism class write and publish a global education issue of the school newspaper. The paper included articles about projects in various classes throughout the school, particularly those classes taught by teachers who were participating in CHI sponsored activities.

Special Projects Initiated by CHI

As was indicated previously, CHI offered small grants to teachers who submitted proposals which were judged by a panel of teachers to be worthwhile global education activities. In addition, CHI directly sponsored an "Orange County in the World" (OCW) project modeled after "Columbus in the World," originally developed at the Mershon Center at Ohio State University (Alger, 1974). As a result of these direct interventions, a number of global education projects were carried out in network schools. The following are examples of such projects:

> Two first grade teachers at La Puente Elementary School carried out an OCW project entitled, "Community Members and Their Origins." Students were taught to interview community members and report on their interviews to the class. They also were encouraged to invite community members to the class as speakers. Students learned of the great ethnic diversity in Orange County and they learned about the customs of a variety of ethnic groups.

> A sixth grade teacher at Buena Vista School, along with a colleague who taught learning disabled upper elementary students, designed a unit on endangered species. Each child gathered data on and reported about an endangered animal in California, the United States, and in some other part of the world. Students not only learned about the animals, they learned a good deal of geography, also. A feature of the unit was a trip to the San Diego Zoo where the students had a special behind-the-scenes tour featuring endangered species. The grant from CHI paid for the field trip and instructional materials.

> Three teachers of regular and bilingual seventh grade science classes at Columbus Middle School developed a nuclear energy unit which received a CHI grant. Students were introduced to the pros and cons of nuclear energy and were shown how nuclear energy in one country can affect people in other countries of the world.

> A seventh–eighth grade ESL teacher at Birmingham Junior High first introduced her students to a variety of folk tales from books in the school and CHI libraries. She had them

interview individuals in their own ethnic communities and write their own folk tales based upon what they had learned. This was an OCW project.

A small grant was given to the English department of North High for the purchase of large world maps for each of the sixteen English classrooms. While this support was not directly for a unit of study, it was felt that such maps would assist students in learning the geography related to the literature they were studying and it would develop in the students an increased sense of place.

A small grant was given to the guidance department of Central High in response to a proposal written by four counselors. The purpose of the grant was to purchase computer software which could provide information to students about peace and international studies programs available to them in colleges and universities in the United States.

What is presented here is just a sample of the school-based projects developed by faculty members at network schools, on their own initiative or with the encouragement of CHI. These were not necessarily the best. They were chosen to show the range of things which were done. There were many other outstanding projects.

Before moving on to a new topic, we need to return for a moment to the issue of international festivals, and, we might add, to culture studies in general. It has been suggested that such festivals and studies are at a relatively low level in helping to develop cross-cultural understanding or global awareness (Bennett, 1986). To respond to this criticism we need to return to our definition of global education. The reader will recall that it had two parts, the first of which had to do with understanding of problems, issues, and systems which cut across national boundaries. The second part had to do with cross-cultural understanding, including the ability to take the perspectives of others. Festivals and simple culture studies, of themselves, do not necessarily develop in individuals the behaviors implied in this definition. However, they are a good beginning place. They deal, as in the network schools, with the real-world issue of growing ethnic diversity in the school population. They tend to be noncontroversial as compared, say, to studies of political systems or war and peace issues. If done correctly, they can lead to further, more sophisticated perspective-taking activity.

It is this *potential* for further study which we would like to focus upon rather than arguing the merits of festivals or culture studies. Such studies must get beyond a focus on otherness and uniqueness and must get into actual perspective-taking activity. Festivals can serve, not so much as culminations of culture-study units, but rather as beginning places for getting at the various issues, problems, and systems that cut across boundaries. If that is how they are used, they can be of real significance. We cannot say that festivals were used in this way in every network school, but this more critical use was present in some, and in others we hope it will develop as more time and thought goes into the process of globalizing the curriculum. That is the goal, at any rate.

Engagement and Resistance

In chapter 3 there was a discussion of conditions for engagement, those conditions which seem to be right for the growth of global education in a school. These included such things as a small group of people who already believe in the movement, and/or a significant number of people who feel that global education holds promise for the development of cross-cultural understanding in their school settings, which are becoming more and more ethnically diverse. That was a discussion of *institutional* readiness to become involved with global education.

In a similar fashion, the idea of "conditions for engagement" can be used to examine *individual* readiness to become involved with global education. The experience in the four-year network project leads us to hypothesize that the readiness of individual faculty members to participate in global education activity can be predicted based upon a set of identifiable factors which relate to the meanings they give to global education (see Figure 4.1).

Those faculty members most willing to engage with global education in the network project were ones who were open to the ideas of the movement right from the start. Many already were infusing their curriculum with a global perspective. The reader will remember that some teachers said things such as "We've just been waiting here for you to come." Such people, we found, were also

Engagement with Global Education

- open to the idea of global education, open to exploring new things, will do extra work
- wants to be involved with "new" ideas, willing to do extra work
- open to the idea of global education, sees that it relates to local school need for cross-cultural understanding
- open to the idea of global education, needs to be shown exactly "how to do it"
- open to the idea of global education, needs to see the relevance for own subject
- open to the idea of global education, needs to see that it will not take a lot of extra work
- needs to see that global education is politically safe

Resistance to Global Education

- too busy with other innovative ideas
- can't understand global education
- believes that traditional subjects are more critical, sees global education as a frill
- doesn't want to be bothered with anything new
- believes that global education is un-American and/or a secular humanist plot

Figure 4.1. A continuum of individual teacher engagement with and resistance to global education.

open to exploring new ideas and they were quite willing to put in extra time planning, teaching, and evaluating what they were doing. In chapter 3 it was suggested that overseas living and childhood knowledge of international events were often characteristic of such people, also.

There was also a significant group of individuals who engaged with the CHI global education project because it was a new idea and they either saw it as having potential to change curriculum and/or instructional practices in general, or they simply liked new things. The first principal of Mesa Junior High specifically said that he saw the project as having the potential for changing the behaviors of teachers he considered instructionally weak.

The third group of people who readily participated in the CHI global education project were those who were interested in doing something about the school's need to develop better cross-cultural understanding among its students and who saw a potential in global education for assisting with this goal. Many of the network schools were undergoing changes in the ethnic makeup of their student bodies. There were people who did not see this link even after it was pointed out by CHI staff. Evidently, it was not part of the meaning which *they* attached to the notion of global education. Unfortunately, this was also true of a few of the principals in the project. As will be pointed out in chapter 6, progress at their schools could have been considerably enhanced if they had been able to make this connection.

There were people who joined the project some time after it had been under way and who had waited because they just were not sure of exactly what they were supposed to do in their own teaching. Some of those who fit this description but did ultimately participate did so after they observed early adopters in their teaching and/or after they began to examine specific lesson plans or units brought to their schools by CHI staff members. In this fairly large group were some teachers who had been involved with one or more of the many other innovative programs that come along quite frequently in American schools and who in some way got burned because the particular innovation was not well thought out or lacked classroom specificity. It is this group of people who remind us that we too easily label teachers who do not immediately accept proposed innovations as "resistant to change." Wanting to see how something works is not resistance. Looked at from one perspective, it is simply common sense. It is incumbent upon so-called change agents, internal or external, to be able to show how a new idea can be implemented in a particular classroom setting.

Initially, there were large numbers of teachers who, while they were attracted to its ideas, thought that global education was something for the social studies classes or, in the case of primary teachers, thought that it was for the upper grades. These people had to see that there were also ways to infuse a global perspective into *their* curricula. In the final analysis, however, there were actually more English/language arts teachers who participated in the network project than there were social studies teachers. This occurred as a result of the provision of appropriate materials, the conducting of workshops, and the giving of small grants.

There is another significant group, described in chapter 5 in the discussion of competing demands, who are open to the idea of global education but who are reluctant to take on new ideas because they perceive that they do not have the time that it will take. The change agent who attempts to convince teachers that it will not take extra time is either being dishonest or naive. It *will* take time. To begin with, teachers have to understand what a global perspective is. They need to learn about global issues. Further, they need to learn how to add a new perspective to what they already do or they need to learn how to teach new lessons. Often—and this is critical—adding a global perspective to a curriculum means learning how to teach differently. When you look at the examples of activities described from network schools earlier in the chapter, it is obvious that such things as cooperative learning, simulation, and community survey are important pedagogical strategies. Not all teachers know how to use such techniques, but to be successful global education teachers they will have to learn them. Those who are interested in convincing teachers to globalize their curricula must be prepared to show how the time spent learning new content and new pedagogical techniques can make their work easier and more interesting (for example, students involved in active learning tend to be more interested in what they are doing and, thus, are less apt to be discipline problems and are more apt to achieve well).

There are a few faculty members who are skeptical of global education because they are afraid that community members see it as un-American or as a form of secular humanism. Such people might, themselves, be open to the idea, but are simply afraid of the reactions of others. In Orange County, California, where the network project took place, there have been from time to time over the past forty years attacks upon schools by various ultraconservative groups concerned with a variety of issues. For this reason, some of the network faculty members were understandably cautious. This issue was discussed at some length in the previous chapter. Suffice it to say here that those interested in having school people involved in globalizing efforts must be able to demonstrate the need for the movement and its importance to America's future.

The point to this discussion of engagement and/or resistance is simple. It is inappropriate to label people as resistant to change simply because they question global education (or any other innovation, for that matter). People often have good and legitimate questions about new programs. It is incumbent upon the change agent to find out what these questions are and what meanings are being attached to the new ideas. As Eicholz (1963) pointed out nearly three decades ago, once those meanings are understood, individualized strategies can be designed for approaching those who question.

Conclusion

In this chapter, an attempt has been made to show the relationship between the *meanings* attached to global education by faculty members in the CHI network schools and those teachers' *activity.* Meaning and activity are not linear commodities; one does not necessarily follow the other. Rather, they are interactive, developing together. If this is so, and it seemed to be in this project, then it seems fair to hypothesize that those interested in bringing a global perspective to the curriculum of a school might do better to encourage immediate activity based upon initial individual meanings rather than trying to impose or attempt to arrive at a common meaning or definition of global education as an initial activity in a project.

Further, given that meaning appears to be modified through activity, it seems appropriate to suggest that change agents might do well to continually and thoroughly assess the meanings being attached to global education by participants in projects or by those who appear to be resisting participation. It is hypothesized that from such assessment, intervention strategies can be planned which are appropriate to the growth of individuals, groups, and entire faculties. Such growth, it is assumed, is in terms of both understanding and action; and, perhaps, it is such growth which is implied in the answer to the question, "What does it take to bring a global perspective to the curriculum of a school?"

References

Alger, C. F., *Your City in the World/The World in Your City: Discover the International Activities and Foreign Policies of People, Groups, and Organizations in Your Community* (Columbus, Ohio: Mershon Center, Ohio State University, 1974).

Bennett, M. J., "A Developmental Approach to Training Intercultural Sensitivity," *International Journal of Intercultural Relations* 10 (2) (Summer 1986).

Blumer, H., *Symbolic Interaction: Perspective and Method* (Englewood Cliffs, N.J.: Prentice-Hall, Inc., 1969).

Duggan, S. J., and S. Thorpe, "Obstacles to Global Education," paper presented at the annual conference of the American Educational Research Association, (San Francisco, April 1986).

Eicholz, G. C., "Why Do Teachers Reject Change?" *Theory into Practice* 2 (December 1963): 264–68.

Fullan, M., *The Meaning of Educational Change* (New York: Teachers College Press, 1982).

Global Perspectives in Education, Inc. (now called American Forum), *Data Base*, 1979 edition of *Intercom*.

Hanvey, R., *An Attainable Global Perspective* (Denver: Center for Teaching International Relations, 1976).

Havelock, R. G., *Planning for Innovation through Dissemination and Utilization of Knowledge* (Ann Arbor: Institute for Social Research, University of Michigan, 1971).

Shiman, D., and D. Conrad, "Awareness, Understanding, and Action: A Global Conscience in the Classroom," *The New Era* 58 (6) (December 1977): 163–67.

Study Commission on Global Education, *The United States Prepares for its Future: Global Perspectives in Education* (New York: American Forum, 1987).

5

COMPETING DEMANDS AND
THE USE OF TIME IN SCHOOLS

We always seem to come back to competing demands—schools and teachers are simply asked to do too much. When something new comes along, no matter how worthwhile, the system doesn't make it easy to "make space" for it—in the schedule, or in the work load, or even psychologically.

—CHI staff discussion memo

Responses to CHI's global education project at the very beginning suggest that many teachers are quite receptive to new programs which they view as worthwhile. In school after school, the field notes reveal a good deal of initial interest and it is fair to say that in all of the schools some teachers, both individually and in groups, began to make plans for infusing global perspectives into their teaching. They identified themes on which they wanted to work, and started to think concretely about the kinds of help they would need.

Other teachers held back a bit—we were told, in a variety of ways, that they were "waiting for the hook"—but when they realized that (in this project, at any rate) there was no hook, they too began to get involved. In every school there were some teachers who already taught with a global perspective. For the majority, however, the necessary starting point involved obtaining information and forming an understanding of global education as it might apply to their own daily classroom work. This process was dealt with at some length in the previous chapter. For the most part, this information-seeking stage could be accomodated without too much difficulty, primarily because it was something teachers initiated on their own, and at their own pace. Whether it was at the beginning of the project, halfway through year 2, or whenever, the first step invariably involved asking CHI staff for teaching materials or reference books on certain topics related to the already prescribed curriculum for which that teacher was responsible. Many teachers also shared such materials with each other, passing them from hand to hand or making copies to share.

Barriers to Participation

As teachers moved through this information-seeking stage and into the networking and implementation stages, though, they ran into trouble. The excitement of working on something they recognized as important for children, and the momentum generated by the sense of involvement with a task they had chosen for themselves—the "ownership" so crucial to teacher morale—came up against the overwhelming reality of competing demands. As long as the teachers were simply *thinking* and *planning*, things were fine; as soon as they tried to actually *do* something, pressures from every direction worked to thwart their efforts.

Not Enough Time

Page after page of the CHI field notes contain apologies and perfectly valid reasons why teachers couldn't give the global education project the time they would have liked to give it. The teachers in CHI's eleven network schools worked tremendously hard, and did so with a generosity and cheerfulness that was truly remarkable. For the most part, teachers in all American schools perform willingly the tasks required of them, and many go further, voluntarily taking on additional duties. Even if they *don't* take on extra work, however, the tasks required of them have proliferated so dramatically in recent years that merely doing one's job requires almost superhuman patience and endurance. Day-to-day life in most schools, for most teachers, is a grueling ordeal: too much to accomplish, for too many students, with too few resources, in too little time, and at far too fast a pace. Listen to the voices of the teachers themselves:

> There's just too much to do in one conference period—I've got to run; can't stay and look through the materials today. Sorry!

I'm sorry to run in and out like this. There's a parent waiting in my room, I've got an assignment to complete, and I'm already late for another meeting!

Fred M. came in during lunchtime very hurriedly and barely said hello, indicating he hardly had time for lunch.

After the meeting, Carlos stopped us in the parking lot and told us that this is a particularly hectic week. Probably, he said, everyone is still burned out from yesterday's after-school SIP (School Improvement Program) meeting, which ran quite late.

Our new principal, like everyone else at this school, is finding that his attention is required in too many places at the same time.

Our meeting was very rushed because of some lunchtime commitments the teachers had with a group of students who were working in an adjacent room.

In the questionnaire which the teachers in all of the schools filled out for us at the end of the fourth year, we asked them to estimate how many of their colleagues simply felt too busy to become involved with the global education project. Out of all respondents, 61 percent estimated that the number of staff who felt they were too busy with other things was "large" or "very large;" another 32 percent estimated that "about half" of their fellow teachers felt too busy to participate in what many of them still, after four years, viewed as an extra. As a matter of fact, this latter group was closer to the mark: of the 342 teachers who responded to this question, 52 percent said that they had been either "somewhat involved' or "very involved" with CHI, and 48 percent—"about half"—identified themselves as never having participated. Of this group, 73 percent identified "lack of time" as the thing which most got in the way of their becoming involved. Twenty percent also said "large classes," which may be another way of saying "lack of time."

It is worth noting that even those teachers who *were* involved with global education efforts found lack of time to be a significant problem: 86 percent of that group selected "lack of time" as the thing which hindered them the most. (Other possible responses never even came close: 28 percent checked "large classes" and 21 percent checked "lack of money," 12 percent checked "lack of instructional materials," and 7 percent checked "CAP/CTBS testing" [standardized tests].)

Getting Together

There are more demands competing for teachers' (and principals') time, attention, and energy than can possibly be accomodated in the hours available. It proved all but impossible to schedule meetings at times when everyone who wanted to be there *could* be there, even when the group was just a small planning group:

> The meeting was to take place at 2:45, but only Barry was able to be there. Santos explained that he and Edna had unexpected things to take care of....

> In the second group, only two people came. Jack told us that there were two other events going on at that same time, and that the other four teachers we'd expected had to attend those.

Common planning time for teachers during the school day seems like such a logical ingredient of school success, but historically it has not been considered important for teachers to have time for substantive professional communication as part of their job. The exigencies of scheduling in most secondary schools preclude common planning periods by department, and most elementary school teachers don't have a break from teaching *at all* during the school day. At both levels, teachers interested in working together on something are forced to try and meet before school or during lunchtime and, as we have seen, it is usually next to impossible to get the whole group together. This was true during the entire four years of the project, and did not change for the better even when the school's commitment to global education intensified and more teachers became involved. Indeed, as more teachers got involved it only compounded the problem, for all of the many other competing demands were still there, even if global education had moved up somewhat on the priority list. Let's take a look at everything that was going on in our network schools in *addition* to the regular curriculum, bearing in mind that every one of these makes some claim on a teacher's attention and that many make substantial demands on his or her time as well:

Drug intervention   Standardized testing
Teen pregnancy   Accreditation self-studies and site
Child abuse awareness   reviews
On-campus violence   Extracurricular activities

Hunger, malnutrition
Self-esteem programs
Suicide intervention
Gang control
Dropout prevention
At-risk programs
Racist incidents
Guaranteed guidance
  services
Career counseling
Work-study programs
Curriculum revision
  cycles
Textbook adoptions
Advanced placement,
  gifted programs

Chapter I programs
SIP (School Improvement
  Programs)
Cooperative learning
Critical thinking
Clinical teaching and supervision
Mainstreaming
Integrating the LEP (Limited
  English Proficiency) students
English as a second language
Computer literacy
Writing across the curriculum
Global education
Special education, IEPs etc.
Literature-based curriculum
Science Fair

One of our eleven schools, an elementary school, was closed by its district at the end of year 3 due to declining enrollments. In exit interviews with the staff of seventeen, we asked "What other competing demands were there at your school while the global education project was there?" The following were mentioned: new curriculum work, extracurricular activities, district workshops, testing, the "specter of closing," mentor-teacher responsibilities, work to obtain advanced degrees, parent conferences, professional association duties, child abuse program, textbook adoption tasks, personal crises, and "just being a teacher."

Demands Come from Every Direction

State

Teachers in the CHI network schools were acutely aware of expectations and pressures which originated at the state level. These included major curriculum revision work, statewide standardized testing, and the beginnings of a restrictive teacher performance evaluation process. One district administrator expressed the view that the state has "dumped on the schools" with all of its demands, and several more expressed concern that moves by the state department of education to assume greater control of education decision-making would, ultimately, prove detrimental to the teaching-learning process.

> "Linda said that Chapter I reading teachers are pretty much locked into a state-regulated curriculum that allows little room for adding global perspectives, aside from the few multicultural short stories which are already part of the course.

For many teachers it was standardized testing which most restricted their professional judgment in curriculum matters. In the questionnaire administered at the end of year 4, thirty-one percent of the responding teachers agreed that "I do not feel free to experiment with my curriculum because of CAP/CTBS testing," and the field notes contain entries such as these:

> As we talked a bit, I felt comfortable asking Pura if I could sit in on one of her classes. She said that right now there is nothing interesting to see because she is preparing her kids for the state CAP tests at the end of the month. In fact, on top of her school load and teaching two nights of adult classes a week, she is also taking a class from the district, to help her teach writing in order to prepare her students for the state proficiency test.

> An ESL teacher spent some time talking with us, and indicated an interest, but said that since the CAP test requirements were changing, she didn't yet know what kinds of materials would be appropriate.

> As for the upcoming workshop (on global environment issues), the science teachers won't be able to come because of testing schedules.

Schools wishing to receive SIP funds from the state also had to prepare needs assessments and funding proposals, according to specified guidelines, and were required to document compliance with the program and go through a site review process every three to five years. These programs placed extraordinary demands on teacher time beyond the normal work day, but teachers went ahead with them because they meant good things for kids in the long run. (It is interesting to note that one of the departments at Pacifica Middle School wrote some global education objectives right into their SIP plan during year 2. In this way, what might have been a competing demand was turned into an opportunity.)

Secondary schools in California are also subject to periodic regional accreditation association reviews by the Western Association of Schools and Colleges (WASC). All three CHI high schools had to go through this process during the time they were involved with the global education project. Tremendous amounts of teacher and administrator time were required for departmental and schoolwide self-studies, and extraordinary psychological pressure attaches to the actual visit of the site review team. During "WASC years," many other school programs are put on the back burner for a while.

District

School districts themselves are also responsible for many of the competing demands felt by teachers—demands which effectively prevent them from doing the curriculum development work that they really would prefer to be doing. (Admittedly, it is sometimes difficult to separate district demands from state demands, as one often extends out of the other. This was especially true during the late 1980s, when districts felt incredible pressure from the state to demonstrate "accountability for excellence".)

The question of district support for the eleven schools in this project is an especially interesting one in view of the fact that each district superintendent had given his or her approval to the project, had appointed a contact person at the district office as a liaison for CHI, had suggested which principals might be most receptive to the project, and had agreed to provide ten to fifteen days of release time (i.e., pay for substitute teachers) annually for each school which chose to participate. Substantial support is indicated by these commitments—indeed, in several districts, some teachers expressed amazement that we had received this much official backing.

And yet, as the four years passed, it became clear that nothing further would be done at the district level to enhance the project's chances of success. In fact, some districts were even forced to withdraw their funding of release time during years 3 and 4 because of budget cutbacks involved with declining enrollment and inflation. Meanwhile, each participating school was still expected to meet all other demands imposed by its district administration. If global education was able to gain a toehold in this environment, well and good. If not, well, the district hadn't gone *too* far out on a limb, or made *too* much of an investment in it.

Teachers felt the pressure of competing demands from the district level in a variety of ways:

> Gary proceeded to tell us how his time just then was totally occupied with developing a new Economics course for the district, and that he really needed to choose a new textbook by next Tuesday. Also, that he had to organize a district-wide Economics workshop for six weeks later....
>
> David told us he arrives at school at 6:00 A.M. in order to prepare for his classes and to do the paperwork the district requires....
>
> "The district asks so much of us. There's no flexibility any more; the curriculum is all filled up."
>
> "We have two weeks of parent conferences coming up, so no time for extra meetings until after that."

Competing demands imposed by the district can be well illustrated with an anecdote from Central High School. In May of year 2, a planned teacher in-service day was originally earmarked as a global education day, and a group of teachers got busy making arrangements for speakers and workshops. In a series of planning meetings with a group of Central High teachers and administrators, however, the district office's agenda kept intervening and the plan for the in-service day was revised several times. Ultimately, global education ended up with *only half an hour,* while large chunks of time had to be allocated for a district speaker on teen suicide intervention and a session on preparing for the upcoming accreditation review. This was very frustrating for the CHI staff, but they realized that these other concerns were also important to the teachers.

Sometimes the district superintendents were very open about their own priorities:

> Dr. M. did talk about his new plan to have teachers certified in Spanish, ESL, and multicultural awareness. He wants this to be mandatory for all teachers, and is now talking with his bargaining unit about it.

The District Ethos

In addition to specific expectations established by the district, classroom teachers also feel enabled (or constrained) by the complex phenomenon which we call the "district ethos." As each school has its own special culture, or unique personality, so too each *school district* has a culture of its own, its "ethos." Chapters 6 and 7 will deal with the culture of the school and the leadership style of the principal, the two school-site factors which, more than anything else, determine the success or failure of an innovation at a given school. But insofar as both of those critical factors are partially reflective of the type of district in which the school is located, we do need to stop for a moment to take a closer look at the *district* culture, or ethos.

The following six components of the district ethos emerged in the course of this study: *first, the management style of the super-intendent.* The old "authoritarian/democratic/laissez faire" range of management style comes to mind, but breaks down when one attempts to apply it to real school districts: evidently very few superintendents can function with a truly democratic management style (even if they would want to, which is by no means clear). In fact, as we looked at the eight school districts involved with the CHI global education project, we found mostly *varying degrees of authoritarianism.*

At the most extreme end, one superintendent ran his district like a very tight ship, tolerating little or no deviation from pre-scribed rules and practices. He did it quietly, behind the scenes, calling no attention to himself and often depending on subordi-nates to enforce his policies. He knew they would understand just what he wanted. Caution and conservatism were expected of every-one, from top to bottom, and risk-taking was definitely out: "The teachers at South High School really believe that the people in the upper echelons of their district are not sympathetic to your type of project at all." The teachers in that district would joke about being in a military organization: "This district is the *army,* and they let you in—amazing!!!" As a matter of district policy, no school in this district was permitted to have shortened days for teacher in-service activities, which greatly exacerbated the problem of competing demands and available teacher time.

Less extreme were two superintendents who seemed personal-ly comfortable with a much more loosely coupled organizational structure. Each was definitely in control of his district, but a cer-tain amount of risk-taking and innovation was considered accept-able and this message was understood throughout the system.

These superintendents visited their schools often and related in an easygoing way with subordinates. There was no feeling of lock-step behavior being required.

The *second* component of the district ethos which we observed was the extent to which the district insisted on *standardized practice* across all of its schools. At one end of this continuum we found a school district which imposed quite a high degree of standardization. For example, one principal told us, "My teachers are used to the school district and school site organization being very structured, and therefore expect a similarly structured, centralized program from CHI." It was in this district that all social studies and science classes in grades 1–6 were taught by ITV (instructional television) programs. Teachers had manuals showing them exactly how to supplement these TV lessons. Beyond allocating ten release-time days for teachers involved with the global education project, the district did little more to ensure that La Puente Elementary would achieve success in globalizing its curriculum, and required the school to meet the same expectations required of all the other schools in the district.

This matter of not making any exceptions, of treating all schools exactly alike and not allowing pilot projects any time or resources not available at all schools, is fairly common. A development at Mesa Junior High illustrates this point. The seventh grade social studies–centered core curriculum at Mesa is described earlier in this book (chapter 3). This program, developed by a group of teachers with the full support of their principal, was unique in the district. It was popular with students and had considerable parent support. Nevertheless, within two years the district was putting pressure on the principal to insist that his teachers return to the standard seventh grade curriculum.

The *third* component of the district ethos was the district's *service orientation*. By this we mean the extent to which a school district acts upon the assumption that its primary function is to serve and *help* the schools, as opposed to somehow giving the impression that the schools are there to meet the expectations of the district. A good example of the *helpful* service orientation, insofar as the global education project was concerned, was the effort made by two of the participating districts to continue providing release time for their teachers to attend CHI workshops, even after district-wide budget cuts had made money very tight. The district ethos was one of cooperation: "times may be tough, but let's just put our heads together and see how we can make this happen."

Some school districts seem to lack any sense of service to their schools. Instead, district personnel get caught up in the needs of the district and assume that the needs of the individual schools are subordinate to those. It can easily happen that the district is completely unaware of an event or situation which is quite important in the life of a school (or to the success of a project which is important to the teachers at that school). For example when, after two years of problems in working with the faculty at North High School, a special global education mentor teacher was finally appointed, the CHI staff was greatly encouraged. The teacher was experienced, well respected by his colleagues, and supportive of global education. He could have made a tremendous difference to the success of the project at North High, but, three days into the new school year, the district office made him an offer he couldn't refuse, and he was gone. It was no one's *fault*—the district had decided it could use him and had not thought to inquire as to how important he was at the school. (Nor had the principal, as it happens, stepped in to say "Hey! We really need him here!" but that's another story, one that will be told in chapter 7).

Fourth, part of the district ethos has to do with *communication*—specifically, with the flow of information. *Does* it flow, in fact? Do people throughout the system feel that they have access to the information they need in order to do their jobs well?

> At the July 24 meeting, the assistant superintendent promised that he himself would tell the principal of Pacifica Middle School about the release-time days promised for year 3. But as of September 17, the principal had still heard nothing....

In addition to the reliability of information flow, the *directionality* of communication is also part of the district ethos: do people in the system feel that the information flow is all one way, from the top down? Or is there a sense that it is two way, that information can also flow from bottom to top? *And if so, does the top listen?* Evidence of this did occur once in a while, particularly from the mid-management level on up, or sometimes laterally. For example:

> The Assistant Superintendent had the principal of University Elementary School give a report on the global education project there to the other elementary school principals in the district.

At the end-of-the-year report to our contact person at the North Unified School District office, the assistant superintendent asked the teacher who had spearheaded the new global telecommunications project at North High, who was present at the meeting, if she would be willing to do a short presentation about the project for the next board of education meeting.

On the whole, however, it was more common to find information flowing just one way: from the top down. District administrators would notify principals, at meetings and in memos, of district expectations and the principals would pass this information along to teachers, at meetings or in memos. This downward flow of information ensures that the district ethos permeates the entire local system. The significance of this organizational communication pattern for the CHI global education project is that, although district-level administrators had given permission for the project to be tried in one or two of their schools, global education became a *district* priority for only one of the eight school districts. For each of the other seven, it remained a strictly localized pilot project in which the district itself had little real investment. These districts did not disseminate information about global education downward throughout the system, and the extent to which such information flowed *upward* from the project schools was determined solely by the initiative of principals or of groups of teachers at the schools who were proud of their global education efforts and took steps to "get the word out" to the rest of the district.

The way a school district *treats its workers* constitutes the *fifth* component of the district ethos.

If you had presented CHI at the very beginning as having some strings attached—like saying that a five-page report would be due upon completion of grant projects, or that you had a specific curriculum you wanted us to implement—more teachers would have shown an interest in and felt comfortable with you, because *that is what they are used to.*

Several teachers expressed concern that because the district was not treating them fairly, they did not have the heart to continue their after-school and before-school activities.... They were not working on their grant projects as enthusiastically as they might have been.

Nancy felt that she had earned a sabbatical and that she badly needed some time to get her professional "batteries recharged." But her district discourages people from applying for leave by refusing to guarantee that they can come back to the same school afterwards, or even to an equivalent position. Teachers see this as a punitive policy.

The *sixth* and final dimension of the district ethos is the *locus of decision-making.* There are decisions that appropriately must be made at the district level, but there are also decisions which may be left to the school site administrator; and some school districts seem to have difficulty in distinguishing between the two:

We were told that the district superintendent is concerned that there are too many teachers out of the classroom as a result of their involvement in so many projects. The teachers seemed to feel that they and their principal should be the judge of that.

While the American system of public education, structured as it is, cannot and probably should not allow *complete* decentralization of decision-making to the school sites, the *extent* to which any given school district tended to centralize the decision-making process, and the *nature* of the decisions which were delegated or not delegated to the school sites, are an important aspect of that district's culture, or ethos.

At a time when site-based decision-making is being promoted, the question is how can a district establish a climate that encourages creativity at the site level while at the same time guaranteeing equal opportunity and maximum results in all schools? (K.Tye, 1991, p. 172)

None of these six dimensions stands alone as the prime determinant of the complex phenomenon which we have called the "district ethos"; they are inevitably interrelated. Where the decisions are made, for example, can reveal much about the flow of communication within a district and probably also about that district's expectation that educational practices be standardized across schools. Likewise, the district's service orientation is likely to be closely related to the way it treats its subordinate workers. And, finally, the superintendent's educational beliefs and personal management style have an enormous impact on all the rest.

We conclude this discussion of the district ethos with a hypothesis. While basically stable, the characteristic ethos or culture of a school district *can* change. It is especially vulnerable in times of economic stress, and at such times may move toward the more centralized and standardized end of the continuum. Single-school initiatives are likely to be severely circumscribed by budget cutbacks, and all the schools of a district will be given the same set of guidelines for belt-tightening. Whatever the district ethos may be at any given time, it is always a fundamental part of the contextual press felt by teachers as they carry out their responsibilities.

School Site

School principals also impose demands. They have priorities of their own, usually based on their understanding of state and district expectations, but sometimes grounded in their own interests. Some principals want to make a wealth of opportunities and choices available to their teachers, so they "let everything in":

> "Our principal has about four million programs going at this school, and he pushes every one of them."

Others try to focus their teachers on just a handful of special projects:

> Mr. C. told us of his interest in computers and of his intentions for using computers in his school. He was very proud that all of his teachers knew how to use computers.

> Mr. K. is a staunch supporter of cooperative learning techniques and has given workshops and presentations on the subject. He was unhappy to be meeting with a good deal of resistance from his staff in this area.

> "Our principal wants this school to be recognized for its academic 'excellence,' so he gives most of his attention to things like the Advanced Placement program and how well our students do on standardized tests. In fact, he even taught a class himself, to help students prepare for the PSAT. He likes it when we all pull together to make sure our school gets the highest CAP scores in the district."

The principal is *the* key person at the school site when it comes to competing demands from outside and from above. Boundary maintenance is one of the tasks that a principal *must* perform, and how he or she does so (or fails to do so) can have a significant impact on faculty morale. In chapter 7, we will look more closely at this and other aspects of the principal's behavior, particularly as they reflect, support, or (very rarely) stand as a buffer against the district ethos discussed above.

Whether they are initiated by the district, the principal, or the teachers themselves, all-school projects inevitably form some part of the yearly life of a school and these, too, compete with everything else for teachers' time and energy:

> Today was the second day of three days of a fundraising project.... The whole school was trying to raise $1,500 for additional computer software. The gym teacher told us that today probably wasn't such a good day for us to come—and so it seemed.

> The principal had asked us to be in the lounge from 2:00–3:30 P.M. Unfortunately, he told us as we were setting up that he also had an art workshop scheduled for the teachers from 2:45–3:30. He apologized profusely for the double meetings, and said that it couldn't be helped.

> International Awareness Day might not go this year because of the number of additional activities going on at the school.... Part of the problem is that Maggie and Eva don't have the same conference period, and they have too many additional responsibilities after school.

Personal Choices and Private Lives

Teachers have to do a great many things which they might *not* do if they had a choice, but it must also be acknowledged that they do some things because they *want* to. Many of the school projects and programs which were competing with global education for the time and attention of teachers had been *willingly chosen by the teachers themselves*. For many teachers, the work on global education was a fairly high priority; for others, it was sort of a mid-range priority; and for some it was not a priority at all. Other projects, roles, or responsibilities were more important to them. (Part of CHI's challenge was to convince such teachers that infusing some global perspectives into their teaching need not displace their other interests, but could in many cases enhance them.)

A good number of the teachers who were interested in global education were also involved in building the Model United Nations program; this was definitely their first priority.

We were told that Gary, who was really interested in the project, was not there because he was a track coach and was at a meet.

"Being here and teaching, this is what we *do;* we need to be here. The kids lose too much when we're gone. I'm not going to go to any more workshops this year if they're during school hours."

Both Joyce and Karen said that the teachers were really swamped and would find little time to do anything with CHI because of the Thanksgiving and Christmas holidays coming up.

"I'm coaching the academic decathlon team, mentoring a first-year teacher, advising the yearbook and the National Honor Society, coaching tennis, and getting a Masters degree. I'm the union rep for this school, and I do my share of departmental curriculum work. That's about all I can handle this year."

And finally, of course, there are the pressures that teachers bring with them to school from their personal lives. Often, these are among what psychologists have recognized as life's most stressful events—the illness of a child, the death of a parent, marital problems, moving to a new home—but they can also be the normal daily aggravations and unexpected minicrises which can be counted on to interfere with what had been planned:

Actually, what with one thing and another, we didn't get started until about 2:30, and two or three interested teachers weren't there—it was payday, and they had to get their checks to the bank before 3:00! On top of that, two other teachers had left early (one felt like she was coming down with the flu).

Linda flew through the library, stopping to tell us that her babysitter had gotten sick and that she was late to school because she'd had to take her daughter to another sitter.

This last item raises the issue of gender and its relationship to participation in an innovative program such as this one. Although, overall, more women than men teachers participated in this project, the women did acknowledge that they felt pressured by an extra set of competing demands imposed by their dual role as working parents. Also, we noticed that at several schools men—although they were in the minority overall as far as participation was concerned—stepped forward to *take the lead* in many of the global education activities which took place. At North High School and Columbus Intermediate, women played the leadership roles, and at the remaining schools the leadership seemed to be distributed about evenly between women and men. The role of gender in the successful institutionalization of an innovative program would be an interesting area for further research.

Teachers' Defense Mechanisms

Given the intensity of daily life in schools, how do teachers protect themselves from the barrage of perceived demands which press on them from every direction? The concept of teachers' resistance to change has been dealt with in chapter 4, but the idea of defense mechanisms in the face of normal job overload is somewhat different. We observed six kinds of behavior which might be described as adaptive. Arranged along a continuum from dysfunctional to functional, these were:

- burnout
- refusal
- avoidance
- withdrawal
- negotiation
- selective participation

Burnout isn't really a defense mechanism, but rather a consequence of *not* having had (or made use of) other sorts of "buffer behaviors." Our reason for including it here will become clear when we discuss the resilience level of a school.

> We got started about ten minutes late and sure enough, the teachers sat cross-armed, challenging George to excite them enough to wake them up, to tear them away from the papers that some of them were correcting during the beginning of his presentation.
>
> As I looked over their faces before we spoke to them, they seemed tired, and bored, and captive.

> The vice principal announced a new program which was meant to help students who were doing poorly—a "buddy system." This would require an additional amount of teacher time, and the teachers responded poorly. Several commented pointedly on how difficult it would be to find the time.

Refusal can take a variety of forms. It can be overtly negative, as in the first example above; or more passive, as in the third example. In any case, it's refusal when teachers—individually or collectively—say, or imply by their behavior, *"No! Not one more thing, no matter what!"*

Avoidance is a defense that was used with a great deal of finesse by many teachers, as a response to a variety of pressures. In connection with this project, it ranged from those teachers who simply chose not to deal with the project at all—they did not talk to CHI staff, and they did not discuss it with their colleagues; when they *had* to attend a staff meeting that was focused on global education, they let what was said go in one ear and out the other—to those who continuously, for the entire four years, professed an intention to become involved—but never did. Perhaps they never really believed that it wouldn't add to their burdens, as was suggested by a teacher who *was* relatively active with the project: "They still think that if they participate, then they'll owe you something."

Withdrawal was a necessary defensive move for some teachers who were active for awhile—attending CHI workshops, participating in school-based activities like "Orange County in the World," or working on a minigrant project—but then found themselves overwhelmed with other demands and having to make some choices. Many teachers who withdrew from their former visibly active participation, however, continued to use what they had learned in their teaching. So it cannot really be said that they withdrew from their original commitment to teach with a global perspective.

> Several of the teachers wanted assurances from the administration that, if they go for this project, it wouldn't jeopardize their accountability in other areas.

Negotiation was a healthy strategy utilized by teachers who felt that they were in a reasonably strong bargaining position, or had a fairly good working relationship, with their principal. Knowing full well that they couldn't do everything they were being asked to do and recognizing at the same time that the principal and the district evidently had some commitment to the concept of global education, they wanted to be certain that the administration would support them *by loosening up the expectations in some other areas* if they became involved in CHI activities. Scholars have written much, in recent years, about the "negotiated reality of the classroom"; here we have an example of what must be seen as the "negotiated reality of the adult work environment" of a school, a construct which deserves further study.

Selective participation is the most functional of the defense mechanisms used by overworked classroom teachers. Given the universe of possibilities (see the list near the beginning of this chapter) teachers make realistic choices of how to allocate their outside-the-classroom time. This kind of self-protective behavior, however, requires that the teacher be able to say no, to decline involvement; or to reorganize priorities so as to phase out something in favor of something else. Unfortunately, both of these behaviors are difficult. Saying no comes especially hard; strong cultural norms press teachers to be compliant and to do their best at *everything* they are asked to take on.

The Resilience Hypothesis

A school is a complex place, its unique personality (or its "culture," if you prefer) is comprised of many interrelated components. But surely one of these is the general area of faculty morale, and it is in this area that teachers' uses of the various defense mechanisms are pertinent. Based on our experience with the eleven CHI network schools, we hypothesize that *the defense mechanism used by a critical mass of teachers at any given school has a direct relationship to the overall morale and resilience levels of that school.* In other words, the way in which a significant number of the teachers deal with competing demands constitutes a major dimension of the climate of that school.

If enough of the teachers feel burned out, their unhappiness will create a certain type of atmosphere. If many feel belligerent—undervalued, poorly treated by their district, taken advantage of—their active resistance will affect everyone. If a significant proportion feel confident, competent, and self-sufficient, this too will create a characteristic environment; one that is adaptive and resilient. Teachers who feel that the problems of their school are overwhelming are unlikely to invest much time in trying to solve them (although they *will* complain about them a good deal). Their defense mechanisms in the face of competing demands are more likely to be avoidance and resistance. On the other hand, teachers who are upbeat and who use strategies like negotiation and selective participation are more likely to see their school's problems as manageable, and to be willing to invest some time in efforts to solve them.

The other aspects of a school's unique personality, or culture, are the subject of chapter 6. Resilience has been briefly discussed here because it is intrinsic to the topic of competing demands: We needed to know not only what those demands were, but how teachers in the project schools dealt with them.

Contemplating the Larger Picture

It seems beyond question that the educational system is seriously overloaded; but why? How did this happen? A variety of possible reasons come to mind, and *all* of them are true: (1) The complexities of schooling reflect the complexities of modern society—system overload is an unavoidable by-product of twentieth-century postindustrial cultures; (2) there has never been agreement, within our society, on the specific purposes we want our schools to accomplish, therefore we have no criteria by which to include some things and exclude others; (3) it is the nature of bureaucracies to expand, taking on new duties and creating new niches for their workers; (4) any new developments related to the socialization and training of the young are automatically delegated to the school, as the institution which has been charged with this responsibility.

We would like to suggest a fifth possibility, one that is grounded in our original notion of the deep structure of schooling. The reader will recall that the "deep structure" consists of those basic values and assumptions which are shared throughout a society, and which shape the educational system of that society in its most fundamental aspects; and also that the deep structure is *extraordinarily* resistant to change. System overload can reasonably be viewed as an institutional way of resisting change; the organization simply *keeps everyone too busy* to ask such important questions as "Why are we doing this?" and "What are our real purposes here?"

It can safely be said that such conversations are absent from life in schools; the norms of the school culture and the pressures of competing demands combine to ensure that there is no time for them. Teachers are thus kept at a distance from the locus of decision-making, kept *out* of the dialogue, and kept powerless to change the institution within which they spend their days. For some, of course, this is just fine. All they want to do is shut their classroom door and teach "their kids." But for others, the situation is felt as repressive and demeaning. They may not articulate this as the reason for their discomfort, but the constant battle with competing demands certainly contributes to their growing sense of deprofessionalization.

Conclusion

In this chapter, we have taken a close look at the daily lives of teachers, and the pressures they feel as a result of the demands made by the state, the district, and at the school site; as well as the competing demands arising from their personal lives and out-of-school responsibilities. Particular attention was given to the district ethos, or climate, and six components of the district ethos were examined; it is clear that the superordinate system, rather than *helping* teachers do their job, is usually the source of many of the competing demands which diffuse a teacher's attention and leave her—or him—feeling exhausted, isolated, and unappreciated. This led us to consider a possible typology of teacher defense mechanisms and, ultimately, to suggest a hypothesis about resilience as an element of the culture at each individual school.

In chapter 6, we will take a closer look at the culture of the school as it affects the change process, using three case studies— South High, Columbus Intermediate, and Caldwell Elementary—to illustrate various aspects of school culture.

References

Tye, K. A., *Global Education: From Thought to Action* (Alexandria, Va.: Association for Supervision and Curriculum Development, 1991).

6

THE UNIQUENESS OF THE SINGLE SCHOOL

In chapter 1, the notion of the *unique personality* of a school was introduced. We pointed out that each school has its own history, community traditions and mores, and internal factors such as teacher-administrator relationships, number and intensity of problems, and classroom climates. We also suggested that there is a *deep structure* of schooling which is determined by the basic values and assumptions that are widely shared throughout a society and which shape the educational system of that society in its most fundamental aspects.

The point has been made that, while the deep structure cannot change independently of a significant and prior change in the society as a whole, the unique personality can change, sometimes quite rapidly. It is both receptive to planned change efforts and responsive to unplanned events.

Because many of the unique personality variables of the single school are manipulable, it seems wise to focus improvement efforts at this level. Thus, the assumption was made in the CHI global education project that, while the facilitating behaviors of superordinate agencies (district, state) and individual classroom teachers were important, what was most critical was to get concerted action at the local school site.

Perceptions of Involvement: A Typology

The story of what occurred in the eleven schools is told in various ways in the first three chapters of this book. In chapters 4 and 5, while the story of what happened continues to unfold, there is a shift to telling *why* certain things took place. In this chapter, we continue the effort to explain what happened in the CHI project, and why. The question is "What were some of the critical aspects of the unique personality of the school that contributed to and/or impeded efforts to bring a global perspective to its curriculum?"

As a way of getting at answers to this question, we first examine various perceptions of the amounts and kinds of involvements school people had with the CHI project. We then look at a number of short case studies of project schools which illuminate the reasons for these levels of involvement.

The CHI staff usually met at least once a week during the four years of the project to review field notes, discuss memos, and share perceptions about events, programs, problems, and issues in network schools. Such meetings led to subsequent intervention and research activity. They also caused the staff to come to know these schools quite well.

By the end of the four years, the staff knew in which schools there was widespread faculty involvement with global education and where, on the other hand, such involvement was more limited. Also, based upon knowledge of the schools, CHI staff felt able to make a collective, qualitative judgment about such involvement. That is, they felt comfortable in estimating the degree to which each school was developing curricula infused with a global perspective.*

Discussions of amounts, kinds, and quality of faculty involvements with global education activity led CHI to the development of a simple typology. Schools were divided into three groups and are ranked from most involved to least involved:

Group 1

Buena Vista School (K–8)

Caldwell Elementary School (K–6)

Mesa Junior High School (7–8)

At these schools, the majority of the faculty were involved in CHI activities, many a great deal. Much of what was taught was infused with a global perspective. Teachers clearly understood what a glob-

---

*For those who are skeptical of the ability to judge qualitative dimensions of school activity, the authors suggest the reading of Elliot Eisner, *The Enlightened Eye: Qualitative Inquiry and the Enhancement of Educational Practice* (New York: Macmillan, 1991).

al perspective was, and most acted upon that understanding. Most, if not all, students could be expected to graduate with a heightened global awareness and understanding.

Group 2
Central High School (10-12)
North High School (9-12)
Birmingham Junior High (7-9)

At these schools, a significant number of the faculty was involved in CHI activities, some a great deal. Global perspectives were being infused into many of the classes, but while most teachers acknowledged a heightened global awareness, not all understood what a global perspective really meant. Many students could be expected to graduate with an increased global awareness and understanding, but many would not.

Group 3
University Elementary School (K-6)
Columbus Intermediate School (6-8)
Pacifica Middle School (7-8)
La Puente Elementary School (K-6)
South High School (9-12)

While a number of people at these schools may have participated in CHI activities, only a handful translated such participation into any actual classroom teaching. While most teachers acknowledged a heightened awareness, only a small number understood what a global perspective really meant. A majority of students could be expected to graduate without an increased global awareness and understanding.

Basically, the perceptions of teachers in the network schools agreed with the CHI staff views stated above. There were some differences, however. Table 6.1 shows the school-by-school response of teachers to the question "How much were you involved with CHI global education activities during the past four years?" The number and percentage of those who reported some level of involvement are reported in the first two columns and a similar report is made in the next two columns for those who indicated that they were "never involved." Schools are organized into the typology devel-

oped by CHI, thus facilitating a comparison between CHI and
school faculty perceptions of involvement.

**Table 6.1: A comparison of CHI staff and
individual school faculty perceptions of teacher involvement
with CHI global education activities.**

| | *Teacher's perceptions of their own involvement* | | | | | |
| *CHI typology of* | *I was involved* | | *I was never involved* | | *Totals* | |
faculty involvement	*Number*	*%*	*Number*	*%*	*Number*	*%*
<u>Very active faculties</u>						
Buena Vista School*	–	–	–	–	–	–
Caldwell Elementary	13	72	5	28	18	100
Mesa Junior High	19	68	9	32	28	100
<u>Somewhat active faculties</u>						
Central High	18	53	16	47	34	100
North High	34	41	43	55	77	100
Birmingham Junior High	17	59	12	41	29	100
<u>Slightly active faculties</u>						
University Elementary	13	81	3	19	16	100
Columbus Intermediate	16	33	32	67	48	100
Pacifica Middle	9	47	10	53	19	100
La Puente Elementary	15	83	3	17	18	100
South High	22	42	31	58	52	100
Totals	176	52	164	48	340	100

*Buena Vista was closed at the end of year 3 of the project because of declining enrollment.
The questionnaire was administered in year 4. Other data from Buena Vista will be reported
later in the chapter, however.

Of particular note were the high rates of involvement perceived by
faculty members at University and La Puente elementary schools.
The fact is, these were small schools and because there was an informal system of rotation at workshops a large percentage of faculty
attended. Also, some people assumed involvement because consultants made presentations at staff meetings. As stated in the typology
descriptions, however, little actually changed vis-à-vis the infusion of
a global perspective into classroom curricula and teaching.

A more closely matched set of perceptions resulted from
responses to an item which asked teachers to rank the effects of

their involvement (on a five point scale from "a lot for the better" to "a lot for the worse," and including "not at all") on their personal understanding of global education, their teaching, the curriculum of the school, and so forth.

With the exception of University Elementary School and, to a lesser degree, Birmingham Junior High, faculty perceptions of how much involvement with CHI had affected their personal understanding of global issues and events were closely matched with the CHI typology of faculty involvement. That is, CHI staff and school faculties pretty much agreed upon how much global understanding existed at each school. The range was from nearly three-fourths of the staff at Caldwell Elementary perceiving that involvement had affected their understanding of global issues and events, to only one-third at South High. The mean for the ten schools was well over fifty percent.

We really could not explain the perceptions at University and Birmingham except to say that either many faculty members overestimated the level of global understanding at those two schools or things happened there of which we were never aware. We are pretty sure it was not the latter.

In most schools, a larger percentage of teachers felt that involvement affected their understanding of global issues more than it did their actual classroom teaching and curriculum. This pattern of greater understanding than action was expected. However, there was less of a drop-off than was expected. The range was from just above three-quarters of the teachers at Buena Vista who perceived that their classroom teaching and/or curriculum had been effected by involvement with CHI to only one-quarter of the teachers at South High who felt this way.

Teachers saw the impact of CHI upon the entire school as about the same as its impact upon their classrooms. At the high end, Buena Vista teachers perceived that the teaching of over three-fourths of the staff had been affected by involvement with CHI, while at South High the perception was that only about twenty percent had been affected. About one-half of the teachers across the eleven schools felt that the teaching of others and the curriculum of the school had been affected by involvement with CHI.

Patterns described thus far held up when we looked at teacher perceptions of the effects of their involvement with CHI on students. At the higher end, approximately sixty percent of the facul-

Table 6.2: A comparison of CHI staff perceptions of faculty involvement with teacher perceptions of the effects of that involvement (all disciplines, all grade levels).

CHI typology of faculty involvement	Number Responding	My teaching/ curriculum better	worse	no effect	My understanding of global issues better	worse	no effect	The curriculum of the school better	worse	no effect	Students' understanding of global issues better	worse	no effect	Students' attitudes toward others better	worse	no effect
Very active faculties																
Buena Vista School	(16)	–	–	–	–	–	–	–	–	–	–	–	–	–	–	–
Caldwell Elem	(27)	75	0	25	81	0	19	75	0	25	67	6	27	73	0	27
Mesa Junior High	(27)	62	0	38	73	0	27	72	0	28	72	4	24	75	0	25
Somewhat active faculties																
Central High School	(31)	58	0	42	71	0	29	68	6	26	74	0	26	58	3	39
North High School	(72)	51	0	49	61	0	39	55	2	43	60	3	30	51	3	46
Birmingham Junior High	(29)	59	0	41	76	0	24	67	4	29	63	7	30	52	7	41
Slightly active faculties																
University Elem	(15)	67	0	33	80	0	20	60	0	40	67	0	33	80	0	20
Columbus Intermed	(44)	34	2	64	48	0	52	46	0	54	48	0	52	41	0	59
Pacifica Middle	(15)	40	0	60	47	0	53	43	0	57	57	0	43	62	0	38
La Puente Elem	(16)	50	13	37	53	7	40	43	0	57	57	0	43	46	0	54
South High	(43)	31	0	69	40	2	58	28	0	72	32	0	68	30	3	67
Total	(308)	50	1	49	60	1	39	54	1	45	58	2	40	52	2	46

Teacher perceptions of the effects of their involvement with CHI ties at Caldwell Elementary, Mesa Junior High, Central High, and Birmingham Junior High perceived that such involvement had affected student understanding of global issues. At the low end, only one-quarter of the teachers at South High agreed with this.

With the exception of University Elementary School, where the estimate seemed quite inflated, a similar pattern existed regarding estimates of the effects of involvement with CHI upon student attitudes toward others. Rankings of teacher estimates at the schools were the same.

Throughout all of these perceptions of the effects of involvement with CHI, teachers at South High remained the most negative. This was not surprising to CHI staff since they ranked South lowest in terms of its amount of involvement. In retrospect, however, it is too bad that a follow-up survey of students was not done there. The reader will recall that a group of teachers there had conducted a survey about racial attitudes and had given feedback to their colleagues about those data. The data were pretty negative, and there was a tendency on the part of some staff to deny its validity. Further, feedback to the faculty was given at the staff meeting where a consultant had angered some staff by being critical of CIA activity in Central America. Even so, despite the negativity of many staff members at South at that time, there were some teachers who did take the opportunity to discuss those data with students. It would have been interesting to have followed that up with a survey of students.

It seems appropriate at this point to look more closely at South High School, along with some of the other schools, as a means of seeing how the unique personality of the school affects an attempt to globalize the curriculum.

The Culture of the School: Three Case Studies

South High School

South High served about 1750 students in grades 9–12. Sixty-five percent were Anglo, fifteen percent Hispanic, and fifteen percent Asian. The remainder were Black or of other ethnicity. While many Asian groups were represented, the majority were Vietnamese. Only four percent had limited English proficiency (LEP).

While family income data were not available, it was estimated that one quarter of the students came from low income families and the remainder were middle class. The number of students from minority and poor families had begun to increase in recent years. Until a decade ago, the school had served only Anglo, middle class students. At the time of the study, South High was similar to many of the schools built in the 1950s in southern California. These served bedroom communities made up of somewhat aging tract houses which were occupied by older middle class couples or a variety of younger families of various ethnicities who were in lower income jobs or who were just beginning their careers. The neighborhood, and thus the school population, was in transition. Leadership in the city was aware of the changes taking place in their community. There was an active human relations council and members of the school board were involved with it.

The teaching staff was not in transition, however. Of the seventy-one teachers on the faculty, sixty-eight were Anglo and only three were Hispanic. The average length of service was fourteen years, the longest of all schools in the network. A little over half of the teachers were male.

The principal was in his first year at South when the project began and was there for all four years. He had been transferred from another high school in the district and, in a way, the transfer was perceived as a promotion. He was enrolled in a doctoral program at a nearby university and, CHI was told, was "being groomed" to move to the district office. He seemed to be mostly concerned with maintaining things in good order: curriculum, discipline, procedures. He was, at times, a bit negative about the faculty, commenting that they had "been around" for a long time and that they were pretty set in their ways. He was minimally supportive of the global education project, generally complying with CHI's requests, but having to be reminded frequently about things that had to be done—for example, selecting teachers to participate in workshops, scheduling CHI at faculty meetings. It was clear that the project was far from being a high priority for him.

The school district, itself, was fairly large and quite bureaucratized. The superintendent had been in that role for some time, was well respected by the majority of the community, and ran the district with more or less an iron hand. One did not get the impression that curricula were standardized any more than in other places, but it was quite clear that operating policies and procedures were to be followed to the letter. Periodically, throughout the project, teachers would comment that they wanted to be sure that what CHI proposed was okay with the district. There was also some question in teachers' minds about district sanction of global education as a concept. One statement was, "They let you in—amazing!"

The school program was typical of American high schools. Most students attended for six fifty-plus–minute periods. There was also an early 'zero" period and a seventh period when a few classes were offered. Teachers taught five classes and had one planning period. The curriculum was mostly standard academic subjects with students more or less grouped into college-bound and non-college-bound classes. There were some shop, homemaking, and business classes offered, but there was really no vocational track available. In years past, the number of college-bound students had been a good deal greater.

The school was the original high school in the district. It had several older Spanish- style buildings which were attractive and in good repair. The remainder of the school plant was pretty typical of southern California high schools, mostly single story, finger construction, covered walks outside, lots of windows. Departments were housed in separate wings, thus keeping teachers isolated from each other for most of the day. There were not many places for teachers to congregate.

Generally, in the hallways and classrooms, students moved about or sat in an orderly fashion. At nutrition classes and lunch, students tended to congregate within their own ethnic groups. There was some racial tension, to which we shall return.

The school was adequately maintained. There was little evidence of graffiti or things discarded on the ground. Rooms were kept locked unless there was a class in session. Administrators were frequently out and about on the campus. There was hardly the fortress mentality which pervades many inner city schools. On the other hand, there was nothing much to distinguish this school from any other.

The response of the faculty to the initial presentation about the global education project was neither extremely positive nor extremely negative. Just over one-quarter of the teachers responded to the initial interest inventory, another fourteen percent said they were not interested at that time, and fifteen percent responded with negative comments or said that they needed more information (one of these ultimately developed quite a significant perspective-taking project). Several of those who were critical indicated that the initial presentation was not specific enough. They wanted to know "exactly" what was expected. Nearly half of the faculty made no response at all.

The following are a few of the initial comments of teachers which give a flavor of expectations and/or thinking at South High at the beginning of the global education project:

> "I'm a math teacher and I'm not knowledgeable of global education. I enjoyed your presentation and would be interested in your resources and ideas on global education for my math class."

> "I would like to incorporate the teaching and writing of research papers with the issues of global education [into my teaching]. Depending upon individual student interest, many topics would be addressed."

> "In my ESL classes I have ten countries represented. In some cases, the need to learn English is the only common factor they realize. I would like to introduce materials about why people immigrate to the U.S., covering the Vietnam and Korean wars specifically. Some of this material needs to be shared with other South High School students who deeply resent the presence of these immigrants."

> "Through my International and Humanities clubs, I enlist the aid of all my students in supporting worthy causes. In the early 70s my students raised over six thousand dollars to aid projects in a slum village in India."

> "I would be interested in observing others who also stress this theme in their classrooms. I would like to see the information available from your organization."

> "I would have a time problem attending workshops/conferences."

> "I'm sure you know that there is a great amount of trouble ahead in education. Sorry, I've lived through several purges and I can see where a word can cause another. Sorry, I'm keeping out of this."

> "I felt the presentation was formless. The presenters did not give any clearly defined projects for us to associate with.... The faculty members in the staff room have discussed the presentation and feel the same way." (This was in a memo sent to the principal the

day after the initial presentation; the teacher was a social studies teacher.)

"We use translated editions of Mesopotamian, Greek, Roman, French, English (early). I also use a VCR (things I have taped from my own TV) and wonder how I taught effectively before I had this resource."

Seventeen teachers indicated that they would attend a second, follow-up meeting at which they would attempt to define some themes for South High School based upon initial faculty response to the project. Nine actually showed up for the meeting (They had been scheduled into two groups by the principal because some were at school from 7:00 A.M. until 1:30 P.M. and others from 8:00 A.M. until 2:30 P.M.)

The nine teachers represented a variety of subject areas: social studies, math, science, English, special education, industrial arts, and business. There was also a counselor in attendance. It was explained that the other teachers who had indicated interest were, in fact, still interested but all had some other demand upon their time. By contract teachers were required only to stay fifteen minutes after school, so this particular meeting was seen as being on their own time.

While a handful of teachers recognized the nature of our changing world and the need for the development of a global perspective, most did not. At this point, too, only a few of them saw the relevance of the CHI project to the changing demography of the school and the need for the development of perspective-taking skills. Those teachers who did become involved with CHI were outstanding individuals who were, in general, respected by the rest of the faculty. They were not the key opinion leaders within the faculty, however. They did not particularly shape thinking at the school.

Competing demands upon teachers' time appeared to be a consistent problem in the network schools as it is in most schools. Upon closer examination, however, there was really little evidence that it was a problem at South High School. There was no evidence of any major curriculum project at the school. There were few district-wide staff development programs. The fact was, aside from a small number of highly dedicated teachers who constantly worked hard to improve their teaching, there was a large group who taught their classes from 8:00–2:30 and did little else. The following responses from teachers to the interview question "What would it take to globalize the curriculum of the school?" give some sense of the prevailing norms which governed becoming involved in an innovative program such as the one described in this book:

> "An atomic bomb. I really don't know. Maybe a new staff. Some have been here four hundred years."

> "A lot of new blood. CHI may never be successful at South High, not that I don't want you to be successful."

> "Part of the problem here is that we have an older faculty like myself who are comfortable with what we are doing"

> "Must come from the district, or the State Department of Education. Teachers don't want to change unless they get paid for it."

> "Change in faculty. Need enthusiastic teachers who are intellectually curious."

> "Teachers who had classes in teacher training institutions—teachers who are steeped in it."

> "I haven't thought about it. I'm not sure I want it globalized. The term *globalized* can be interpreted in so many ways."

In chapter 3, we describe the outstanding job done by a small group of faculty in carrying out a study of racial attitudes at South High. Further, we describe the early release-day faculty meeting at which a consultant spoke about the special needs of immigrant children and youth. It was at this meeting that a number of faculty members became incensed because the consultant criticized the Central Intelligence Agency. There were staff members at the school who had seen the global education project as un-American right from the beginning. The episode at this faculty meeting during the third year of the project only confirmed their opinions.

The problem with this incident was not the controversy that it caused. There were some teachers who indicated that this controversy was a good thing because it got people talking to each other. What was too bad was that it gave many of the faculty the opportunity to deny the fact that there was a problem of racial prejudice at the school and, thus, not take any responsibility for doing anything about it. The incident with the speaker overshadowed the presentation of the prejudice survey data in many teachers' minds. For example, in response to an interview question "Is global education at all a political issue at this school?" one teacher responded, "No, I haven't seen any evidence. What I remember is a speaker denouncing the U.S.A." The real issue, racial prejudice, was lost. Another teacher responded, "No. If anything, some staff members felt it was an inroad on class time—asking old staff to retool." Table 6.3 shows the results of the student survey conducted at South High in early 1988.

Table 6.3: Survey of student racial attitudes at South High School (1,302 respondents).

Selected questions	% Yes	% No
1. Are most students at our school friendly to everyone?	53	47
2. Are all teachers respectful of all students regardless of race?	62	38
3. Do some students at our school dislike other students because of their race?	77	23
4. Do students feel safe on our campus?	77	23
7. Are there gangs at our school?	67	33
8. Are some students afraid of other students because of their race?	62	38
9. Have you ever seen students at our school treated with disrespect because of their race?	73	27

Approximately three-fourths of the student body responded to the survey. Of that number, fewer than one-quarter felt that the campus was unsafe. Even so, the responses to the other questions clearly show that the school had a problem that would probably only get worse if not attended to. During the 1988–1989 school year, CHI's year 4, the principal of the school was seriously ill and was not able to follow up with the project. The original committee members attempted to get an expanded group to join them in continuing to plan for dealing with the problem. The original group had had some release time provided by a small grant from CHI during the previous year. A new grant for this year was not guaranteed. For whatever reason, not enough people came forward to continue the project in 1988–1989 and it was dropped.

There were a number of other good global education projects carried out by individuals or groups of teachers at South High. For example, one U.S. history teacher did a unit on immigration, utilizing the backgrounds of his students. Two science teachers carried out a fairly sophisticated study of environmental interdependence and actually had students look at the effects of environmental degradation upon biological, cultural, economic, and political systems. Yet another social studies teacher videotaped selected immigrant students as they told their stories of reaching the U.S. The counseling office developed a computer program with information about peace and international studies programs available in colleges and universities in the U.S.

Perhaps the most important missed opportunity at South was a program which was proposed but which never came to fruition. The principal, concerned about the fact that academic preparation seemed to be declining, was interested in developing a study-skills course for entering ninth graders. There were such courses in two other high schools in the district. In a meeting with one CHI staff member, the principal indicated that a course such as this really needed to have some content for it to be interesting to students. Having CHI assist with the development of such a course was discussed and informally agreed to. Periodically, CHI checked with the principal to see when planning for such a program might begin. There always seemed to be some reason why it couldn't get started: there were too many other things going on, the right teachers needed to be found, etc. Unfortunately, after two years, the principal decided to drop the idea, ostensibly because the course was not working well at one of the other high schools.

On the end-of-project questionnaire, South High ranked last on five of the eight "school climate" items, to which teachers responded on a six-point scale from "strongly agree" to "strongly disagree." On average, South High teachers mildly *disagreed* with the following statements:

> "Information is shared between teachers from different departments, teams, or grade levels."

> "Staff members are flexible; they can reconsider their positions on issues and are willing to change their minds."

> "The staff is continually evaluating its programs and activities and attempting to change them for the better."

These data support the perception that this staff had a number of people who were both professionally and politically conservative. Certainly, the consultant who was retained by CHI in response to the request of the multicultural committee at the school should have been warned about this and advised to avoid inflamatory comments.

More important, however, there were a number of people who did become involved with the project and there were many more who might have if they had been identified and approached in some helpful way. In retrospect, what CHI should have done was to find out the specific reasons for people's noninvolvement and then design appropriate, individualized strategies to approach them. The use of a framework such as the resistance framework described in chapter 4 perhaps would have helped.

Additionally, in retrospect, the multicultural committee should have been given more support, particularly after their initial presentation of data, so that their work could have continued. A few days more of release time, along with the provision of reading materials and/or appropriate consultation would probably have led to more progress in dealing with the problem of racial prejudice at the school.

Finally, the idea of a study-skills course using global education content was a good one and should have been pursued further. One of the authors of this book did develop just such a course for college freshmen, and it served its dual purposes quite well. In this case, there needed to be some confrontation with the principal about the fact that, while he purported to be supportive of the project, much of his behavior indicated that such support was minimal. As much of the literature on school improvement and/or global education suggests, the principal is critical to the change process (Boston, 1991). In chapter 7, we shall examine the role of the principal in some depth.

Caldwell Elementary School (K–6)

Caldwell had an enrollment of approximately 530 students. About one-third of these were Asians, including a large group of Koreans, a number of Indians, several Japanese, and a few of other nationalities as well. Nearly forty percent of the students were Anglo, with some of those being limited-English speaking (LEP) immigrants. About ten percent were Hispanic: Mexicans and a few Central Americans. There were small numbers of blacks and Middle Easterners, also. Twenty percent of the entire student body were designated as LEP. The school, indeed, was a mini United Nations.

School personnel estimated that sixty percent of the families served had 1986 incomes of between forty thousand and sixty thousand dollars. Twenty percent had incomes lower than that and an approximately equal number were higher. There apparently were few very poor or very rich families in this attendance area.

All but three of the faculty were female, and their average length of service was ten years. Three were Asian, three Hispanic, one black, and the remainder were Anglo. There was an active affirmative action plan in the district and an effort was being made to increase the number of minority teachers at the school.

There were two principals at Caldwell during the life of the project, and each served for two years. They were both supportive of the global education project and clearly saw its relationship to the multiethnicity of the school population. While both principals also had priorities other than globalizing the curriculum, this did seem to be high on their lists.

Both principals were quite clear about their goals for the school, although each had slightly different goals and they had distinctly different styles. The principal during the first two years was quite interested in technology and the arts. He was supportive of and quite well liked by the staff, who saw him as somewhat nondirective. The principal for the final two years of the project, on the other hand, was seen as interested in cooperative learning, literature-based reading, doing away with ability grouping, and involving faculty more in curriculum decision-making. She was seen as being more directive and, in her first year, there were a few teachers who felt a bit pressed by her. That seemed to work itself out pretty well, however. Both principals were quite concerned for parent education and involvement and, as part of that, cross-cultural understanding. The first principal, along with two upper-grade teachers, had developed a computerized community bulletin board.

The district was fairly large and unified, and had a deserved reputation of being quite innovative. However, during the four years of the project, there were four different superintendents. The initial superintendent, who had been in the district for several years, sanctioned CHI and global education. As it turned out, so did the elementary assistant superintendent. (That was not the case with the secondary assistant superintendent, but that story will be told in the next chapter.) After the first superintendent left to take an attractive job in another district, an acting superintendent was in place for a brief while. He was followed by a third superintendent who was quite supportive of CHI and its activities. After two years, he resigned under pressure over issues not related to the project and was followed by yet another superintendent who truly had his hands full but who gave at least verbal support to CHI and its work. It was the significant support and continuity of the elementary assistant superintendent which ultimately was of real significance to this project.

In many respects, Caldwell was not a typical school. The middle class, multiethnic student population has already been described, and so has the innovative reputation of the district. The district was relatively new, having been unified out of three other districts. The population was growing and many of the schools and teachers were relatively new, also. There was a sense of excitement and professionalism here that was harder to come by in some of the other, older districts faced with problems brought about by declining enrollments.

The school plant itself was fairly new and organized into semi-open-plan pods with four carpeted classes to a pod and a central library/meeting area. The administration area was separate and accessible to teachers. There was a faculty area where teachers from all grade levels could congregate. Outside walks were covered and there was an outside, covered lunch area for students. The entire building was attractive both inside and out, and was well maintained. More important, perhaps, the interactions at the school were friendly and relaxed. Caldwell was a pleasant place to be for children and adults.

At the beginning of the project, the principal arranged a meeting at which CHI staff members met with him and four upper-grade teachers. It became quite obvious that the use of computers was primary in their minds. They wanted to know if we could get an international company such as TRW, AT&T, or IBM to provide them with equipment for an international telecommunications project. The teachers spoke of various systems which were already in existence, but they were interested in developing their own. CHI staff spoke of possible UNESCO (United Nations Educational, Scientific, and Cultural Organization) connections. The principal shared his interest in developing a community-history project with a data base developed at the school. CHI staff described the "Columbus in the World" project. The Caldwell group expressed interest in getting literature in Spanish, Korean, Chinese and/or

Hindi. They also showed an interest in simulations and were pleased to note that CHI already had a large collection. At first the two groups, CHI staff and Caldwell faculty, seemed to be talking past each other. On one side there was an overwhelming interest in the potential of the computer and on the other, a lack of knowledge about computers and their potential but an interest in global perspectives. Finally, when the conversation got around to simulation materials and *then* when the focus shifted to a discussion of connecting Caldwell via telecommunications with a school or schools in other parts of the world, a real bonding was made.

Actually, the project got off to a slow start at Caldwell. Some of the upper-grade teachers were not at the initial faculty meeting because they were at camp with their students. Only a half-dozen teachers attended the follow-up session to identify school-wide themes. However, teachers attended network-wide workshops and did a good job of reporting back to the entire faculty (this was supposed to happen at all schools, but didn't). An expert in educational technology, Dr. Terry Cannings, helped the upper-grade team establish a computer linkage with three schools in or near Sydney, Australia, and *all* classes, including the kindergarten, had pen pals there. Gradually, through materials visits by CHI staff and through other means, more and more teachers were drawn into global education activities. For example, materials from Educators for Social Responsibility were provided to one teacher interested in peace studies. CHI's support of the school's International Month, held each January, very much helped to strengthen the relationship also. In the end-of-project questionnaire, nearly three-fourths of the teachers indicated that they had been significantly involved with the project. When everything is taken into account, all classes were affected to one degree or another. Conditions were ideal for globalizing the curriculum at this school. In summary, those conditions were:

1. a student population with ethnic diversity from families interested in and actively supportive of the school;

2. a faculty who looked upon this diversity as a positive factor rather than as a problem and which was open to finding new ways to do their jobs better;

3. principals who were supportive, goal focused, and who actively worked to make the project successful;

4. a supportive district administration;

5. a small amount of resources to be applied to the work at hand.

There were other conditions, as well. The norms of openness on the part of faculty have already been mentioned. Other aspects of school culture probably also came into play. The school was small, communication was good, goals were clear, administration and teacher collaboration was basically positive, and faculty satisfaction was high. Measures of school climate from the end-of-project, reflective questionnaire were higher at Caldwell than at any other school except Buena Vista.

There were as many competing demands upon the time of Caldwell teachers as there were at any of the other network schools. When asked what things got in the way of globalizing their curricula, over forty percent said "lack of time." Even so, none of the teachers ever said that they could not participate in the project because they were too busy with other things.

The computer linkage with Australia has been described elsewhere in this book. So has the International Month. There were other outstanding projects at Caldwell, also. There was an international music project in first grade. Special education students had a pen pal project with students in England and a multicultural study, fifth and sixth grade students did an extensive study of Central America, second and third graders had a peace and multicultural study, and so forth. In the final year of the project, 1988–1989, two new primary teachers submitted a grant proposal to develop an integrated language arts–social studies program focused on literature from around the world. The grant was approved. The teachers had been encouraged to make the submission by the principal and by other teachers who had received previous grants.

The curriculum at this school became quite globalized. In retrospect, CHI probably could have done more to support the efforts of this faculty, but the teachers did not seem to feel this. In fact, their end-of-project responses to what happened were quite positive. In response to the question "What do you believe it would take to globalize the curriculum of this school?" a typical statement was, "Most teachers are doing this already. Keep on providing release-time workshops, grants, and word of mouth." In response to the question "Would it have made any difference if CHI had been more directive and structured in its approach?" the following statements were of interest:

"It would have stifled our creativity. We don't need anyone making additional demands. It was good to be trusted as a professional."

"The last thing we want is to write an awful lot of additional paperwork. Had the teachers felt demanded upon, we would not have done it.... Thus, because of flexibility, I got involved."

"It would have been just the opposite. It would have scared teachers away. [Loose structure] allowed teachers to become more creative. Teachers have so many 'have to's' from the administration and district. Your heart is in it when you're allowed to choose."

Columbus Intermediate School

Columbus served just under thirteen hundred students. Approximately eighty-five percent were Hispanic, eleven percent Asian and three percent Anglo. Nearly one-third of the student body had limited English proficiency (LEP). It was estimated by school personnel that ninety-eight percent of the families served by the school had an income in 1986 of twenty thousand dollars or less.

Approximately sixty percent of the fifty-seven teachers at Columbus were female, and the average length of teaching service was ten years. Just under eighty percent were Anglo while almost twenty percent were Hispanic. Most of the schools in the school district served similar populations, and they were trying very hard to increase the minority representation in the teaching force.

The school program was typical of those in intermediate schools across the country except that English as a second language (ESL) and reading programs were quite large by comparison to other departments at the school and to similar departments at most intermediate schools. All subjects were taught separately and students had a fifty-minute first period (including home room) and six other forty-five-to-fifty-minute periods. They also had a fifteen-minute morning nutrition period and approximately one-half hour for lunch.

Columbus certainly did not fit the stereotype of a barrio school. The facilities, while crowded, were new, bright and open, well kept, and very pleasant. The initial impression one gained upon entering the school was that this was a relaxed and enjoyable place to be. Office staff were helpful and friendly, adults spoke to students with respect, and students moved about easily. One teacher reported early in the project, "Substitutes say this is their favorite school in Orange County because of the friendly staff and kids."

There was a change of principals after the first year of Columbus' involvement with CHI and global education. While that could have had some impact on teacher involvement, it did not seem to. While it was not perceived by CHI or the faculty that global education was a major priority for either principal, it was clear that both of them were supportive of the project. They complied with all CHI requests and both communicated favorably with teachers about CHI-sponsored activities. On the other hand, well into the second year of the project, the *vice* principal was not aware of what the project was attempting to do.

The district tended to be more bureaucratic than most with which CHI worked. There was a high level of centralized curriculum development and teachers were conditioned to follow prescribed courses of study, allocations of time, rules for field trips, and myriad other policies. While the project had tacit district approval, it did not have strong endorsement as, for example, at Caldwell. This was further compounded by the implied and overt pressure on teachers to improve statewide achievement test scores through alignment of their curricula with district prescriptions which, in turn, were aligned with state frameworks. Something new, such as global education, was seen by some as contravening this tight curriculum coupling. The district level ESL office never saw the potential of this project for its program.

As one would expect, there were competing demands upon teachers' time at Columbus. In addition to the pressure to give a good basic education to ESL students, the school had a tradition of competition, both athletic and academic. Teachers were expected to help students participate in a variety of local, state, and national contests. Campus safety was a concern and there was a special gang prevention program. Individual teachers were involved with various district curriculum projects. The second principal began a new PTA and pushed hard on parent conferencing and community-involvement activities—science fair, back-to-school night, advisory committee. Dropout- and drug-prevention programs were important and long-standing. There were some teachers who worked part-time teaching evening adult ESL classes, also.

The initial reaction of the Columbus staff to the idea of global education was basically positive. At the end of the meeting when the project was introduced, twenty-one teachers individually shared their interest with CHI staff members. Most people easily made the connection between cross-cultural awareness and global awareness. In many of the other schools in the project, the demographics of the student population were changing to include more minorities and poor. In most of them, faculty members were having some trouble adjusting to these changes. At Columbus, this was not true. On the contrary, the student body there was minority and poor and always had been. Most faculty members were committed to serving "their" population, were searching for better ways to do that, and seemed proud of what they were doing. In fact, on the reflective questionnaire at the end of the project, the mean response at Columbus to the agree/disagree item "Most people find their job rewarding in other than monetary ways" was among the highest of the eleven schools in the project. This was of particular note since a few of the means for other climate items as perceived by teachers were among the lowest in the network—clarity of goals, administrator and teacher collaboration, flexibility of staff.

Despite this seeming initial interest and, on balance, the positive ambiance of the school, Columbus Intermediate School had one of the lowest involvement rates of any of the network faculties. The CHI staff rated it as only "slightly" active and, by their own report, two-thirds of the teachers were never involved. The explanation, as one would expect, is complex. To begin with, the school joined the network in year 2 as a replacement for a school which had dropped out. Also, during the course of the project, there was a contract dispute between teachers and the district. Such disputes occurred in five of the eleven network schools and *negatively affected project participation in all five.* Teachers simply are less apt to be active in anything they perceive as extra just before, during, or just after such disputes. Fortunately, an agreement was reached fairly quickly, there was little acrimony, and the effect was not too bad.

Early in the life of the project, one small group of teachers became attracted to it and, in a way, adopted it as theirs. This group was not necessarily in the mainstream of the faculty, and some people who expressed sympathy to the idea of global education also indicated that they did not wish to participate because of the apparent ownership by this group. This attitude was intensified after some of the early adopter group were less than successful in developing an early project which had some visibility at the school.

Another reason for the low rate of involvement at Columbus was that CHI's intervention activity was probably too laissez faire. Three quite good school-based projects, involving several teachers, were developed during the second year of the school's participation. To begin with, three well-respected science teachers received a small grant from CHI and developed a nuclear energy unit which gained a good deal of positive recognition from the faculty. Second, and also supported by a small grant, a group of seven teachers and the principal (among them some very popular people) developed an all-school International Week Celebration which included song, dance, ethnic dress, and sport. The entire school participated. Third, five students chaperoned by a teacher-leader on the faculty, were helped by CHI to participate in a week-long program of cross-cultural awareness at Las Palomas de Taos, New Mexico. The experience was outstanding and the student enthusiasm upon returning to Columbus was quite contagious. The following summer, another five seventh-graders went to the Taos workshop with the same teacher. This time, some money was raised at the school to help defray travel expenses for the group.

Thus, by the end of its second year in the project, this school seemed to CHI to be poised to move forward in many directions. However, there had not been an assessment of engagement/resistance. If there had been, it would have been recognized that those people open to the idea of global education and/or who saw its relationship to cross-cultural understanding, and who were willing to work a bit extra, were really the only ones who were participating. Some others did not really understand global education; for them it had no meaning. They certainly did not see a link between global awareness and multicultural awareness. Others needed to see that participating with CHI would not take too much extra work. Some needed more help with "how to do it," for example how to infuse a global perspective into a basic subject. There were a very few people who just didn't want to be bothered. This potential for moving ahead and the lack of strong resistance were evidenced in teacher responses to a question on the end-of-project questionnaire which asked them whether or not they had been discouraged by anyone from participating in CHI activities. Most said no, with only three responding affirmatively as follows:

> "I've heard discouraging remarks from the perpetual cynics, but those remarks aren't directed against CHI specifically."

> "Some don't want their set opinions challenged so they don't participate."

> "There are people who don't want to do anything else other than their day-to-day work."

What CHI did was to continue its normal activity: school visits, offering of grants, provision of workshops, and so forth. Not only did involvement not increase, it actually dropped. In retrospect, it seems quite clear that initial enthusiasm should not have been mistaken for long-term commitment and/or as a sign that the project was "on its way." Frequently, this second, or post-initial, enthusiasm is the most critical to any attempt to change a school, and assessment and some individualization of strategies is critical. This certainly was the case at Columbus.

Conclusion

At all three of these schools—South High, Caldwell Elementary, and Columbus Intermediate—the principals were crucial to the progress of the project. In all cases, they were cooperative and responded to requests for assistance from CHI. However, the degree to which global education became a high priority for each one varied considerably. At South and Columbus, it was never really seen by the principals as a vehicle for integrating other school goals. At Caldwell it was; and the project flourished. Much of the literature on school change tells us how vital the principal is to the change process. Let us turn now, in chapter 7, to an examination of the role played by principals in the global education network project.

References

Boston, J., "School Leadership and Global Education," in K. Tye, ed., *Global Education: From Thought to Action* (Alexandria, Va.: ASCD, 1991).

Eisner, E., *The Enlightened Eye: Qualitative Inquiry and the Enhancement of Educational Practice* (New York: Macmillan, Inc., 1991).

7

THE PIVOTAL ROLE OF THE PRINCIPAL

Principal Leadership Today: Key Theories

The literature of educational change has pointed consistently to the principal as the key person in the school improvement process. The CHI study confirms that position. Network principals played significant roles vis-à-vis the globalization of the curriculum of their schools. This chapter attempts to tell the story of just how significant those roles were. Before the data about network principals are presented, however, let us briefly look at what some of the more thoughtful theorists have had to say about leadership, school change, and the principalship.

As a beginning point, it should be noted that one can be a school administrator without being a leader (the reverse can be true, also). The classic distinction made by James Lipham (1964) over twenty-five years ago best explains the administration/leadership contrast. Lipham points out that a leader is primarily concerned with the creation of new structures or procedures for achieving group or organizational goals while the main function of the administrator is simply to utilize existing structures and procedures to achieve exisiting institutional objectives. He describes the leader as disruptive of the current state of affairs and the administrator as a stabilizing force.

In a school setting, it would be rare to find an individual consistently playing one role. Ideally, a school leader *chooses* to alternate between roles as the situation dictates. It has been pointed out, for example, that the principal who regularly utilizes existing structures such as staff and/or team meetings and weekly bulletins to promote open communication is performing an administrative function. If, however, such existing structures (meetings and bulletins) are not adequate to bring about the desired communication, as a leader, the principal might choose to create new ones such as a coordinating council of some type, a communications laboratory, release-time meetings, or informal dialogue (Novotney and Tye, 1973).

Leadership is not a phenomenon which can be easily analyzed and/or quantified. The question of what consititutes good and effective leadership has been studied for many years. Perhaps the most comprehensive current summary of such studies is that of Bernard Bass and Robert Stogdill (1990). Prior to 1945, it was believed that all leaders shared certain identifiable personality traits. This ideas is now considered inadequate because so many different kinds of people can and have demonstrated leadership ability. It is impossible to identify certain common traits which leaders have and others lack.

Scientific management theory emerged early in the century and had organizational efficiency as its goal. It held that good leadership was that which best organized work and workers so as to maximize production. This viewpoint was totally task oriented and focused upon the needs of the organization. While this view of leadership is known to be inadequate because it overlooks the human elements of organizations, it continues to recur. We have neoscientific management today as a school of thought, for example, and the so-called accountability movement in education is based upon scientific management principles despite the fact that those principles have been found wanting (Taylor, 1911; Callahan, 1962).

Human relations leadership developed in the 1920s as a reaction to the impersonality of the scientific management approach. Based upon the assumption that the interpersonal relations in an organization determine its effectiveness, the goal of the approach was seen as producing worker satisfaction. Thus, the focus was on the needs of individuals in the organization (Mayo, 1945).

Beginning in the 1950s, a growing number of studies turned their attention to leader *behavior*. This was parallel to the powerful overall behavioral movement in psychology and education, which held that all observable phenomena could be understood by (1) breaking them down into their component parts, and (2) studying the parts.

Behavioral studies in the area of leadership led to a number of useful models. The simplest one identified three basic approaches to leadership in the behavior of leaders who were studied: (1) *authori-*

tarian, which is characterized as directive and task oriented; (2) *democratic,* which is seen as participative and process- and relationship-oriented; and (3) *laissez faire,* which is said to be nondirective and lacking in formal leadership (Lewin, Lippitt, and White, 1960).

Douglas McGregor (1960) developed the now famous Theory X and Theory Y model in which he posits that Theory X leadership resembles authoritarian behavior and is based on the assumption that the power of the leader comes from the position he or she occupies, and that people are basically lazy and unreliable. Conversely, Theory Y leadership resembles democratic behavior and assumes that the power of leaders is granted to them by those they lead, and that people are basically self-directed and creative if properly motivated. In addition, the theory suggests a self-fulfilling prophecy: If leaders behave toward people in the organization as if they are lazy, uncreative, in need of control, and so forth, they become so. On the other hand, when treated as creative, self-directed, and so forth, they are seen to take on these characteristics.

Subsequently, Chris Argyris (1971) identified two sets of leadership behaviors which he calls A and B. He distinguishes these from Theory X and Theory Y attitudes and suggests that A behaviors usually (but not always) go with Theory X attitudes. Pattern A includes not owning up to feelings, not being open, rejecting experimentation, and not helping others to engage in these behaviors. It is characterized by close supervision and a high degree of structure. Pattern B leaders, on the other hand, are seen to behave in more supportive and facilitiative ways. They are thought to own up to their feelings, they are open and experimenting, and they help others to engage in these behaviors. Argyris posits that such behaviors tend to create organizational norms of trust, concern, and creativity.

A series of behavioral studies of leadership were initiated at Ohio State University in 1945 and resulted in the development of the Leader Behavior Description Questionnaire (LBDQ) (Stogdill and Coons, 1957). The two major dimensions of this instrument are "initiating structure" and "consideration," with each of those divided into six subdimensions (e.g., production emphasis, persuasiveness, and superior orientation for "initiating structure," and demand reconciliation, tolerance of freedom, and tolerance of uncertainty for "consideration"). The critical thing about these studies is that they identify distinct dimensions of leadership which can be described separately or in combination.

At the Survey Research Center at the University of Michigan, a series of studies likewise identified two distinct dimensions of leadership behavior: "employee orientation" and "production orientation." Using these concepts, Rensis Likert (1961) conducted a series of studies and determined that employee-centered leaders have better performance records than those who are job centered. He found that "supervisors with the best records of performance focus their primary attention on human aspects of their subordinates' problems and on endeavoring to build effective work groups with high performance goals."

Ultimately, through his studies, Likert (1967) developed a continuum of management styles in organizations. System 1 he characterizes as a task-oriented, highly structured, and authoritarian style; System 4 as a relationship-oriented style based upon teamwork and trust. He presents Systems 2 and 3 as intermediate stages between the two extremes. Systems 1 and 4, respectively, approximate Macgregor's Theory X and Theory Y.

Behavioral approaches to the study of leadership have been influential in shaping our thinking about organizations. However, current theory has moved beyond these earlier theories to include consideration of the *situation* as well as the behaviors of both leaders and followers.

Perhaps the earliest situational theory was that of Robert Tannenbaum and Warren Schmidt (1958). They propose an interrelationship among follower behavior (e.g., needs for independence, readiness to assume responsibility), forces in the leader (e.g., personal value system, confidence in group members), and forces in the situation (e.g., the problem, pressures of time) which call for different leadership behaviors as circumstances dictated. These behaviors are seen as ranging from, on one hand, the leader identifying a problem, considering alternative solutions, choosing one of them, and telling followers what to do to, and, on the other, the leader giving the group the power to make a decision and agreeing to live with the outcomes.

Fred Fiedler is widely known for his "leadership contingency theory" (1967). According to this theory, three variables have to be considered by a leader who is deciding what behavior is most effective at a given time. These are: (1) his or her personal relations with the members of the group, (2) the amount of structure in the task, and (3) the degree of position-power the leader has. Fiedler developed eight possible combinations of these variables and ultimately concluded that task-oriented leadership was more appropriate when the situation was either very favorable or very unfavorable, and the relationship-oriented style of leadership is more appropriate when the situation is neither one nor the other, but is somewhere in between.

The situational theory which is most applied currently to the research and practice of leadership in education is that of Hersey and Blanchard (1988). In this model, the terms *task behavior* and *relationship behavior* are used to describe concepts similar to *initiating structure* and *consideration* of the Ohio State studies. The four basic classes of leadership behavior are: High task and low relationship, high task and high relationship, low task and high relationship, low task and low relationship. In addition, they have introduced another dimension which is important to the situation. That is the *maturity* of the group with which the leader is working. The notion is that the *effectiveness* of leaders depends upon their selecting the appropriate class of behavior in light of the maturity of the group. The major difference between this theory and most others already discussed is that in this theory any of the basic styles may be effective or ineffective, depending on the situation. In other theories there is generally the assumption that there is one consistently *best* leadership behavior.

The leadership theories discussed thus far are normative. That is, they address the issue of what leadership *should* be: how leaders should behave. The question, of course, is, "How *do* leaders behave?"

Argyris (1962) suggests that bureacratic-pyramidal values, comparable to Theory X assumptions discussed earlier, dominate most organizations. He states that such values lead to poor, shallow, and mistrustful relationships which, in turn, result in decreased interpersonal competence. According to Argyris, today's organizations are usually created to achieve goals that are best met collectively. However, management most often determines how these goals are to be achieved. Thus, the design comes first and individuals are to be fitted to the job. The design is based upon four concepts of scientific management: task specialization, chain of command, unity of direction, and span of control.

Hersey and Blanchard summarize this view of Argyris's as follows:

Management tries to increase and enhance organizational and administrative efficiency and productivity by making workers "interchangeable parts."

Basic to these concepts is that power and authority should rest in the hands of a few at the top of the organization, and thus those at the lower end of the chain of command are strictly controlled by their superiors or the system itself. Task specialization often results in the oversimplification of the job so that it becomes repetitive, routine, and unchallenging. This implies directive, task-oriented leadership where decisions about the work are made by the superior, with the workers only carrying out those decisions. This type of leadership evokes managerial controls such as budgets, some incentive systems, time and motion studies, and standard operating procedures, which can restrict the initiative and creativity of workers. (1988, p. 61.)

Those who wish to know what it takes to bring a global perspective to the curriculum of a school need to be aware that Argyris's description is pretty accurate when applied to today's schools. The implication is quite clear. Not only does the curriculum need to be changed, but our basic ideas about the management of the institution of school need to be rethought as well. It is one thing to *talk* about school-based management, restructuring, teacher empowerment, and the like. It is quite another to expect people to actually give up power and control over such things as budget and curriculum. Very few school administrators today see their roles as ones of facilitating the work of others. Most see themselves as making the decisions that others carry out. Current notions of scientific and Theory X management are such a part of the deep structure of schooling that they most often go unchallenged.

Our school systems are bureaucracies. As such, they encourage and reward vertical orientation, and consequently most school principals tend to behave as administrators rather than as leaders. They utilize existing structures or procedures to achieve existing goals set by the superordinate system and they are rewarded for this vertical orientation. We are reminded of a presentation of a well-respected superintendent of schools several years ago who was addressing a group of principals at a conference on school innovation. He exhorted them to "change anything you want, just don't rock the boat." As absurd as this admonition is, it demonstrates the tremendous pressure placed upon principals to conform to the dictates of the superordinate system.

Goal Orientation of Principals

When teachers in the eleven network schools were interviewed at the end of the global education project and asked, "What goals are high on your principal's agenda?" the answers most often given were "academic success," "good test scores," "the advanced placement program," or some other response supporting the finding that academic preparation, generally, was the highest priority for principals. They know that academic success is basically what society wants from its schools. They also are keenly aware that their own performance is often judged by their superiors on the basis of their school's ranking on key academic indicators such as CAP, CTBS, or SAT scores, the percentage of students reading at or above grade level, the percentage of students enrolled in foreign language classes, higher math, or college placement sciences, and so forth.

Table 7.1 shows that the general area of campus safety (discipline, drug intervention, gang awareness, programs for at-risk youth, and dropout prevention) ran a very close second, trailing academic preparation by only one percentage point. It is not surprising that teachers viewed school safety as being high on their principal's agenda: keeping the campus under control and maintaining an environment in which teaching and learning can take place is, in fact, generally understood in our society as being the primary responsibility of the principal. Those who do this well are much appreciated—by teachers, parents, and certainly by their superiors in the district office.

Responses that might be categorized as "public image" were the next most often mentioned goals. "She wants the school to look good to the community," "He wants us to make him look good," "She doesn't want to make waves," "He really wants the school to do well on the WASC accreditation review," and ""Good PR with the parents and community," were typical answers. Some teachers implied that their principal would do whatever it might take to make the school seem to be all the things that it was supposed to be.

Eighteen teachers (eight percent) thought that global education was part of their principal's agenda and many of those noted that it was a "midrange" priority. This is a sobering statistic for those interested in global education and points to the need, as

Boston (1991, p. 98) suggests, for global educators to assist principals to clarify their own vision. Likewise, it points to the importance of assisting principals to see how global education might serve as a vehicle for the accomplishment of a variety of school goals.

Table 7.1: Teacher responses to the interview question, "What goals are high on your principal's agenda?"

Number giving response	*Response*
43	Academic success, good test scores, etc.
41	Campus safety, discipline, etc.
35	Public image
22	Good social environment, student self-esteem, etc.
19	Curriculum issues
18	Global education
16	Don't know what my principal's goals are
12	Changing ethnicity of students, LEP, etc.
9	Middle school concept
8	To have things run smoothly, everyone gets along
5	Sports programs
5	Support for teachers, staff morale, etc.
4	Cooperative learning
3	"What's best for kids"
240	Total

In chapter 6 we wrote that the CHI staff came to know the network schools quite well. For example, they felt comfortable in estimating the degree to which each school was developing curricula infused with a global perspective. For the purposes of this chapter, it should be noted that they came to know the principals of the eleven schools quite well, also. The following kinds of data were collected from and about the principals:

1. Informal observations during visits to the schools, including planned staff meetings, interactions in the faculty lounges, and scheduled meetings with principals about global education activities at the schools.

2. Informal observations at network-wide administrator meetings for principals only and at other meetings with district administrators and representative teachers.

3. Structured interviews with principals about global education activities at their schools.

4. Informal observations of principals at network-wide teacher in-service activities.

5. Structured interview and questionnaire responses from teachers about their principals.

On the basis of these data, it was hypothesized that the critical indicator of principal leadership was what came to be called her or his "goal style." With regard to goals for the school, the principal was seen as *focused, diffuse,* or *coping.*

The *focused* principal seemed (1) to have a few, carefully selected goals for the school, and (2) to work diligently to accomplish those goals. Such principals were able to articulate clear visions of *what* schools were supposed to do and *why.* They also seemed able to find ways to cause their schools to approximate these visions. Being able to go beyond the simple concern for what works and/or how to keep school is what seemed to distinguish focused principals from others. Sergiovanni (1987) points out that the ability of leaders to communicate their values and beliefs to others in a way that provides meaning is highly significant in the shaping of a school and its culture.

There were eleven schools in the network. Six of them had principal changes during the four years of the project. Thus, there was a total of seventeen principals who worked with CHI. Of this number, six principals were seen as focused. Two of these clearly articulated goals related to global education, two felt strongly about development of multicultural awareness because of the demographic changes occurring at their schools, one had strong progressive ideals and saw active learning and integrative experiences as critical to quality education, and one had firm convictions about academic excellence. Except in the latter case, to which we shall return in a bit, these were the principals who saw the value of global education as a means toward furthering their own goals. Because of this, they supported the CHI project most vigorously. It was these *focused* principals who seemed to most clearly understand the meaning of global education and who could see how it could help them achieve their own goals. Further, it was these schools which ultimately came closest to bringing a global perspective to the curriculum.

The manner through which this process occurred is amply demonstrated by the following field note from October 1987, written by a CHI staff member after an informal meeting with one principal:

> As we walked out with [the principal] to get a master schedule, he further told us about his international experience: his daughter was going to school in England and she somehow was connected with a group of international students from various countries. She was helping them become accustomed to the U.S. culture. Thus, these students were coming in and out of his home a lot.
>
> He also said that his was a very religious family and that he had some experience with right-wing fundamentalists who are opposed to global thinking....
>
> He also shared that it took him a number of years to decide how his personal thoughts and feelings differed and/or fit into some of these ideas and that now he knows his own personal balance in this area....
>
> He's done his homework in thinking through what he believes.

Focused principals often had more than one goal. However, the number was generally limited and, in every case, *very* well articulated to teachers, community, the district, and others. In many instances, if the principal had been in place for awhile, many teachers had been hired who were in sympathy with these articulated and focused goals. In fact, three of these principals, in end-of-project interviews, pointed to the hiring of teachers sympathetic to their goals as a major accomplishment.

Another five principals were seen as having a *diffuse* goal focus. That is, they worked at keeping themselves at least somewhat informed about trends in schooling and they frequently articulated school goals in terms of such trends. The result was often a large variety of goals, often changing, and sometimes even in conflict.

At Central High, for example, in the third year of the project, a full day of student free release time for teachers had been planned for several months for global education in-service. Little by little, additional items came to occupy the agenda. Even after CHI personnel arrived at the school, they found more changes in the day's program. Two weeks before the meeting a speaker on teenage suicide was added to the program. A presentation on the state education budget was felt to be important enough to take an hour, forty-five minutes went to information on progress toward the upcoming accreditation, and the principal felt it necessary to present an "end of year activities update." After all was said and done, half an hour went to global education.

Commenting on this same principal, one of the long-time staff members said: "[This principal]...tries to have a lot of opportunities available to the kids. In fact, he has about four million programs going on at Central and he pushes each of them. This is a wonderful opportunity for the kids and the teachers."

Each of the network principals who seemed to be in this category spoke in favor of global education to his or her faculty, often with enthusiasm. As time went on, it became apparent that several other competing goals also were articulated. Many teachers at these schools told CHI staff that they initially responded cautiously to the project because they saw their principal as attracted to fads and they just didn't have time for "every new thing that came along." At these schools, the idea of *competing demands* was quite prominent and such demands were often pointed to as a reason for nonparticipation in global education. These principals seemed less able to see how global education might relate to other goals and, in fact, even seemed less apt to truly understand what global education was. They appeared to be attracted to it, at least in part, because it was seen as an innovation.

The final six principals were seen as having a *coping* goal focus. Their behavior was similar to that of the *administrator* described earlier by Lipham. That is, they focused on managing the school, on seeing that things ran as smoothly as possible. Little, if any, concern was expressed by these principals for substantive issues.

To one degree or another, coping principals tended to only respond to directives from their districts. They certainly were loath to initiate anything without checking first with superordinates. In the end-of-project survey, teachers clearly felt that these principals' goals were those supported, rewarded, and/or dictated by the district administration.

Field notes also showed that such principals often placed district rules and requirements ahead of school-site needs or wishes. Examples of such notes were:

> He apologized for not being at the department chairs meeting he'd promised to attend, citing a district meeting which interfered.

> She wanted to screen all the minigrant proposals before teachers submitted them to CHI to be sure that no one was planning to do anything that would "make waves" at the district office.

> "Teachers said the principal was the one who had "let the project in" at their school. Several said they didn't really believe it when they were told that participation would be their decision. They always look upward for cues as to expectations and rewards.

These principals seemed not to initiate new programs on their own. They tended to react to things *as they came along.* They expressed support to their faculties for the CHI project, at least in the presence of CHI staff members, However, in every case, these were the principals who frequently did not follow through on commitments and/or who needed reminders about activities and things which needed to be done.

As it turned out, the five schools in which these six people were principals were the ones which accounted for the lowest levels of teacher participation in the project. In some cases, teachers expressed very negative feelings about these principals. For example, the following statements were recorded:

> He is just marking time, waiting to retire.

> He'll do whatever makes him look good to the district and the parents.

> He just wants things to run smoothly. He doesn't want to "stir things up."

Such statements, alone, do not prove anything. However, when seen as part of a pattern of resistance to new ideas, lack of enthusiasm, and the like, they give an indication of the culture of a school. In chapters 3 and 6, the importance of school culture to the globalization of the curriculum was discussed and others have emphasized the inseparable relationship between leadership and culture (Sarason, 1982; Schein, 1985).

The idea that the style of goal orientation of the principal is critical to his or her leadership and to the culture of a school is suggested here as a hypothesis to be tested further in other settings. It seems related to the behavioral theories of leadership discussed at the beginning of this chapter. Further, it seems to combine the normative outlook of those theories and the descriptive and pragmatic orientation of situational theories. The latter are quite useful but tend to emphasize management behavior to at least the partial exclusion of important value questions—for example, "*Why* should we teach certain things?"

District Ethos and the Principalship

The concept of district ethos was explored fully in chapter 5. It was pointed out there that most school systems treat their schools in fairly standardized ways and that communication and expectations tend to be top-down. This is very much like the bureaucratic design described earlier by Argyris with its neoscientific management concepts of interchageable parts, task specialization, chain of command, unity of direction, and span of control.

The *interchangeable parts* nature of school districts, for example, was dramatically demonstrated in this study. Six of the eight districts in the project had conscious policies of rotating principals every so often. No single policy can more assure principal loyalty to the superordinate system rather than to the school than this one. Such systems require that middle managers, as principals are often called, behave as administrators rather than leaders and they encourage *coping* rather than *focused* behavior. In fact, focused and/or leadership behavior, in some instances, can be seen as threatening to the system.

Situational leadership theories do not now adequately take into account this pervasive, deep-structure characteristic of our school systems. Many of those which speak of school-based managment, decentralized decision-making, empowerment of teachers, and the like, do not either. Further study of goal orientation should show us the degree to which it is even possible to create schools which are truly able to be innovative, and in which principals, with their faculties, can choose and pursue their own relevant goals.

One leadership theory which has not been mentioned thus far seems appropriate to consider here. That is distributive or functional leadership (Johnson and Johnson, 1987). Based upon a substantial body of research on small group behavior, it suggests that group goals (tasks) are best accomplished and group members are better satisfied (maintenance) when leadership acts are carried out according to (1) the needs of the group and (2) the strengths of its members (Bales, 1950). This theory, closely related in orientation to the Ohio State and Michigan studies cited earlier, has much relevance for any discussion of principal leadership. It suggests that, while on the one hand a formal leader such as a principal should have well articulated and focused goals (a vision of how the school should be), such goals will be better accomplished if they are shared by other members of the staff and if these other members also perform leadership acts as appropriate. This cannot happen if neoscientific management principles dominate in a school district and individual schools and their faculties are treated as interchangeable parts. Global educators should not be naive about this matter. They must assess the management philosophy of the school district and determine appropriate strategies for bringing a global perspective to the curriculum of a school. This would involve such things as getting special consideration for a school to practice real teacher involvement in decision-making, getting dispensation for the school from district curricula and even testing, and even confronting district administrators about their management styles.

Two Case Studies

While each of the principals of the eleven network schools had an interesting story, the authors of this book decided to develop the story of two in some depth in order to demonstrate many of the concepts discussed thus far in this chapter. Both had what has been called a "focused goal orientation": they had a few carefully selected goals for the school which they clearly articulated and which they worked diligently to achieve.

They differed greatly in many respects, also. One was the principal of a small K–8 school with declining enrollment. The other headed a large, comprehensive 9–12 high school. One fully supported global education. The other, while he professed support at certain times (e.g., in meetings with district superordinates in attendance, and when confronted by CHI staff about happenings at the school), actually and consistently behaved in ways that were detrimental to bringing a global perspective to the curriculum of the school.

Marla Chambers and Buena Vista School

School Description

Buena Vista, a K–8 school, had a gradually declining enrollment of approximately 450 students in 1986. Slightly more than three-fourths were Anglo, a bit more than ten percent were Hispanic and about twelve percent were Asian. About six percent were classified as limited English proficiency (LEP) students. The school served many students from single-parent families and in many of the two-parent homes, both parents worked.

School personnel estimated that in 1987 nearly half of the families served by the school had an income between twenty thousand and forty thousand dollars per year. Nearly thirty percent had an annual income of over sixty thousand dollars. Thus, while there were very few really poor, there was a bimodal distribution of incomes among families served.

Six of the twenty regular teachers were male and five of those taught seventh and eighth grade classes. All were Anglo and they were a relatively young group with an average of just less than ten years of service.

The school was in a relatively small elementary district. The superintendent and other district administrators were supportive of the project both on philosophical grounds and because thay had worked with key CHI staff members in a prior school improvement project. The district had a reputation as innovative and as one where a good deal of decision-making had been decentralized to the school-site level.

The Buena Vista District had undergone rapid growth during the 1960s and 1970s, but by the time of the project was suffering from declining enrollments. As was the case with a number of the other project districts, this declining enrollment pattern had led to budget problems and other stresses, including some labor-management tension. While this tension was less in Buena Vista than in some other districts, it was a factor.

Largely because of its small size, but in part due to a conscious philosophy, the district was less bureaucratic than most. Decisions could be made fairly quickly and there were fewer administrative policies and regulations about which to be concerned.

Buena Vista School was unique in the CHI network in that it was K–8. The district, which was an elementary district, had never created separate junior high schools despite periodic pressure to do so. Instruction for seventh and eighth graders was departmentalized with students and teachers both having six periods. This intermediate-level program was fairly standard, with students having English–language arts–reading, social studies, math, science, fine arts, practical arts, and various electives including computers and Spanish.

At the elementary level, there was some multigrading and cooperative teaching. Two teachers were responsible for all grade one and grade two students, and classes were often organized with students from both grades. A similar organizational plan existed for students in grades four and five. Students were regrouped in various subjects in these classes. While the one third grade class and the one sixth grade class were separate from other classes in the school, there was a great deal of informal collaboration among most teachers at Buena Vista.

The building was a modern, one-level unit with a partially open, flexible floor plan. Students were grouped into kindergarten, primary, intermediate, and seventh and eighth grade "pods" which were arranged in an imperfect square around a central outdoor patio. Most of the classrooms, particularly the ones in the primary and intermediate areas, had a feeling of openness; most had only three walls, allowing for a common space where students and teachers could move about on carpeted floors which helped keep things quiet. The library learning center, a frequently used resource for teachers and students, was centrally located with easy access from all classrooms.

The school had a warm and friendly atmosphere. Even though many parents worked, they were frequently visible at the school. Attendance at special evening activities and cooperation with teachers regarding the children's programs was outstanding. Students were treated with respect. It seemed a good place to be.

Global Education at the School

By the end of year two of the project at Buena Vista School, nineteen of the twenty-five faculty members had participated in one way or another in global education activities. Of special note were four minigrant proposals: (1) two teachers developed a five-week study of environmental interdependence for grades 4, 5, and 7; (2) two other teachers developed a course in Spanish language and culture for grades 6–8; (3) one teacher developed an ethnic foods unit for grade 7; and (4) two teachers developed a study of ethnic, cultural, and religious diversity in Orange County for grades 7 and 8.

The level of participation at the school remained at about eighty percent during the third (and, as it turned out, final) year of the project. Unfortunately, the school was closed at the end of the 1987-1988 year because of declining enrollments in the district. Along with regular activities such as use of library materials, speakers, attendance at network workshops, and participation in the International Sports Day, there were five special projects: (1) a grade 1 and 2 study of folk literature, poetry, and music around the world; (2) a collection of library books dealing with cultural commonalities among families of the world for grades 7 and 8; (3) an endangered-species unit for the middle grades developed by a sixth grade teacher and a teacher of learning handicapped students; (4) a special global education section developed in the library, and (5) an all-school "Our Earth" display which included interdisciplinary activities at all grade levels. This project actually came about as a result of faculty participation in the network-wide "Your Community and the World" project described elsewhere in this book. The fact was that the curriculum of this school, by the end of year 3 of the project, was well on the way to being "globalized."

The Principal

Marla Chambers was in her second year as a full time principal when CHI approached first the district and then her about participation in the global education network project. Prior to that she had been a teaching vice-principal for two years at Buena Vista, teaching seventh and eighth grade social studies as well as providing leadership to the school. For seven years before that she had also taught middle school-level social studies.

Chambers had a personal background which gave her an orientation toward global studies. She had been in a junior year abroad program in Sheffield, England. She had student taught there and, subsequently, had taught for a brief time in both British primary and secondary modern schools. She had travelled extensively in Europe, Mexico, Canada, and the United States. As she was growing up, there was a good deal of discussion of world events and politics in her home. As she said in her exit interview with CHI personnel, "I come from an 'aware' family."

From the beginning of the project, it was apparent that Chambers had a clear vision of what global education was. She made an immediate connection between the perspective-taking dimension of it and the local need for multicultural understanding brought about by changing demographics at the school. However, globalizing the curriculum was *not* one of her original goals for Buena Vista. Also, and while she was aware of the district approval of CHI's program, she was concerned that demands would be made upon staff members which might stretch their ability to remain focused upon the fairly clear school plan which she and the teachers had developed together.

In chapter 5 the concept of boundary maintenance, keeping things out or letting them into the school, was introduced in reference to principal behavior. This can be positive: a principal screens demands upon teachers, seeing that they (1) do not impinge too much upon faculty time and (2) are related to the identified goals of the school *or* can influence those goals in valued new directions. It can also be seen as being negative: no new ideas are allowed in except those imposed by the superordinate system or, on the other hand, every idea which comes along is presented to the faculty as something of value to include in the instructional program.

Chambers was a classic case of a positive boundary maintainer with regard to the CHI global education project. On the one hand, she was very aware of the many demands already placed upon Buena Vista teachers, was concerned about *exactly* what new demands would be made, and realized that the *meaning* of global education was not clear to many of the teachers. She wanted to go slowly at first.

Chambers' strategy with teachers was to assist them to understand the meaning of global education, to help them see that the project would not place undue stress upon their time, and to concentrate on making global education an integrating force for the various goals already identified for the school. These goals included development of basic skills in students as well as development of a positive self-concept and responsible and active citizenship. Further, and because of the changing demographics of the community, her goals included an emphasis upon multicultural awareness and perspective taking.

From her first exposure to the project, Chambers saw its potential for facilitating these goals, particularly the development of multicultural awareness. Some of the other principals saw this potential, too. Some never did. In acting upon this potential, Chambers made sure that adequate resources were available (e.g., release time for teacher in-service), she was a spokesperson for the school to the district, she protected teachers from extraneous demands, and she frequently participated along with faculty members in network activities. This behavior-modeling showed teachers just how important she thought global education really was.

In theoretical terms, what was observed at Buena Vista was a principal who was goal focused, who demonstrated appropriate initiation and/or production behavior on the one hand and consideration and/or employee orientation on the other. She had the ability to gauge situations correctly and apply motivational strategies as appropriate. Because of the high level of maturity of the faculty, she almost always used a delegating or participating leadership style (Hersey and Blanchard, 1988).

While she did not articulate it with exact terminology, Chambers understood the importance of *meaning* to a new movement such as global education. More than once at the beginning of the project she commented that some of the concepts would seem vague to teachers for awhile because "we are still forming our perspectives in this area of education."

Chambers' role in making the project a success at Buena Vista was acknowledged by both her superordinate, the district assistant superintendent, and the faculty. The assistant superintendent, for example, said in his final CHI interview:

> Her role was critical. Chambers was the key player. She sees how things interconnect. She is intuitive herself, and she helps others see relationships. She has the ability to make linkages and the skill to involve and support others. She is a good coordinator. She has vision, gestalt.

In their end-of-project interviews, teachers were asked "What role has your principal played in involving you in CHI activities?" Typical responses were:

> "Marla was very encouraging and very good at involving teachers. She would make sure the staff knew about upcoming activities and would match people up with CHI activities. She knew who was interested in what."

> "She played a critical role. She was firmly convinced that it was a good program. She allowed us time at staff meetings to share what we learned at workshops. Sometimes she allowed us as long as fifteen minutes to share CHI experiences."

"Marla went out of her way to expose the faculty to the project. She played a large role."

"She was such a big proponent of CHI. She tried to get at least one teacher to each of the CHI activities. She paid for a substitute. She kept us informed of what CHI was doing at each of the staff meetings."

While it was important to the project and to global education that Chambers was supportive of CHI programs, it was far more critical that she saw where this all fit into the entire program at her school. This is what the assistant superintendent meant when he said she had "gestalt."

The data above suggest that Chambers had outstanding leadership skills. Even more important, however, she held a clear vision for the school. Fortunately, this vision included the possibility of the development of a global perspective. In a very important piece on such development, Boston (1991) says:

> A key task for an organizer in an outside agency promoting a more global perspective is to help school leaders clarify their own vision for an education which reflects the changing nature of the world. Once a vision is clarified and strategies identified which move toward that vision, outside resources and support systems can be used more effectively to help achieve the school's goals. The outsider can be facilitator, coach, information source, but cannot carry the vision for the school or exercise leadership within it.

This, then, leads to one of the major hypotheses generated by this study. If we are interested in real school improvement, not simply in cosmetic change, a major focus for the outside agency and the superordinate system has to be upon helping people at the school site, foremost among them the principal, to clarify and develop their *own* vision and meaning. Such vision and meaning cannot successfully be imposed from above or from outside.

Eric Norman and North High School

School Description

North High School was the largest school in the CHI global education network with approximately twenty-four hundred students in grades nine through twelve. The student population was ethnically diverse. Just under one-half were Anglo, while nearly one-quarter were Asian. Approximately fifteen percent were Hispanic and about twelve percent were black. The number of minority students was beginning to grow fairly rapidly, particularly the number of Hispanics.

The community served was basically middle class, with annual family incomes in 1987–1988 falling between thirty thousand and sixty thousand dollars. However, many of the growing number of Hispanic students came from families with lower incomes.

About sixty percent of the nearly one hundred faculty members were male and the average length of service for teachers was approximately ten years. It was a relatively young group as senior high faculties go. There was a strong affirmative action program in the district and in 1987–1988 the ethnic breakdown of the North High faculty was: Anglo, 63 percent; Hispanic, 13 percent; Asian, 7 percent; black, 5 percent; other, 2 percent.

North High was in the same school district as Caldwell Elementary and that district was described in some detail in chapter 6. It will suffice here to remind the reader that the district was large and had a reputation for being innovative, but that it had had four different superintendents during the four years of the global education project. Support of the project (or lack of it) by district-level administrators varied greatly and that is an important part of the story which shall be told here.

The school had a seven-period day, with students attending six classes from periods one through six or two through seven except for the few on a shortened day schedule. Teachers generally taught five classes although a few taught more for extra pay. Department chairs had one period of release time for planning. The athletic director had two.

The North High curriculum was typical of large, comprehensive high schools in the 1980s in which the emphasis had come to be on academics at the expense of more vocationally oriented subjects. Of the 448 courses offered at the school, 307 (69 percent) were academic courses—English, social science, mathematics and computer science, science, foreign language. Vocationally oriented courses included 66 in practical arts and 15 business courses, for a combined 18 percent of all offerings. There were 28 physical education courses (6 percent), 24 in the fine arts (5 percent) and 8 activity courses (e.g., newspaper, drill team, pep squad, student government) (2 percent). This was, in fact, an unbalanced curriculum, perhaps adequately meeting the needs of the college bound but far from meeting those of a growing non-college-bound population. Once again, it should be noted that this was a pretty typical set of offerings arising from the so-called reform movement of the 1980s set off by the *Nation at Risk* report (National Commission on Excellence in Education, 1983) and promoted by many educational leaders and politicians across the nation.

Students were clearly tracked in the academic subjects. English and social science courses were labelled as basic, general, college preparatory, honors or advanced placement. In mathematics and computer science, science, and foreign languages, only honors or advanced placement labels were given to some courses. Theoretically, basic, general, and college preparatory students could be found together in other classes in these disciplines. In reality, student self-selection caused homogeneity. You would find very few non-college-bound students in Algebra II or German III, for example.

Eric Norman was the principal at North High School for the first three years of CHI involvement there. He was quite proud of the academic orientation of the school and often bragged about the "fast growing" advanced placement program he was developing there. More will be said about this a bit later. It should be noted here that at the end of his tenure at the school in 1988, there were actually only 15 AP classes, (a total of 3 percent of all offerings). In addition, there were 16 classes designated as "honors" (3 percent) and 45 as college preparatory (10 percent). As was noted earlier, many of the regular offerings which had no special track designation really served the needs of the college preparatory students—world geography, chemistry, psychology, trigonometry. There was even a course entitled "Fine Arts for the College Bound."

The fall 1988 schedule listed such practical arts and business courses as auto mechanics (4 classes), work experience (5 classes), word processing (5 classes), industrial arts survey (3 classes), co-ed foods (3 classes), graphics (6 classes), clothing (1 class), drafting (2 classes), electric repair (1 class), typing (3 classes), office machines (1 class), and accounting (2 classes). There were other offerings as well for the total of 81 classes (18 percent of all offerings) mentioned earlier.

An examination of course offerings also gives some idea of the extent to which the globalization of the curriculum had taken place at North High. Twenty-six of the 67 social studies class offerings in 1988 were in U.S. history. There were 14 world history classes, 2 European history (both AP), 4 economics classes with international content, and 1 world geography class. Even with a large Asian student population and a location near the Pacific Ocean, there were no classes on Asian history, geography, and/or culture. This was a pretty ethnocentric set of offerings which could not be said to prepare students well for life in an interdependent world. Courses in the science department, in addition to being quite limited except for college-bound students, also reflected little global content.

In terms of a global perspective, there were bright spots, however. There was a very active Model United Nations program which, while there were only 2 classes, had a substantial impact upon the student body through its activities. A small number of teachers in the English department worked hard to teach literature from around the world. Finally, there was a strong foreign language department which offered classes in six languages and which focused upon culture as well as language. There were 27 classes of Spanish, offered to college-bound and non-college-bound students. There were also classes in Portugese, French, Latin, German, and Japanese. We shall discuss the foreign language department and some of their activities a bit later.

The school plant was relatively new. There were no open classroom spaces. There were work spaces for teachers and the school was arranged into "houses." Thus, English teachers were in one building, science in another, social studies in another, and so on. The principal and several teachers commented (and complained) about the great difficulty of communication at the school because of its size and construction. The "house" arrangement is quite common in American high schools and lends itself to the "factory with interchangeable parts" ideas of neoscientific management discussed in an earlier section in this chapter.

Global Education at the School

By the end of the third year of the project at North High School, thirty-three people had participated in one way or another. That was approximately only one-third of the faculty. In the end-of-project survey, when teachers were asked, "How much were you involved with CHI global education activities during the past four

years?" seventy-seven teachers on the faculty of a hundred responded. Of those, 56 percent said "never" and only 8 percent indicated
that they had been very active. The remaining 36 percent replied
that they had participated "a few times." Interestingly, in response
to another question, "At this school, the number of staff involved in
global education is...," 80 percent of the respondents said "not very
large" or "small." However, no one answered "none." Evidently, the
receipt of the project newsletter distributed to all faculty members
and the various faculty meetings where presentations were made
counted as participation.

Eighty-one percent of the respondents agreed with the statement "It is clear to me what global education is," and 88 percent
agreed that "Global education is important and all students should
be exposed to it." Eighty-one percent of the respondents at North
High also agreed with the statement, "I am more aware of global
issues today than I was four years ago," and 71 percent felt that this
was "due, at least in part, to CHI's presence."

In the end-of-project interviews conducted with a sample of
teachers, there were a number of people who indicated that the
project had received little encouragement from the principal who
was there during its first three years. In fact, activities which did
occur were developed solely by teachers without any encouragement (or recognition) from that principal.

There were some minigrant projects which were noteworthy.
One science teacher developed a collection of videotapes which had
a global focus. Five members of the foreign language department
developed a telecommunications project in which students communicated directly with classes in South America and Spain. Later, the
foreign language department, in cooperation with the foods teacher,
developed culture units to share with their sister schools. Further,
this department developed a set of workshops, lessons, and teaching
materials to present to teachers *across the curriculum* which
explored the cultural patterns of the *students* of the school and district. An English teacher developed a four- week literature unit on
the effects of war. This grew directly out of a network-wide CHI
workshop. Finally, a grant proposal was written and funded to supply all English classrooms with world maps. The idea was simply to
help students learn geography while they were studying literature.

By and large, these were sophisticated projects developed and
carried out by dedicated and knowledgeable teachers. CHI staff,

throughout the four years of the global education project, felt that this staff had potential to do outstanding global education work. Unfortunately, that potential was never realized. We turn to a discussion of the school's principal to better understand why.

The Principal

When the global education project was introduced at North High School in 1985, the principal, Eric Norman, was beginning his thirty-third year as an educator. He had begun in a neighboring district where he spent ten years teaching a high school English–social studies core curriculum and three years as a counselor. From there, he moved to the rapidly growing and newly unified North School District were he first taught English and social studies and subsequently became a vice principal at one of the high schools. After five years in that role, he moved to the new North High as vice principal. At the end of one year, he became principal and had been in that position for eight years when CHI arrived on the scene.

At North High, Norman maintained a fairly active professional life. He participated in local and regional administrator association activities and during the time of the project he was quite involved with regional and statewide "effective schools" associations and programs.

According to his own report, there were no discussions of global issues in his family as he was growing up. However, as a child and youth, he was an avid reader and, in fact, somewhat of a family focal point because he "knew so much."

Norman had traveled in Asia and the Pacific both as a serviceman when he was younger and more recently when he visited American high schools at military bases as a member of Western Association of Schools and Colleges (WASC) accreditation teams.

Eric Norman seemed to have a clear understanding of what global education was and why it was important, or so it seemed to CHI personnel initially. The first meeting with him was early in 1985 in the North district superintendent's office. In attendance were the superintendent, two assistant superintendents, and three principals, including Norman. The intent at that meeting was to ascertain interest, on the part of the district and the principals, in global education and the CHI project in particular. Norman seemed positive and spoke positively of earlier efforts in American education to internationalize curriculum. While no commitments were made at that meeting, CHI personnel went away feeling that he was interested. In fact, they believed that he would be a strong advocate for global studies at his school. They were mistaken, as we shall soon see.

That Norman understood global education was clearly demonstrated by the definition he provided to CHI during a subsequent interview:

> The objective of global education is to give students a global view of the world interactions which are increasingly important. What happens to me often has its genesis in other places. Interactions need to be understood.

Norman had a clear goal focus. He articulated a desire to "create academic programs with high expectations...[and] move the school to a more academic stance." He discussed this quite enthusiastically during his exit interview in June 1988 just prior to his retirement:

> We've been successful and it's been a lot of work.... It's different from eight years ago when I arrived. We've received the Distinguished School Award this past year. In 1981–1982 we had one Advanced Placement class; in 1987–1988 we had fifteen. Foreign language has doubled, there are fourteen upper-division classes. There is a problem in getting a good teacher match for the AP classes. Teachers have the same set of assumptions. They've bought into the mission. It is a unified drive. One-half [of the teachers] are now my hires. Parents are supportive. There has been a flip-flop in terms of support.

Norman was motivated in part by a sense of competitiveness with two other district high schools which had reputations for high-quality academic programs. His goals were clear. His actions were in line with those goals and the school was successful as evidenced by the Distinguished Service Award, increased number of AP courses, and general recognition.

However, the AP program, at its peak, served only a relatively small segment of the student body. The tremendous energy poured into this program diverted attention from the demographic changes occurring at the school and the concomitant need to provide appropriate programs for students with special needs—for example, there were *no* ESL classes. Likewise, racial tensions were increasing on the campus and the academic emphasis played a part in heightening these because many Asian students seemed to do better and, thus, benefit from the academic emphasis. Finally, and despite his belief to the contrary, the majority of the staff had not "bought into" the goals expressed by Norman. Some that he had hired, and particularly those who taught AP classes, were pleased with the emphasis, however, as we shall see, there was a good deal of faculty dissension.

Marla Chambers at Buena Vista was described as a principal who exhibited boundary maintenance behavior which protected teachers from too many competing demands and, at the same time, helped them to smoothly infuse global education into their curricula. Eric Norman, on the other hand, was an example of a principal who consciously acted to keep global education out of the school. He was devious in doing so and his story is quite interesting.

The reader will recall that in the meeting with the superintendent Norman had appeared knowledgeable and enthusiastic. CHI staff had great respect for that superintendent, the accomplishments of the district and, going into the project, Eric Norman. Things changed.

At the beginning of the first meeting with Norman at North High, he made it quite clear that he was not very enthusiastic about the project. Specifically, he said:

1. That he was an "old-timer" and had been around during the first go-around of global education, which he felt had failed.

2. There were just too many projects in which his school was involved.

3. The district (and state) was very "centrix" [centralized] in curriculum, especially in U.S. History, allowing teachers little freedom to pick and choose what they taught.

4. His own focus was American civilization, and "sheer academics."

As that meeting progressed, Norman appeared to change his position somewhat. He spoke of having a faculty member coordinate the project (he, himself, was too busy), he pointed out the need for America to avoid being isolationist, and he suggested that CHI staff members should meet with the teacher coordinator (who was supposed to have been at this first meeting but was not contacted) and with department chairs at their next regular meeting.

In succeeding weeks, Norman kept himself aloof from the project. The teacher coordinator also coached after school and failed to keep appointments that were scheduled with him. Two meetings with department chairs were poorly attended because the principal failed to communicate with them about the project.

Finally, late in the fall, Norman was confronted about his lack of support. At this meeting, he acknowledged the importance of his role, but stated that he could not participate directly because the district had given him too many things to do. During that meeting, he asked if CHI had funding from the National Endowment for the Humanities. He said, "I like humanities projects." That meeting ended with the scheduling of a full faculty meeting to introduce the project. At this initial faculty meeting, Norman was very positive in his introduction of the project. Many teachers made favorable comments about global education. The meeting seemed very positive. From there, the project proceeded slowly at the school. Seven different teachers attended CHI workshops during year one, and twenty-two teachers checked out materials from the CHI library. However, the teacher contact person and the principal still did not get involved.

During the second year, a new contact teacher was selected by Norman. He was promised release time, but got none. Also, he did not get the teaching assignment he was told he would get. Consequently, he was quite discouraged and negative about Norman. Under the circumstances, he did a pretty good job of acting as liaison between CHI and the faculty.

Also, during the second year, the Model United Nations (MUN) sponsors came in contact with CHI, used resources, and took part in some activities. At this point, Norman was somewhat negative about the MUN and its people. It is interesting to note that in his exit interview two years later, however, he gave them high praise. In the intervening period, they had won state and national awards and brought much positive publicity to North High. (Good public relations is a sure way to get the support of many administrators. See, for example, Tye, 1990).

At the end of the second year, a sample of eighteen teachers was selected for interviewing by CHI. In summary, findings were:

1. Teachers did not always know about CHI sponsored activities. Even when they did know about them, many did not wish to participate.

2. Teachers felt isolated in their departments and perceived campus-wide communication to be poor.

3. There was a general feeling that the principal was *not* supportive of global education. One teacher said, "He'd have a Great Books curriculum if he could."

4. Morale was not very good. However, teachers generally were positive about the students, colleagues, and the school.

Norman also was interviewed at the end of this year. The lack of significant progress at the school was pointed out to him and he was asked if the project should be withdrawn from North High. He indicated that he wanted it continued and that he would find a teacher who could do a better coordination job. When asked how important he felt global education was, he responded, "I don't agree with William Bennett. I don't see it as a political position. It's an academic problem. We need to move the country away from its xenophobia."

During the third year of the project, Norman's last year before retirement, MUN was thriving and the foreign language department began two telecommunications projects, one with a CHI grant and one on its own through GEMNET, a national telecommunications network. A series of teacher liaisons worked with CHI until finally a strongly motivated member of the foreign language department took on the responsibility.

In his final interview in June 1988, Norman concluded by saying:

> You [CHI] will persevere. The trend is toward global education despite William Bennett et al. It makes so much sense. I was partly responsible for the project not succeeding here. Kids need to be globally literate.

This contrasts with the following note he had sent to one of the Model U.N. teachers about global education:

After reading your lengthy memo of today I find that we have a basic difference of opinion. I support, in effect, Secretary Bennett's approach to the study of social science. You do not. What I am talking about is the UPS [University Preparatory Studies –AP] curriculum, not the MUN curriculum. MUN is a co-curricular program at this school. It has not been infused into the curriculum that I know of, at either the state or district level. The enrichment that we have chosen in the UPS program we control, and I feel very strongly that I want that enrichment to be in the humanities area and not in the global education area. No amount of aggressive arguing of opinion will change my point of view on this at this time.

CHI did not know about this memo until the end of the project and, thus, did not confront Norman. Recall that he was asked at various times whether or not the project should withdraw from the school, and each time he said no. At about the time he sent the memo to the MUN teacher, he also told CHI that Bennett was wrong about global education.

One could draw the conclusion that Norman finally changed his view at the end of the project. That may have been true but is unlikely. The evidence seems to suggest that he did not believe in global education, that he purposely sabotaged the project, but that he consciously attempted to give the appearance that he was trying to be cooperative.

As was pointed out in chapter 5, the ethos, or climate, of a school district has a lot to do with the behavior of principals and, thus, the climate of its schools. The evidence is pretty clear that Norman's own value system explained much of the deceptive and contradictory behavior described here. However, some of that behavior may have resulted from what was going on at the district level during the project.

Recall that the initial meeting with principals in the North District was held in the superintendent's office. At that meeting, it was clear that the superintendent was in favor of the project and, in fact, knew one of the codirectors of the project quite well. Eric Norman behaved accordingly and was positive. The assistant superintendent for secondary instruction, Mr. Fox, also seemed supportive at this first meeting.

Early in the first year of the project, that superintendent left the district for another superintendency. After the superintendent left, Fox questioned the project (never directly to CHI, however) on the grounds that it was "leftist." Norman never spoke of this until quite a bit later and it was a complex issue because there were other things involved; for example, Mr. Fox saw CHI as being in competition with another global education project at another institution in the area. That other institution happened to be his alma mater.

Norman was friendly with this assistant superintendent. However Fox, too, left the scene. After a brief time with an acting superintendent, the district appointed a permanent replacement. One of his early actions was to demote Mr. Fox to a nonline, less important administrative position. The new superintendent also promoted the assistant superintendent for elementary instruction, Dr. Klein, and put her in charge of both elementary and secondary instruction. She was quite a knowledgeable person who had always been a strong supporter of global education and the project. At this point, Norman's behavior became more cooperative. Further, Dr. Klein was also instrumental in supporting the foreign language teachers in their development of the telecommunications projects.

Norman retired at the end of the third year of the project and a new principal worked with CHI during the fourth and final year. While it cannot be said that the curriculum of the school became globalized, many things did happen. The new principal acknowledged the potential of global education to assist him with one of his goals: the development of multicultural understanding. The MUN and telecommunications projects flourished. More teachers came forward to participate in grant proposals and workshops. A project with folk literature developed in the English department. Perhaps most important, the new principal inserted a line in the "Goals and Objectives Statement" for the school which specifically mentioned global education as a new curriculum thrust and discussed its potential for creating interdisciplinary planning and teaching.

Conclusion

Eric Norman seemed to understand the meaning of global education. However, while he gave one definition to CHI personnel and discussed the importance of the movement with them, at the same time he communicated a negative view of it to others. What was going on? Norman wasn't a political ultraconservative nor a religious fundamentalist opposed to global education. He had a clear goal focus: academic excellence.

Norman's behavior, in fact, was pretty typical of many of today's school administrators. On the one hand, he was caught between his own often conflicting perennialist and liberal educational values—the former reinforced by the cynical political rhetoric of the 1980s and the latter by the idealistic, and sometimes unrealistic, notions of his younger years during the early–post-World War II era. On the other hand, he operated in a bureaucratic system—schooling—which constantly demands a kind of neoscientific, pragmatic behavior ("make it work at whatever cost"). At one level, this caused one teacher to observe: "He is hot and cold about what he supports; he wavers." At another level, he both supported and blocked CHI's global education work at North High School.

The hypothesis arrived at earlier, derived from the data about Marla Chambers at Buena Vista, is reinforced by this case: Real school improvement depends upon helping people at the school site, particularly the principal, to clarify and develop their own vision and meaning. Such vision cannot be imposed.

Unfortunately, CHI never attempted to help Eric Norman with such clarification. Given all of the circumstances, it would have been difficult, at best. However, there was one opening which was not adequately pursued. Norman, as part of his academic orientation, was interested in the development of an alternative to the International Baccalaureate (IB) program for North High School.

For some reason, Norman was not happy with the regular IB program and wanted to develop an alternative. He had given some thought to this and had designed a program which would include such things as a full-year course in non-Western cultures, a minimum of four years of foreign language as measured by an advanced placement exam or proficiency, comparative government, fine arts appreciation, and community service. Topics to be covered in the program, if it were adopted, were to include such things as the causes, practices, and effects of war; nationalist and independence movements, decolonization, and the emergence and problems of new nations; economic developments and social changes in the twentieth century; and the establishment and work of international organizations. To say the least, these were global education topics. Had CHI worked with Norman to develop this IB program, his values may have been clarified in the process and the curriculum of *all* students ultimately may have been affected.

In the process of assisting leaders with the clarification of their values, it becomes important for global educators to assess a number of factors which have been dealt with in this chapter. Knowing a principal's background, for example, is critical. It seems that travel and even childhood experiences can have some bearing upon attitudes toward and the valuing of global education. In the case of a leader who has a limited background in international affairs, the outside agent must provide some very basic education in the form of readings, workshops, conferences, and even travel opportunities.

In addition to personal background, the concept of focus, discussed earlier, needs to be assessed. If a principal is focused and the focus includes global education, the interventionist has little to worry about. If, however, the focus does *not* include global education, there is some educating and influencing to be done. If, as was suggested earlier, a principal has a diffuse or coping style, the role of the interventionist is to assist with helping him or her to become more focused.

It is also important to assess the leadership behavior of the principal. Does he tend to behave as a leader or as an administrator? Does she vary her task and relationship behavior appropriately according to the situation? Are Theory X or Theory Y assumptions pervasive at the school? The assessment of such leadership factors should also assist the interventionist and principals with the planning of various types of in-service activities.

Any concern for leadership must also take into account the district ethos. It is appropriate to be concerned with the behavior of principals. However, as we have seen, in school districts where the currently popular neoscientific principles of management prevail, it is unlikely that principals will hold anything other than Theory X assumptions or perform as anything other than administrators. In such situations, in which the idea of interchangeable parts is so strong, to encourage principals to do otherwise might jeopardize their jobs. In such cases, and there are probably many, interventionists must work first with the superordinate system to assure that principals actually will be given the latitude to become leaders in their schools and not simply be expected to administer what has been mandated from above.

In the final analysis, then, we are led back to the hypothesis which was stated earlier and which arose from the consideration of the pivotal role of the principal. That hypothesis simply states that if we are interested in real school improvement, not just cosmetic change, a major focus for the outside agency and the superordinate system has to be upon helping people at the school site, foremost among them the principal, to clarify and develop their own vision and meanings. Such vision and meanings cannot successfully be imposed from above or from outside. The task for the global educator is to assist school leaders to see that their vision reflects the changing nature of the world and to support them in every way possible as they work to bring a global perspective to the curriculum of the school.

References

Argyris, C., *Interpersonal Competence and Organizational Effectiveness* (Homewood, Ill: Dorsey Press, l962).

———, *Management and Organizational Development: The Path from XA to YB* (New York: McGraw-Hill, 1971).

Bales, R., *Interaction Process Analysis: A Method for the Study of Small Groups* (Reading, Mass.: Addison-Wesley, 1950).

Bass, B., and R. Stogdill, *Bass and Stogdill's Handbook of Leadership: Theory, Research, and Management Applications* (New York: Free Press, 1990).

Boston, J., "School Leadership and Global Education," in K. Tye, ed., *Global Education: From Thought to Action* (Alexandria, Va.: ASCD, 1991).

Callahan, R., *Education and the Cult of Efficiency* (Chicago: University of Chicago Press, 1962).

Fiedler, F., *A Theory of Leadership Effectiveness* (New York: McGraw Hill, 1967).

Hersey, P., and K. Blanchard, *Management of Organizational Behavior: Utilizing Human Resources,* 5th ed. (Englewood Cliffs, N.J.: Prentice Hall, 1988).

Johnson, D., and F. Johnson, *Joining Together: Group Theory and Group Skills,* 3d ed. (Englewood Cliffs, N.J.: Prentice Hall, 1987).

Lewin, K., R. Lippitt, and R. White, "Leader Behavior and Member Reaction in Three 'Social Climates,'" in D. Cartwright and A. Zander, eds., *Group Dynamics: Research and Theory,* 2nd ed. (Evanston, Ill: Row Peterson, 1960).

Likert, R., *New Patterns of Management* (New York: McGraw Hill, 1961).

——, *The Human Organization* (New York: McGraw Hill, 1967).

Lipham, J., "Leadership and Administration," in *Behavioral Science and Educational Administration,* sixty-third yearbook, National Society for the Study of Education, part II (Chicago: University of Chicago Press, 1964).

Mayo, C., *The Social Problems of an Industrial Civilization* (Boston: Harvard Business School, 1945).

McGregor, D., *The Human Side of Enterprise* (New York: McGraw Hill, 1960).

Novotney, J., and K. Tye, *The Dynamics of Educational Leadership* (Los Angeles: Educational Resource Associates, Inc., 1973).

National Commission on Excellence in Education, *A Nation at Risk* (Washington, D.C.: Government Printing Office, 1983).

Sarason, S., *The Culture of the School and the Problem of Change,* 2d ed. (Boston: Allyn and Bacon, Inc., 1982).

Schein, E., *Organizational Culture and Leadership* (San Francisco: Jossey-Bass, 1985).

Sergiovanni, T., "The Theoretical Basis for Cultural Leadership," in *Leadership: Examining the Elusive,* 1987 ASCD yearbook (Alexandria, Va.: ASCD, 1987.

Stogdill, R., and A Coons, *Leader Behavior: Its Description and Measurement,* research monograph no. 88 (Columbus: Bureau of Business Research, Ohio State University, 1957).

Tannenbaum, R., and W. Schmidt, "How to Choose a Leadership Pattern," *Harvard Business Review,* vol. 36, No. 2, March–April 1958, pp. 95–101.

Taylor, F., *The Principles of Scientific Management* (New York: Harper & Brothers, 1911).

Tye, K., *Global Education: School-Based Strategies* (Orange, Cal.: Interdependence Press, 1990).

8

THE INTERVENTIONISTS

Unfortunately, by the time we get it right...it will be the end of
our project and we will be able to look back and say how it
should have been.

—Kathy O'Neil, Staff Member

It's only human to want to get things right the first time, but
in a developmental undertaking such as this, one must come to
terms with the notion that the project staff—regardless of their
skills, abilities, or prior experience—will be learning as they go to
some extent. Some people are likely to be uncomfortable with a
change strategy which has objectives that are emergent rather than
predetermined, and activities which are nonlinear, to say the least.

In this chapter we will present what we learned about the role
of the consultant/interventionist from an outside agency who is
faced with the task of helping teachers to learn, practice, and ultimately to institutionalize a new curricular program. To do so, we
will rely heavily on the thoughts of the CHI field consultants themselves—Ida Urso, Kathy O'Neil, and Joy Phillipsen—as recorded in
the field notes or obtained from end-of-project interviews.

Three Interconnected Functions

Intervention

CHI staff members delivered resources and services to teachers in the eleven schools, spending the majority of their time helping teachers, both individually and in groups, as they planned,
taught, and evaluated lessons incorporating a global perspective.
They also devoted considerable time to interacting with teachers

who were not yet actively involved with the project, since one of the cornerstones of the CHI philosophy was that global education should remain open to all and should never come to be seen as belonging just to those few who got involved early on. Only in this way would it be possible to reach the goal of infusing global perspectives throughout an entire school.

> Because CHI is a "frontier operation," not a formal bureaucratic organization, roles have not become institutionalized, and there is a flexible division of labor, with some blurring among participants. There is general agreement that it's OK to be "ad-hoc-ing it" in dealing with the visits to the schools, and that all are alert to the developing process. (R. Lessor, CHI resident sociologist, memo to staff, spring 1986.)

Although Lessor was correct in this observation, to some extent there *was* a division of duties amongst the staff. The project was small enough so that everyone was aware of what everyone else was doing, and there were some activities in which everyone participated—for example, preparing for theme workshops and putting out the newsletter—nevertheless, other tasks were taken on by those best suited or most interested. Thus, the field staff estimate spending from sixty to seventy-five percent of their time on school site visits (including preparation and follow-up) and far less on local, state, and national networking, but it was just the reverse for the codirectors. One of the codirectors also took responsibility for finances and fundraising; the other chaired the weekly staff meetings and helped other staff members with day-to-day problem-solving as needed.

Some decisions that were made about resource allocation had a direct bearing on staff workload and task assignments. For example, during the first two years the amount of time that the two field consultants were actually able to spend at the school sites was limited by the amount of time they found they had to spend in building up and organizing the curriculum materials library in order to make it useful and accessible to teachers. It became quite clear that this was not the most effective use of their time and talent, and that the project really needed the help of a professional librarian. Following a staff discussion of budget priorities, a part-time librarian was hired for years 3 and 4. She took charge of the collection and freed up the field staff to devote more of their time to interacting with teachers and gathering data. As it turned out, an unanticipated bonus also resulted from the decision to hire a librarian: she initiated contacts with the librarians in the eleven schools, visiting them herself, and thus drew these key support people into the project in a way that had not happened before.

Research

As was described in chapter 2, CHI staff members spent many hours on the research component of the project: writing and analyzing field notes and generating hypotheses about participant and nonparticipant behavior, about why certain strategies seemed to work while others didn't, and so forth. The focus of this part of their duties, generally speaking, was on the behavior of the *school people*.

Self-Study

The third critical element of the work done at CHI—one which is often omitted from education research efforts—is the *record of the reflection of staff members upon their own behavior as change agents*. CHI staff members devoted a great deal of time to thinking about and discussing the change process as they were experiencing it. Inevitably, this included self-critique as one part of the contextual analysis. The overriding question, "What does it take to globalize the curriculum of a school?" implies not only questions like "How much time? How much money? How many inservice days for teachers? How big a resource library? How much nurturing of administrators? What kind of district support?" and so forth, but also "What kinds of behavior on the part of the external change agents?"

Weekly staff meetings dealt with all three of these fundamental elements of the project—implementation, research, and self-study. Indeed, as the figure on the next page suggests, it is impossible to separate them. The manner and timing of the delivery of resources and services to the teachers—the *interventions* in the ongoing lives of the eleven schools—were affected by both the observations made and the hypotheses generated as part of the research process, and by the strategizing that was done in the search for ways to operate more effectively.

The research model itself was actually an integral part of the intervention strategy as well, because as is described in chapter 2, as the staff moved back and forth between the coding and analysis of field notes on the one hand and the verification of emergent patterns with the teachers at the school sites on the other. In effect a type of *data feedback* process was being used: By sharing their perceptions of what was happening and why, the CHI staff provided information which the school people could use, if they chose, in their own decision-making.

And finally, weekly analysis by the staff of its own effectiveness (as well as their subjective feelings about how things were going at any particular point during the four years) both affected and was affected by the intervention and the research activities. The figure below places the weekly staff meetings precisely where they belong, although the staff was not really conscious of it at the time: in the center, where all three of the critical project functions overlap.

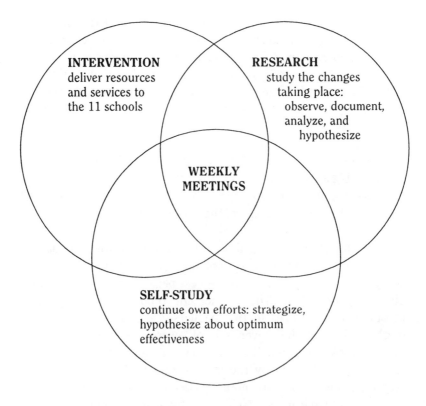

Figure 8.1: Relationship of the three major functions of the interventionist.

Practical Considerations

Dangers of Focusing on One of the Functions

Many "educational change" or "school improvement" efforts undertaken during the past twenty-five to thirty years focused primarily on *Implementation,* and as a result much of what was learned in the course of such implementation was never documented. "How I wish we had kept some records, kept minutes of our meetings, gathered some baseline data!"—these were (and still are) fairly common cries of educators involved in the later stages of innovative programs.

Even after funding agencies (particularly state governments) caught on and began requiring an evaluation component for every project, still it wasn't always easy to discern what of significance had really been learned about changing schools for the better; as a rule, the crucial insights were literally buried in an avalanche of mandatory paperwork. Eventually, school people began to wonder if trying something new was even worth it, given the cumbersome, distracting, and time-consuming compliance requirements.

Practitioners as Researchers, and Vice Versa

The idea that a new program (such as global education) can be simultaneously implemented *and* studied by the same people still strikes some educators as strange; the notion that *the intervention/research agency would observe itself as it carries out its intervention and research activities* may seem stranger yet. Even the familiar concept of formative evaluation doesn't quite cover this notion of self-study by the intervening agency.

While the interdependent and mutually reinforcing nature of these three elements came to seem obvious to the CHI staff, the extent to which it may seem strange to others was made clear when, during the writing of this book, the authors made a presentation about CHI to a group of education researchers. The questions raised made it plain that some in the audience were uncomfortable with the thought that any project would be researched by the same people who were responsible for its implementation. Furthermore, the notion that researchers would also *evaluate themselves* struck them as very alien.

Nevertheless, the authors remain convinced that this tripartite scheme is not only valid and useful, but that in fact it reflects the kinds of multiple activity which characterizes *most* educational change projects, whether those involved realize it or not.

Work Load and Work Environment

We have been speaking in a rather general way about the three kinds of work required of CHI staff members; perhaps it would be helpful to conclude this section with a quick rundown of weekly tasks at a more concrete level.

After the project ended, each of the six professionals involved (the three full-time field consultants, the part-time librarian, and the two part-time codirectors) was interviewed about his or her involvement. When asked to describe a "typical week," all were quick to point out that every week was different. One offered her view that "the work load was always correlated to the next major upcoming activity—energies would flow in that direction until the activity or event was over." She was referring to special events such as theme workshops, school in-service days, CHI Board of Trustees meetings, and administrator conferences; activities which supplemented the day-to-day servicing of the eleven schools and the data gathering at the eleven sites.

During any given week, the field consultants would spend their time (a) in the schools with teachers, principals, and others, (b) at the CHI office, pulling together materials and arranging resources for teachers, writing up field notes, preparing articles for the newsletter, participating in staff meetings, and sharing perceptions with colleagues, (c) networking: making telephone contacts, answering mail, learning about similar projects in other parts of the country, and attending meetings of the Western International Studies Consortium (WISC), of which CHI was a charter member.

The codirectors would do most of these things, too, though not full-time, plus additional tasks referred to earlier such as fundraising, maintaining contacts with school district people, problem-solving, and making presentations about the project to interested civic and professional groups. The librarian's work has already been described. The office manager coordinated purchasing and kept the books, put the newsletter together, made arrangements for special events, and—on a daily basis—generally juggled eighteen balls in the air at once to keep the office running smoothly, so the others could concentrate on their own responsibilities. Finally, a series of student workers helped with basic office tasks and occasionally accompanied the field consultants to the schools as well.

While all of these things were going on, everyone was constantly reflecting upon his or her own performance within the context of changing conditions and needs at the eleven schools, and thinking of ways to do better. In keeping with overall project philosophy, there was considerable freedom for staff members to decide on their own task priorities and to set their own work schedules. It has been observed that one of the purposes of any organization is to "make good work for people," and as was pointed out in chapter 7, employees who are treated with respect and involved in appropriate, job-related decision-making are more productive than employees who are treated as if they are interchangeable parts. Other aspects of the CHI philosophy (the way in which teachers were dealt with, the research methodology that was selected) also reflected a consistently "Y-minded" approach (MacGregor, 1960).

The remainder of this chapter is based on CHI staff reflections about their experiences in the eleven schools over the four years of the project, and sets forth what they learned about their role as agents of change: the skills needed, the strategies tried, the feelings involved, the workload, and so on.

What It Takes to Do the Job

Innovative projects require people with certain personal qualities, skills, and abilities appropriate to the tasks at hand. Some of these can be learned on the job, while others may be a matter of personal style and therefore not really "trainable" (Miles, Saxl, and Lieberman, 1988). In either case, those doing the hiring need to have a well-thought-out understanding of the kinds of people they hope to find.

Insofar as the project described in this book is concerned, the codirectors wanted nothing less than the perfect renaissance global education person: someone with a certain set of personal qualities, with highly developed interpersonal skills and specific kinds of work skills; someone with an in-depth grasp of how schools really work, a solid knowledge of global education content, and some familiarity with the relevant research base and data-gathering techniques. Quickly realizing the futility of such a search, they settled for the most reasonable alternative—they hired a *team* of people with complementary skills and personal qualities.

The discussion that follows, then, is not based on descriptions of individual CHI staff members but rather on the characteristics of the *team* which were important to the success of the project. These have been grouped into six categories, as follows: personal attributes, interpersonal skills, work habits, knowledge of how schools function, content-area expertise, and research skills. Of course, there is considerable overlap between them.

Personal Attributes

For a project of this type, which had a distinctly humanistic orientation, it was necessary to find staff members who shared this view—not merely at an intellectual level, but intuitively. A demonstrated ability to operate in a complex environment, and a tolerance for the ambiguity often typical of such environments, would also be essential. Openness, integrity, concern, a sense of humor, and the special kind of humility which finds expression in a genuine respect for teachers—these, too, would be necessary.

The open-ended, nondirective philosophy of the project demanded staff people who were truly comfortable with a nonimpositional approach. In practice, this meant that they had to forgo being seen as global education experts, instead putting their content-area expertise to use in the service of helping the *teachers* to develop their own expertise. In a very real sense they had to teach the teachers to fish, rather than catching the fish for them. It also meant that they had to allow enough "gestation time." (How much was enough, of course, varied from teacher to teacher and was determined by their work schedules; the pace they were comfortable with; their needs, interests, and concerns; and what global education, and the project itself, meant to them at any given time.) Giving the teachers this psychological space—in the form of time and, as one teacher commented early in the project, by the attitude of "no arm-twisting!" sometimes felt frustrating to the project staff, but they discovered that it usually paid off, in the long run, in a teacher's more genuine readiness to participate.

Finally, staff members had to believe in the purposes of the project itself with a sort of Deweyan whole-heartedness (Grant and Zeichner, 1984). One of them was asked, in her final interview,

"What qualities and skills do you think are essential for someone in this type of role?" She responded, "Enthusiasm for the project, belief in it. It's too hard to do if you don't love it."

Interpersonal Skills

In response to the same question, another staff member observed, "I would emphasize the people skills over the content skills. In education it is too often the other way 'round. You can have all the information in the world, but it won't do you any good if you can't communicate, excite, motivate."

The kinds of "people skills" she meant are perhaps best described in the words of the CHI staff members themselves:

"...relate well to teachers; understand what they go through."

"...able to develop good rapport."

"...be friendly, outgoing, and *diplomatic!*"

"...sensitivity to teachers who do not have the habit of opening up to outsiders—teachers whose guard is up, or who may be defensive."

"...a nonthreatening approach to make people feel comfortable if you're going to interview them or observe in their classroom.... what you tell them beforehand; how you assure them that your purpose and role is as a helper, not a judge."

"...able to work with *all* types."

"...willingness to *really listen* to teachers."

"I learned at our meeting, from a teacher who seemed loud and pushy, that that is her way of expressing her enthusiasm. So, I need to be a very good listener and try not to judge a book by its cover, but rather to gather more information and keep an open mind."

"...able to adjust my behavior to (a) teachers at different readiness levels, and (b) schools at different stages of engagement."

"...able to find the balance between addressing the practical needs of individual teachers, and getting them to see and understand the 'larger picture.'"

The necessary interpersonal skills included a knowledge of how schools work (we will come back to this a bit later), credibilty with teachers and administrators, sensitivity to nuance, the ability to read people and situations correctly, and tact in handling delicate situations, diplomacy and a certain political savvy.

Some of these interpersonal skills may be learned through experience (unlike the personal attributes, which are either part of a person's makeup or not), particularly through prior personal experience in schools. Reflecting upon their work with this project, CHI staff members all felt quite strongly that "experience as a teacher—to know what would work, to be credible to other teachers." was a *must* for staff members of any external agency involved in working with teachers on a new project.

Work Habits

In addition to certain kinds of personal qualities and interpersonal skills, we learned over the course of the four years that a project such as this needs staff members who possess two absolutely critical clusters of work habits. The first of these includes organization, planning, and time-management skills. Serving eleven schools with a staff of just three full-time and three part-time people made these skills especially important. Whether this particular project was understaffed (or overcommitted) will be discussed in the next chapter. In any case, the work load was heavy and the pressure was often intense. Decisions on use of time had to be made daily by every staff member, and no one unaccustomed to organizing and prioritizing tasks would have enjoyed working at CHI.

The second cluster is closely related to the first. It includes a willingness to work hard, an ability—and readiness—to take initiative, and the high energy level needed for both. One CHI staff member added *reliability* to her list of necessary work habits: "Be organized, and follow through; if you promise, make sure you deliver." In the field of education, and especially where new programs and projects are concerned, teachers have often felt a lack of continuity. This element of reliability, therefore, becomes a particularly vital component in the process of building trust between external change agents and school people.

Knowledge of How Schools Function

The importance of past experience in the public schools to the effectiveness of an external consultant in a school change program has already been mentioned. A real understanding of how schools and school districts function, however, requires more than simply having paid one's dues in the classroom—or, for that matter, in a support or administrative position. It requires that a person have taken an active interest in the internal dynamics of the educational *system* in all of its complexity, at least enough to be able to identify the unique personality of a school—to recognize the parameters of possibility and the unspoken norms, assumptions, and expectations present at any given school site. Indeed, the word that comes to mind is *connoisseurship* (Eisner, 1979, 1991).

The level of knowledge suggested by this term was essential for the CHI staff members, who had to be able to walk into eleven participating schools, pick up quickly—and accurately—on what was going on in each one, and act appropriately.

Content-Area Expertise

It wasn't necessary that every member of the team be an expert on international studies, but each person hired *should* show a genuine interest in the subject matter of global education and work quickly to familiarize herself with it. The ability to demonstrate a classroom activity on a concept such as human migration, for example, or to successfully teach a math lesson using data on international trade, can contribute significantly to the field consultant's credibility with teachers.

On the other hand, it wasn't necessary for everyone to become a walking encyclopedia, either. In this particular project, teachers of every subject area and grade level were involved and it clearly would have been impossible for any consultant to meet every need. So, while a knowledge of international issues and systems—and the ability to translate such knowledge into workable lesson plans—was important for all team members, the project budget also allowed staff members to hire real experts to work with teachers on specific topics, on a one-time or short-term basis. Project staff also made a point of finding out *where* resources could be found, both in the schools and elsewhere. In the schools, for example, they learned of teachers who had travelled or lived overseas, in other cultures; who were involved with global-issues organizations such as Greenpeace, the Sierra Club, and Educators for Social Responsibility, or who hosted foreign visitors or exchange students from other countries. Frequently Ida, Joy, and Kathy were able to connect a teacher who wanted information on which to base a global lesson with another teacher who had already done the groundwork and was teaching a similar lesson.

Research Skills

Since this is a research project, should we hire people who are experienced education researchers? But it is also a school change effort—should we hire people who are experienced school-site practitioners? Perhaps we ought to construct a team consisting of some of each. What is the optimum balance, and how do we achieve it? These are questions that must inevitably be faced by anyone who is responsible for hiring staff for an innovative project which includes a research or evaluation component. As one of the CHI field consultants once said, "It really is important for a person to be in tune with classroom life, teacher needs, school dynamics, etc. If you are, that makes it easier to write field notes in a way that more accurately captures the essence of what's going on." Thus, for this project it was decided that people hired for the field consultant positions should be practitioners first and foremost. They should, however, have some knowledge of research methods, be able to draw upon education research in general and to think conceptually about the project.

Although the authors of this book had considerable research background, symbolic interaction theory (the framework selected for the research component of this project) was new and unfamiliar to them and to everyone else on the team, as was the methodology of data collection and analysis associated with it. As described in chapter 2, a sociologist skilled in qualitative research methods—and with a particular expertise in symbolic interaction theory—was hired to train the entire team. The staff of experienced school practitioners went through this research training process together, guided by Dr. Roberta Lessor.

Team responses to these training sessions, which took place at intervals throughout the first three years of the project, were consistently positive:

> "When Roberta came in, it gave us a focus we couldn't have achieved by ourselves."

> "The questions she asked showed she was really interested in it.

The more we shared with her, the more fascinated she became with what we were trying to accomplish; that's what I felt from her."

Although training helped the staff members to master and make use of a specific research methodology, it was soon recognized that many of the qualities, skills, and abilities mentioned earlier in this section were also important to the success of the data-gathering efforts. Understanding how a school system works was helpful, for example; as was sensitivity to context and nuance: the ability to read situations correctly and to capture them precisely in the field notes. Being open to multiple perspectives—recognizing that different people, even in the same setting, will attach differing meanings to the same event—was very important, and the staff members worked hard to check perceptions with a wide range of participants. And, as one field consultant admitted when reflecting back on her experience, "When in doubt, admit you don't know. Especially, avoid interpreting teacher behavior if you're not in a position to double-check that your interpretation is correct. Just describe it, and make a note to check on its meaning for those involved at a later time."

In summary, then, we found that although staff members could be trained in research methodology (coding field notes, recognizing patterns and developing memos, for example), what really made for sensitive data gathering in this project were those untrainable personal qualities, intuitively humanistic interpersonal skills, work habits, and compassionate understanding of schools that had been sought in the original hiring process.

In this case, due to the nature both of the project itself and of the research paradigm that was chosen, it was not necessary (and would probably have been counterproductive) to have a team composed of some people who were practitioners and others who were researchers. That might not, however, be true for all studies of educational change. Those in a position to hire staff for a new program, as we noted earlier, should simply be clear about what they are looking for, and why.

Intervention as an Evolutionary Process

As suggested in chapter 1, schools and school districts are tremendously complex systemic organisms. At the deep structure level, they are tightly connected to the widely-held values of the society they serve and thus are very resistant to change. Indeed, at that level significant change is unlikely—unless the society's values change significantly first.

On the other hand, at the unique personality level each school has a culture of its own—a densely woven fabric of history and tradition, socioeconomic realities, the interpersonal dynamics of teachers and administrators, the characteristics of the student body, and so forth. At this level change is difficult, but possible. It is, however, not an event but a *process* (and, despite the wisest planning, an often unpredictable process) requiring certain kinds of adaptive behavior from those who are responsible for bringing the change about.

In the course of the global education project described in this book, four types of adaptive behavior stood out as being vital to what the staff came to think of as the formative, emergent, or evolutionary process of intervention:

1. being alert to changes in the *meanings* attached to the project by teachers and support personnel in the participating schools;

2. being sensitive to matters of *timing,* in working both with schools and with individual teachers;

3. being a skillful *negotiator:* without being manipulative, providing resources and support in ways likely to help the project to achieve its objectives;

4. being *visible and available* at each school site, and being viewed as a source of support and help.

The fifth adaptive behavior, which is implied in each of the first four above is, of course, *flexibility.* The external consultant must be able to assess unanticipated changes at a school site and alter plans, shift direction, and adjust his or her behavior quickly—and appropriately.

1. Being Alert to Changes in Meaning

In chapter 4, we encountered many examples in which teachers' deepening understanding of the purpose and potential of global education led them to alter their behavior. For example, over the course of the four years, increasingly sophisticated minigrant proposals were submitted, from groups of teachers as well as from individuals. Those teachers who were fairly active in the project and made good use of its services and resources became more knowledgable and more confident at the same time.

Many teachers who chose not to become involved during the first year, or even the first two years, did eventually become active by trying a few lessons, joining a group of colleagues to develop a minigrant proposal, or attending a CHI workshop. These first encounters with the project were important for them. The CHI staff knew that when a teacher expresses readiness to investigate a new program—especially after having held back for a year or more—a good introductory experience can be the key to further participation. Since this project was entirely optional for teachers, the *voluntary buy-in* was crucial. A great deal of time was spent in strategizing about ways in which first encounters with the project, whether in year 1 or year 4, could be made positive, stimulating, and relevant to the teacher's daily classroom life. The field consultants kept an eye on those teachers for whom the meaning of global education seemed to be changing. They became very interested in the internal and external forces which prompt a teacher to say, for the first time, "I want to be a part of this program." The theme *turning points*, closely related to *changes in meaning*, was the subject of several staff memos during years 2 and 3.

The concept of turning points is of far more than research or academic interest, however. It is critical for the interventionist to be able to recognize them and act appropriately. It has been understood for many years that individuals who are exposed to an innovation go through stages of receptivity and involvement as they adopt the innovation and make it a part of their lives. For example, Havelock (1971), building on Rogers' studies of successful innovation in farming practices during the 1940s and 1950s, proposed that an individual begins with initial awareness and information-seeking and then, assuming he or she is satisfied with what is learned, moves on through several levels of trying out the new practice until (if the experience has been positive at each stage) it becomes an internalized and regular part of his or her work life. He also suggested what types of interventionist behavior would be most appropriate at each stage in the adoption process: promote the idea, provide information, demonstrate the new practice, train others to do it, help them in their early efforts, service their continuing efforts, and provide support until they have reached the internalization stage and will continue the new practice on their own.

Although each teacher's decision to participate was a personal one, arrived at as part of an internal adoption process such as the one suggested by Havelock, the role of peer pressure in school settings should not be minimized. We are accustomed to thinking of peer pressure in terms of students, but it seems to be almost as strong a force among teachers. Often it was a *group* of teachers who had a shared understanding of global education that helped to change another teacher's view of the project:

> At this point one of the teachers raised her hand and with anger and indignation in her voice asked what we meant by including "world religions" as a topic of interest. I realized the question was "loaded," and tried to diffuse the anger by telling her, in a mild voice, that these ideas had been suggested by other teachers and that they probably had just meant the study of major world religions in a historical, rather than a theological, context. She seemed a little appeased but still troubled. At this point two of the other teachers spoke up and said that they taught world religions as part of their sixth grade world history curriculum. The tone in their voices indicated they were somewhat chiding their colleague for a concern that was not warranted.

The interventionist must be alert to ways in which other teachers can act as allies in helping to clarify the meaning of the change for others, and constantly seek to create a critical mass of support for the new program. At the same time, he or she must create the conditions which will bring individual teachers along from one stage of adoption to the next. And all of this must be done without coercion.

2. Being Sensitive to Matters of Timing

The concept of turning points is also closely related to the whole area of timing, because it seemed that when a teacher reached a turning point (the "teachable moment"), there was a window of opportunity of several weeks during which the field consultant could act. If that time passed and the teacher had not received the information, materials, or other help which she had been ready to use, her interest would wane.

In most cases, the CHI field consultants were able to recognize these periods of readiness in individual teachers, but in trying to serve eleven schools, inevitably some were *not* recognized. Occasionally, a teacher who felt ready to participate in the project *didn't say anything:* didn't ask for information, materials, or help. Once in a while teachers did send signals, but subtly; and the field coordinators simply missed them. Later, in reading through the field notes, the signals were recognized; but by then the optimum moment had usually passed. The CHI staff began to think of these as *the theme of missed opportunities* and, while there was inevitably some chagrin at having missed them, the staff became sensitive to the need to be continually alert to teachers' changing readiness levels as they moved through the stages of awareness, information-seeking, evaluation, trial, installation, adoption, and internalization (Havelock, 1971).

Another theme that emerged which is closely connected to both *meaning* and *timing* (and, in a way, to *missed opportunities* also) is the theme *fitting together of biographies.* Teachers, like students, bring to the workplace not only their professional histories and work-related concerns but their private lives as well. For dozens of reasons, any given individual just may not be at a point in his or her life when a new program is going to "click." Conversely, that person may in fact (whether or not he is conscious of it) be ready and waiting for some new project to bring excitement and renewal to his work life. Particularly in the early years of the project, a surprisingly large number of teachers said things like, "Where have you been? I've just been waiting for something like this to come along!" or "This project has made me feel excited about teaching again!"

The image of intersecting trajectories seems useful here, though one wouldn't want to be too fatalistic: at some point in our lives, most of us have had the feeling that something happened at *just the right time* or, perhaps, at the wrong time—"If I had only met her five years earlier..." or "If I hadn't gotten involved in that project when I did, I never would have had this new job opportunity," or "I just wasn't ready to learn Spanish then, but I am now." The CHI field consultants noticed that when the life of a teacher and the life of an innovative educational program met and the teacher felt that "click" of recognition—"this is for me"—it meant that the teacher felt some pull towards the *intrinsic* rewards inherent in the project (satisfaction of professional growth, stimulation of new ideas and teaching practices, feeling that one is involved in a worthwhile effort). No longer would the *extrinsic* rewards (getting free materials, having time off to attend workshops, the status of being associated with the new program) be the primary motivating force. (Remember that in the end-of-project teacher survey, seventy-six percent of those teachers who identified themselves as having been "very involved" with global education said that they became so either "because I felt that it was part of an important educational movement," (forty percent) or because "I saw it as a professional opportunity" (thirty-six percent)—both responses which reflect *intrinsic* motivation to participate.)

In studying the delicate balance of readiness for change, the CHI staff realized that fortuitous timing and the fitting together of biographies (or intersection of trajectories) alone were not enough to bring teachers into the project: the *context* in which they worked was also a key factor. At North High School, for example, there was evidence during the first three years that quite a few teachers were interested in being involved with CHI; but they held back because the principal seemed ambivalent about supporting the project, and they didn't want to "get on his bad side" (the story of North High was told in chapter 7). The chronic feelings of stress felt constantly by most of the teachers at Pacifica Middle School prevented all but a tiny handful from *ever* reaching a point of readiness to start trying out—even in a very small way—some global education teaching/learning activities. A context that discourages innovation, then, can stifle even a potentially vigorous interest. More often than not, such a context is one in which the force of *competing demands* is keenly felt by teachers (this theme was explored in detail in chapter 6).

On the other hand, a *positive* environment can help encourage teachers to set aside their reluctance and give something new a try. At Mesa Junior High, for example, the principal asked CHI staff *not* to come into his school until almost the end of the fall 1985 semester—he wanted some "lead time" to do some preparatory groundwork in creating a receptive and positive environment for the project. Consequently, when CHI staff members went to Mesa to do their introductory presentation—months after having done it at most of the other schools—the teachers were ready and interested.

Being sensitive to matters of timing also means tuning in to "the timetables teachers have in their heads," as one staff member put it. A regular schedule of school visits—an "I'll be at your school every other Thursday" approach, for example—was rejected by nearly every faculty.

> "Don't come back until after Christmas," the teachers at La Puente Elementary School told us shortly before Thanksgiving. "There's just too much going on. We'll be ready and waiting for you again in January."

> We were advised by the teachers at Birmingham Junior High as to when to have the meeting, and they were absolutely right.... We need to be even more sensitive to teachers' schedules than we have been in the past, and not impose a "guess-timated" time frame on them.

There is, as every teacher knows, a natural rhythm to the school year; this can work for or against change efforts. An intervention team which fails to acknowledge it (by adjusting their work in the schools accordingly) risks loss of support by teachers, who will feel that the "outsiders" don't *really* understand the work environment in which they, the teachers, must function.

Just as there are cycles of high and low interest and participation within the nine-month school year, there are also identifiable cycles of interest and participation over periods of several years. During the first two years of a new program, the interest builds as teachers seek information and new resources are made available to them. Many new projects also bring people together, satisfying a deep desire for professional networking which many teachers feel but ordinarily do not act upon. The very novelty of the new program attracts some, a sense of its value for students attracts some; and the "in-group" sense of being in the vanguard of an educational movement also is satisfying.

During the third year it is not uncommon for a new program to lose some of its momentum. Norms and traditions, rules and regulations, competing demands, and unexpected developments combine to challenge the time and energy that had been devoted to the new program. The support base may erode as the early adopters move off to become involved in some *other* new project, or as some key participants transfer to other schools and are replaced by newcomers unfamiliar with the program. This difficult year can prove fatal to a project if the problems are viewed as unsolvable or if the project loses key funding just at that point.

If the problems are tackled with enthusiasm and the money doesn't run out, however, a faculty can survive the "year three crisis" and in fact experience a rekindling of interest and participation. Interventionists face the task of designing creative strategies to help teachers move through that inevitable period of decline with the project intact and able to regain its momentum. In the CHI project, it was the awarding of minigrants to groups of teachers for curriculum development projects which sustained the original momentum and, indeed, continued to attract new participants throughout the four years of the project. Ways of initiating newcomers must be developed, and the unflagging and constructive support of the principal is also a critical element.

At each stage of a new project, interventionists must act in different ways. Earlier, the work of Havelock was mentioned in connection with the stages that individuals go through as they try out and adopt a new way of doing something, and it was pointed out that the interventionist must learn to relate appropriately to each teacher, depending upon which stage that teacher is in at any given time. The same general principle holds true for working with schools as units. The first stage, introduction of the project to the faculty, involves clarification of goals and purposes and the provision of information; this is generally followed by a stage of initial acceptance by at least some portion of the faculty and a willingness to "wait and see" by the rest. In the next stage, the burden of proof rests with the interventionists: they must show that they can and will deliver the promised resources and support, and they must demonstrate their own competence and establish their credibility, good faith, and reliability. What they do at this stage must be consistent with what they *said* they would do when they were in the earlier, "selling" stage.

> I am beginning a file, with a cross-reference of teachers' names by subject or grade, from the various schools. This will enable us to cross-reference teachers with each other from the same subjects, and different subjects. I am also forming a request list with the names and schools of teachers, so that we can quickly see where similar interests overlap among schools. I record this at this point because we are growing so rapidly, and I would like for

us to be able to capture most requests and interests, and do follow-up work on them.

As teacher interest builds, then the interventionists must "do their homework." As they do so, however, slowly but surely the burden of proof shifts to the teachers and the school enters a stage in which "the ball is in their court." The intervention team has delivered on its promises, and the next steps are up to the teachers—individually or in groups. This is the point at which teachers begin to integrate the new material or processes into their actual teaching, to work with it and try to make it part of their permanent repertoire. The interventionists don't sit back and relax at this stage, however: they must continue to provide appropriate help as requested, and even to sense what help is needed and provide it even if not asked. The continuing support of the principal is important throughout this stage.

Finally, as use of the innovation spreads throughout the school, the interventionists must nurture the teacher-to-teacher support networks that will emerge. This critical stage lays the groundwork for the project to continue without the need for the constant presence of outside help. In the global education project, once again it was the minigrants which encouraged the formation of these teacher support networks, because with few exceptions the minigrants were awarded to *groups* of from two to twelve teachers for collaborative work on a specific set of lessons or activities.

Being sensitive to matters of timing, then, involved recognizing when a teacher was ready to join, and providing appropriate support; understanding the complex contextual pressures which compete for a teacher's time and energy, and acting accordingly; and having a feel for the rhythm of the school year and for the cyclical rhythm of interest and participation over longer periods of time. The interventionist cannot push too hard, and must sense when to let up for awhile, but on the other hand there are times when a teacher, a group of teachers, or even an entire faculty is ready to move, full steam ahead, and the interventionist must be ready for that as well.

3. Being a Skillful Negotiator

We have referred to the context within which teachers must work, and in chapter 6 we discussed the impact of competing demands in considerable detail. When viewed from the perspective of the external consultant whose job it is to help a school faculty adopt a new program, the reality of those competing demands means that being a skillful negotiator is one of the basic adaptive behaviors connected with the emergent process of intervention. Without being manipulative, the CHI field consultants had to find ways to move the teachers—individually and collectively—as close to the goal (globalization of the curriculum of the school) as humanly possible within the four-year period of the study.

> By themselves, the normal expectations of teaching are extensive. Planning and carrying out five to ten lessons per day, keeping discipline, filing reports, and so forth are duties requiring one's full attention. To that we have added in recent years the notion of accountability. In fact, several teachers asked explicitly of administrators at our introductory meeting of September 30, 1985, if participation in our project would jeopardize their accountability in other areas. Also, many questions were directed at finding out rather precisely what they would be expected to do, how things would work, and how locked in they were. (staff memo on clarification of expectations.)

We noted in chapters 1 and 3 that at these introductory meetings of 1985 many teachers were skeptical, since a project that claimed to have no particular requirements (and no intention other than to provide teachers with the resources they might want) certainly sounded too good to be true. The first task of negotiation, then, was to earn trust and convince the teachers that CHI staff members were prepared to act consistently with what had originally been said.

The second task of negotiation was to work out some understandings about what teachers could expect CHI to provide and what the teachers would do. Again, the goal was to have teachers *voluntarily* take on more and more, over time; but for this to happen, CHI had to meet them well over halfway for the first year or two of the project. "There seems to be negotiation over how much you will do, and how much they will do," observed the consulting sociologist in the spring of 1986, "It's a problem in negotiation and *not* a problem in social control because you don't have any authority over them as you would in a mandated project."

During the entire four years, CHI field consultants did everything they could to provide interested teachers with the resources they needed in order to teach with a global perspective. Reference materials, starter lesson plans, audiovisual aids, chances to share ideas with other teachers, and chances to attend workshops on topics they themselves had suggested—even minigrants, which allowed teachers to buy planning time or teaching materials—all of these were provided; all a teacher had to do was ask. For teachers who couldn't quite see how global perspectives could be added to the curriculum without displacing the district- or state-mandated topics and skills, CHI staff did page-by-page analyses of the California Model Curriculum Standards document and several district curriculum guides. A yellow felt pen was used to highlight those sections of the documents in which global knowledge was either explicitly or implicitly included. The result was visually powerful; flipping the pages of the documents rapidly to show the considerable amount of yellow ink throughout, it was then possible to say "Look, we're just asking you to give us a chance to help you do what you're expected to do anyway" (Phillipsen, 1986).

There were, however, some things which CHI refused to do. Unwilling to create any conditions which could foster dependency, the staff decided that they would not do demonstration lessons in classrooms. Many demonstration lessons were done for groups of teachers during the four years, but it was then up to the teachers to take what they could use and incorporate it into their teaching in their own way and at their own pace. Once in a great while, too, a CHI staff member would encounter a teacher who seemed to want CHI to do it all for her. As one of the field consultants noted at the conclusion of the four years, "My lowest priority was serving those teachers who seemed to be taking advantage of us by getting us to do their work. There weren't many of these, but there were some. Consultants need to be aware of this; they need a little 'street smarts' with some teachers."

A third task of negotiation involved the use of *time*, a teacher's most precious possession. As the project got under way, it seemed that teachers were willing to give it some of their time if (a) they received what *they* viewed as constructive and pertinent help; and (b) the project staff was clearly making an effort to be sensitive to the teachers' time constraints, and trying not to waste any of their time. There were numerous opportunities to demonstrate good faith in this area, especially during the first year as the relationship of the project to each of the schools was being worked out:

The film was twenty-eight minutes long, and because the principal had used up twenty of our allotted forty minutes, we ran over the time limit. This was very frustrating. From this experience, we learned to try and control the time factor more stringently. We need to be very clear about (1) stating the exact amount of time needed for our presentation, (2) running interference for teachers in terms of adhering to the amount of time that *they* have been asked to give, (3) work more closely with principals to respect this time commitment, and (4) have a "plan B" if our time is cut short. I feel that teachers do respect us for staying within the parameters of the allotted time.

A fourth negotiation strategy involved gently but firmly pursuing all expressions of interest. Without being coercive or unpleasantly insistent, CHI field consultants made it somewhat difficult for teachers to drop away from the project once they had begun to get involved: "Another strategy that we use with teachers is one in which we leave no one out. For example, any teacher scheduled to meet with us who cannot show up today receives a note of hello from us, plus the handouts he requested, and an invitation to call us if we can be of further assistance."

The basis of the project was voluntary participation, and the "try it, you'll like it" approach lay at the heart of all of CHI's negotiation strategies. Staff members (who, it must be remembered, had all been classroom teachers themselves) sensed intuitively that commitment would follow successful first attempts rather than preceding them. Indeed, in discussing a study by Crandall (1983), Doll (1989, p. 390) observes

Interestingly, commitment occurred largely *after* implementation, whereas the conventional wisdom holds that teachers become committed first and then willingly implement. This finding suggests that, in cases where curriculum planners know practices will work, they can follow a 'try it, you'll like it' philosophy with teachers. Once teachers have tried the practices and liked them, they will become committed to them.

4. Being Visible and Available

The fourth type of adaptive behavior which the CHI staff found was critical to the evolutionary process of the global education intervention was, simply, accessibility—being visible and available to teachers at each school site, and being viewed by those teachers as a source of support and help. This matter of accessibility can be tricky, however. As suggested in the discussion of being sensitive to matters of timing, teachers didn't want the consultants around *all* the time; there were points in the school year when consultants had to back off a bit. If they did so, they were welcomed back later and complimented for understanding what teachers' lives are like. If they didn't, they risked losing some of their credibility.

Nevertheless, an interventionist mustn't just become scarce on command. There are also times when he or she would be wiser to do just the opposite—to *push a little harder* instead of backing off. One of those untrainable skills mentioned earlier in this chapter is probably the intuitive sense of when to push on and when to back off. But especially at the beginning, when teachers and consultants are still getting acquainted, simply *being there* is very important:

> Site visits were important—getting to know the teachers—the more you're out there in the trenches, the more you can appreciate what teachers and schools are doing. Once they associate you with the project, you can develop confidence, a sense of direction, and a feeling that you *can* make a difference, and all of that helps you grow into your role.

> I wore a name tag this morning, and I think it helped. It's going to be a while before we are known to everyone in these schools.

> At this school, the media center is a much better environment than the teachers' lounge in terms of space, aesthetics, and comfort. Also, it is preferable because it houses the xerox machine, which teachers line up to use—they can visit with us while they wait for it.

> This has been a wonderful morning—I've interacted with a number of people. Upon arriving, I was relocated from the library to the communications room, as they were testing in the library today. I was centrally located and very visible in this room, and really felt a part of the day's activities.

It soon became apparent that for two full-time field consultants to be adequately visible in *eleven* schools—in addition to all of their other responsibilities—would be no easy matter. At one point early in the project, it seemed more effective for them to go out to each school together:

> When we both go out to a school our presence seems to attract people, questions, and introductions. Many times Ida is with one person or group while I am with another. I personally think that this kind of interaction and visibility has more of an impact on the school than the times I have gone there alone. I sense that double exposure and double coverage promotes more change and more growth. Ida and I each take care of different details at the school site, and the result is a job thoroughly done, with more individual time given to teachers.

By the end of year 2 this didn't seem as important, and during years 3 and 4 the two field consultants more often visited the schools alone. By then they were well known to everyone at each site, and either one could accomplish whatever was needed.

> They invited me to join them and a few other teachers for lunch at a local hamburger joint. I decided it might prove useful, so I went.

> I learned today, from the *principal's secretary*, that as of next September, Pacifica Junior High will become a 6-7-8 middle school. It's a good thing we've been careful to nurture our relationships with the front office secretaries!

These changes in deployment of staff for purposes of accessibility to the teachers were all a part of the emergent process of intervention. Before concluding this section of the chapter, one more point about visibility needs to be made: Sometimes, the CHI field consultants learned, being *seen* with certain teachers can interfere with one's success in reaching the rest of the faculty:

> One teacher occupies most of our time with her stories and her pushiness, and this makes it difficult for other teachers to get near the table. They reject her participation, and this may be hurting the project. We saw this happen right before our eyes; even the teachers who have attended our workshops stayed away.

> The principal told us that three of the teachers we were trying to work with are not the most well-respected or well-liked teachers on the staff. He wasn't at all surprised that we don't seem to be getting anywhere.

When it comes to visibility, then, it is important for the interventionists to identify the opinion leaders within each faculty, and find ways of gaining their support for the project. If this can be achieved early on, then it is less problematic to be seen *also* helping the teachers who possess lower status within the faculty's social structure. Again, of course, the ultimate goal is to involve *everyone*, if possible.

The Inner Life of the Interventionist

Confidence

Since for this particular project the decision had been made to hire people who had had classroom teaching experience but who were neither seasoned researchers nor global education experts, per se (though one did have a Ph.D. in international relations), in the beginning self-confidence was low in these latter two areas.

> In the beginning, I was intimidated. Teachers might ask me questions I couldn't answer.

> I worried at first that I couldn't capture the really important things in the field notes I was writing. But working through some sample sets of field notes with Roberta helped a lot.

Confidence was high, however, in the critical area of interpersonal skills, and as the project passed through its first year and the CHI field consultants earned the trust and respect of the teachers and felt welcome and at home in the eleven schools, confidence was no longer an issue.

> Because the teachers knew I had been a teacher, it was comfortable for me...and for them.

> I liked knowing what teachers lives are like. That is something I could contribute.

> Since we know our teachers a little better this year, and since I know the materials now, it feels that the job here has changed, from bag lady to global perspectives resource person. It's nice.

Excitement

As with most innovative programs, the first six months were terrifically exciting. Staff members believed strongly in the value of global education, and were encouraged by teachers' positive reactions to the early information sessions about what the project could provide.

> When I was given that first package of materials to read—I took it on a camping trip and couldn't put it down. It was liberating...and pretty overwhelming. The materials suggested solutions to problems I'd felt powerless to solve. That gave me the courage to articulate to others—friends, family—some of what I'd learned.

> I'm in love with the notion of 'no arm-twisting.' I love not having to "sell" anything. I feel energized when I leave a school.

> It's refreshing to see them sort of melt and smile when they realize that it's really true that we're not there with expectations.

> Teachers' enthusiasm; their real care to do their job well—they really do care about kids—it's a real source of inspiration for me.

Frustration

By midway through year 1, however, the day-to-day pressures of life in schools had tempered the excitement and optimism with a sizable dose of realism. From then on, the project settled into a pattern of ups and downs which kept life interesting, but which sometimes left the staff feeling as if they were on an emotional roller coaster. Since everyone on the staff had been a classroom teacher, however, the inevitable frustrations came as no surprise.

> The hours of preparation do not match the teacher response at times. In the midst of this disappointment, I try to think of a better way of doing these school visits. I remember that our absolutely best teacher response has been on minimum days and at staff meetings.

> When you're an outsider working in schools, you can see how you think things ought to be, but they don't always happen that way, and you have to keep your mouth shut!

> There are so many people in our schools who have yet to look at global education—to open their minds to it. I remember being so aware of walking on eggshells with some people because I realized there wasn't a hundred percent receptivity.

> I grew into the role by constantly trying to recognize and anticipate the obstacles.

Somehow, the situation seems worse. I was made to feel that I was invading their space...it was awfully strange and uncomfortable.

What I learned today is that first on the agenda at Pacifica Junior High is their own trauma. How can we connect with problems like drug traffic and abuse, pregnancy (six this semester), child abuse, gangs, low attendance, hungry children? In spite of all this, the teachers keep plugging along and meeting the challenge of addressing this school's needs.

Often people held up "the system" as an obstacle. This was problematic for me because I sometimes questioned whether the "obstacles" they saw were really there.

There's a tendency to think that the change will happen much faster than it actually does. The progress is very subtle sometimes. You can't just overnight go into a school and have everyone jump up and shout "more, more!" The pebble-in-the-water/ripple thing may be the best you can hope for.

In our minds, we could see a lot of things that could be done, but we simply didn't have the time. For instance, we could have done more with networking teachers to each other and to community resources, but the telephone time to make the connections just wasn't there.

When these things happen, such as very little teacher interest on a given day, Ida and I try to remember that we are also studying what happens, and we simply write it up, figure a new strategy, and move on.

The staff members quickly learned that they could not expect a single strategy to work at all of the schools. As Patterson (1989) warns:

Many of the field agents experienced difficulties which were caused by the interaction between the planned change and the individual characteristics of the school site. The uniqueness of each school required effective consultants to adapt their activities to the local conditions, rather than rigidly adhere to preconceived ideas of appropriate behavior.

Satisfaction

Despite the feelings of frustration and the times when all of the problem-solving and strategizing just didn't seem to work, there were just as many—if not more—moments of real satisfaction during the four years of involvement with the eleven schools. As any classroom teacher lives for the sudden flash of comprehension in the eyes of a student—"Oh—I get it!"—the interventionist is sustained by those times when teachers get interested and involved.

> The group was very attentive and worked very hard to develop clear theme statements. They did not respond to the "ten minutes are up" announcement; they were not stingy about time and they didn't want to leave early. After the session, they were all pleased with their theme statements and want to use them in rewriting their school plan next month.
>
> It felt so nice to see teachers' responses when they felt they were really being heard.

It also felt good to know that the majority of teachers at the eleven schools came to accept and trust the CHI field consultants:

> I just received another invitation to have lunch. They are so friendly here.
>
> When I walked into Mesa Junior High at the start of year 3 it felt good. It was like being "home."

There was tremendous satisfaction, too, in seeing carefully thought out plans work the way they were supposed to work:

> Today feels good because I tried a new strategy...and it worked!
>
> Our hours of planning and thinking through the agenda really paid off.

There were satisfactions, too, in working together as a team:

> The level of sharing among the CHI staff members was excellent. We had the time to sit together and talk about the experiences we were all having. Our staff meetings were probably unique in that respect; we never felt rushed, and the emphasis was on information-sharing and perception-sharing. It had to be that way; we all had to know as much as we could about each site in order to be sensitive to each school.
>
> I found the teamwork very satisfying, though it's more time-consuming because you have to listen to everyone's stories and con-

sider everyone's views and feelings. Even the secretary and the student workers had chances to participate, and their views were listened to carefully.

In this project, the bulk of the actual intervention work at the school sites was done by the three field consultants: Joy Phillipsen, on the team for the first two years, Kathy O'Neil, for the last two years, and Ida Urso, who was with CHI for the entire four years. After the project ended, these women were asked to identify those aspects of the project which they had found especially satisfying:

> I think it makes a tremendous difference for those teachers who actually participate. It can change their motivation, renew them professionally—and it gave me a great sense of reward to be involved with that.

> The outside change agent is such an important catalyst; when it comes from inside, it's just not the same. You *are* a catalyst—you do bring information, ideas, energy that is helpful. You can see how your efforts inspire—you're a breath of fresh air for them.

> Working with the minigrant projects was wonderful. I got to see them from the time they were just ideas, through to the end of their implementation. Teachers responded to having someone take an interest in them, and by following through with the grant projects maybe I helped some teachers to do a better job than they might have done alone.

> CHI was a pivotal experience in my life. I feel like a permanent change took place: It widened my perspectives, and made me feel that trying to be a voice for global education wherever I go *isn't* a hopeless task—the ripple effect really does happen!

Disappointment

During the first three years, feelings of disappointment were connected primarily to missed opportunities—those times when, for a complex variety of reasons, a teacher was ready to become involved but CHI wasn't able to respond adequately. By year 4, however, as the project entered its final phase, and as more and more teachers *did* become involved, there were fewer missed opportunities but a greater sense of sadness about time running out.

> Towards the end, it was difficult to stay as upbeat when I knew it wasn't going to continue.

Globalizing can't happen in just four or five years, so there was a sense of not completing what we set out to do. On the other hand, I suppose this is one of those efforts that's never really "finished."

By the time the project ended, I was just starting to feel that I was able to work with administrators. That is one area I could have done more with if we had continued.

Yes, I felt sorry to know that I wouldn't be working with those schools any more. But I do believe this project made a real difference, and that it touched more people than we will ever know. In the years ahead, as world events unfold, those teachers will think back to the CHI years and understand what it was all about. And some of them will continue to use the global lessons they developed, and others will begin doing it, and it will spread...because it's the right and necessary thing for the children. And for all of us, for that matter.

Conclusion

With this look at the evolutionary process of intervention, the qualities and skills needed for success in such work, and the actual experiences of the CHI field workers, we reach the end of our exploration. In chapter 9 we will summarize what we learned from the CHI project, and propose a set of questions and hypotheses for further exploration.

References

Crandall, D., "The Teacher's Role in School Improvement," *Educational Leadership* 41 (3) (November 1983):6–9.

Doll, R. C., *Curriculum Development: Decision-Making and Process*, 7th ed. (Boston: Allyn and Bacon, 1989).

Eisner, E., *The Educational Imagination: On the Design and Evaluation of School Programs* (New York: Macmillan, 1979).

Eisner, E., *The Enlightened Eye* (New York: Macmillan, 1991).

Grant, C., and K. Zeichner, "On Becoming a Reflective Teacher," in *Preparing for Reflective Teaching* (Boston: Allyn & Bacon, 1984).

Havelock, R. G., *Planning for Innovation through Dissemination and Utilization of Knowledge* (Ann Arbor: Center for Research on Utilization of Scientific Knowledge, University of Michigan Institute for Social Research, 1971), 10/54.

Little, J. W., "Norms of Collegiality and Experimentation: Workplace Conditions of School Success," *American Educational Research Journal* 19 (3) (Fall 1982):325–40.

MacGregor, D., *The Human Side of Enterprise* (New York: McGraw-Hill, 1960).

McDonald, J. P., "When Outsiders Try to Change Schools from the Inside," *Phi Delta Kappan* (November 1989).

Miles, M. B., E. R. Saxl, and A. Lieberman, "What Skills Do Educational 'Change Agents' Need? An Empirical View," *Curriculum Inquiry* 18 (2) (1988).

Patterson, C. J., *The Perceptions, Concerns, and Professional Lives of Curriculum Consultants,* unpublished doctoral dissertation (School of Education, Macquarie University, Sydney, Australia, 1989).

Phillipsen, J., "Model Curriculum Standards Include Global Perspectives," *Thrust* (the Journal of the Association of California School Administrators) (May–June 1986).

9

WHAT *DOES* IT TAKE TO GLOBALIZE
THE CURRICULUM OF A SCHOOL?

We shall not cease from exploration, and the end of all our
exploring will be to arrive where we started and know the place
for the first time.

                                                              –T. S.Eliot

Properly understood, research is a never-ending process: one
question leads in several directions, and in each direction one may
find numerous additional questions. Finding answers to any of
them leads to the discovery of yet others; and on it goes. Similarly,
school improvement is a never-ending process: solve one problem,
meet one need, implement one program, and other challenges
appear as if by magic—everything is connected to everything else.

After four years, CHI's global education project in the ten
remaining network schools officially ended, but many of the teachers who had become involved with the project continued to infuse
global perspectives into their teaching. World events in that year—
1989—were so dramatic that many teachers who had *not* participated in CHI activities during the four years of the project began to
support global education in their schools even though the project
itself was no longer available. The press of competing demands
remains a problem for teachers who are trying to implement a new
program, of course. But informal sampling conducted since the end
of the project shows that, unlike some curriculum innovations,
efforts to teach using global perspectives may be on the *rise,*
whether or not special resources are available. As we proposed in
chapter 1, being globally literate is an idea whose time has come—
in society, and in schools.

As described in chapter 2, the eleven schools in the network were studied in detail throughout the four years. Patterns of teacher and administrator behavior were noted and recorded, questions were asked and hypotheses were proposed, and additional data were gathered until some hypotheses were verified and others were modified or abandoned. By the end of the four years, some questions had been tentatively answered, but new ones had been posed. It was time, nevertheless, to pause and review what we had learned. This book is the result of that review, and in this final chapter we will summarize what we believe to be the most significant points made in the previous eight chapters. These have been grouped into two categories: what we believe we know, and what we are posing as hypotheses for further exploration, by ourselves as well as by others. Readers will note that *the process of educational change and school improvement* is the focus of our findings, and recall that global education was the *programmatic vehicle* used to study the change process.

What We Believe We Know

1.   An understanding of "how the world works" is crucial for everyone, if we are to live well in an increasingly complicated society. Such understanding can be achieved through global education for both children and adults.

The five global systems—environmental, economic, political, cultural, and technological—interconnect with each other and with our daily lives. The Middle East crisis provoked by the Iraqi invasion of Kuwait in 1990 was a perfect example: we were forced to pay much more than we were accustomed to for gasoline because suddenly the steady supply of oil—which is an environmentally scarce commodity anyway—was threatened by the military-political attack of one oil-producing nation upon another. Since our country has not made much of an investment in the development of alternative energy resources since 1980, there seemed no choice but to intervene in the situation in order to protect our national interest.

Thus do economics and politics merge. We, the authors, saw our neighbor's son go off to Saudi Arabia to defend the oil reserves of that nation upon which our nation depends; there was a yellow ribbon tied around our neighbor's sycamore tree. Our other neighbor, an Arab-American with family members still living in Baghdad, was worried sick about their safety. We watched on TV as news commentators speculated about the possible cultural effect of the presence of American servicewomen on traditionally conservative Saudi society. We heard reports of the technologies of war and wondered what lay ahead—poison gas, biological weapons, even nuclear war? There was no doubt in our minds that the world is small now, and that in the words of the old spiritual, "There's no hiding place—." Current events tie our own neighborhood tightly to all corners of the globe. We need to be better informed about the connections between the global systems, and so do our children and grandchildren. Otherwise we will live in a world we cannot comprehend, and if we cannot comprehend it we will lose control over our own lives.

2.   Conditions are right for global education, but there *is* some sociopolitical resistance.

Global education promotes an outward-looking perspective, and historically Americans have been outward-looking primarily during times of relative economic and political security. The enthusiasm and pride with which we supported the Peace Corps in its early years, for example, had its roots in the soil of the safe and secure Eisenhower era: we, who had so much, felt good about ourselves and our ability and willingness to help others.

The nation and the world have been through some wrenching years since then. That ebullient generosity of spirit seems to have given way to a corrosive pessimism, an inward-looking preoccupation with personal well-being, and general apathy about really *doing* something to help the less fortunate. The extent to which Americans have lost faith in the ability of a democratic system to solve social problems can be gauged by the steadily increasing percentage of adults who simply don't participate.

Homelessness, crime, drug abuse, urban crises of all kinds, growing unemployment, decay of the infrastructure, breakdown of the health care system, air and water pollution reaching the danger level, an economy teetering on the brink of collapse—little wonder that Americans feel anxious and insecure as they face the final years of the twentieth century. It is hardly surprising, therefore, that there is some resistance to global education within our society. In chapter 4 we presented some information about this resistance, noting that it is situated primarily within the membership of fundamentalist religious groups and ultraconservative political groups whose philosophical grounding tends to be absolutist in nature. A deeply rooted belief in timeless and universal absolutes, be they religious or political, precludes tolerance of relativist assumptions such as, for example, the need to understand and accept other cultures' mores, values, and beliefs *on their own terms*.

What *is* surprising is the widespread support for global education, given the insecurity of the times. But this support can be traced, we suspect, to a pervasive feeling that the *lack* of a global perspective may be part of what caused many of these problems to get out of hand in the first place. Americans can no longer ignore or deny the connectedness of their lives to events taking place all around the world, nor can they explain away the recent studies which show how ignorant they are about geography and current world events. There seems to be a feeling that the world is getting away from us, and global education offers a way to turn that around—or at least to better understand what is happening and why.

3.   There is a deep structure of schooling.

In chapter 1, we presented a model for thinking about (1) why schools are nearly identical at one level and yet at another level, entirely individual, and (2) why significant and long-lasting change is so difficult to achieve in our schools. This model is the *deep structure/unique personality* schema. Other educators have noted the resistance of the educational system to change, and suggested various reasons for it—Sarason (1982), for example, identified institutional and behavioral "regularities" which are so well entrenched that they operate at the taken-for-granted level of our thinking.

The deep structure/unique personality model emerged from analysis of the data gathered from thirteen high schools as part of the Study of Schooling, directed by John I. Goodlad (Tye, 1985). In this model, the deep structure is defined as those educational practices which are "determined by the values and assumptions that are widely shared throughout our society...[and] shaped by conventional wisdom, by tradition, by vested interests—and by a certain amount of institutional inertia." The deep structure determines the use of space, allocation of time, general approach to students as revealed in policies, programs, and pedagogy, ways of grouping students, decisions about curriculum, and reliance on test scores as measures of success.

Data collected for CHI's study of global education and school change support this notion of a deep structure. In addition to the characteristics just mentioned (use of space, allocation of time, etc.), another component of the deep structure of schooling was found, in this study, to be very powerful: this is the phenomenon of *competing demands*. In chapter 5 this theme was thoroughly explored, and the following hypothesis was proposed: *Competing demands may be the institution's way of resisting change.* System overload—keeping everyone too busy to be reflective—guarantees that the questions likely to challenge the status quo (*Why are we doing this? What are our real purposes here?*) are unlikely to be asked. Whatever the answer, anyone who has ever tried to introduce and institutionalize an innovative program has found that competing demands are one of the primary barriers to success. The new program may be adopted for awhile, but eventually it fades away and is replaced once again by the traditional ways of doing things.

4. Increased bureaucratization and standardization stand in the way of school improvement efforts.

It is axiomatic by now in the literature on adoption of innovation that *people are more likely to implement a change if they have had some personal involvement in the decisions about that change.* Such personal involvement can only take place within one's immediate context: at the school where one works or, possibly, within the school district. Decisions made at increasingly remote levels of the system—county, state, regional, or national—lose this element of personal involvement and, thus, also lose the personal *commitment* to implement the change. This is why mandates for change from the higher levels of the system are less likely to "stick" than are decisions made by each faculty for the school in which they work.

Nevertheless, the twentieth century has seen the increasing bureaucratization of schooling. Centralization and standardization are the foundations of this bureaucratic system, typified by the rapid consolidation of smaller schools and districts into larger units in the years following World War II. Done for the sake of efficiency, the consolidation movement contributed to the transformation of schooling from a local, human-scale operation to a more distant, unwieldy, and faceless one.

Standardization followed centralization more or less naturally, since one of the tenets of large-scale management of schools was that all units in the system should be treated alike. This principle makes it difficult for an individual school to take the initiative for site-specific improvement, or (at best) forces the school site team (teachers and administrators together) to accomplish their goals *within the same framework of constraints imposed on all other schools in the district.* We saw this principle at work in the global education project when, for example, South High School was not permitted to have a half-day in-service because none of the other schools in the district were allowed to have in-services on school time.

5.   The schools, in general, are doing their best to cope with the many tasks set for them by society, but it is not easy.

None of the eleven schools with which we worked for four years could be described as a serene or easygoing place; all were stressed to some degree—some extremely so. Many contradictions coexisting in our society and reflected within the school environment create an atmosphere which seems to lack centrality of purpose. This lack of purposefulness, coupled with the tendency to add more and more expectations to the school's mission (without deleting any) leaves conscientious school people feeling stretched thin and unable to do as good a job as they would like to do. Instead, they are expected to be babysitters, personal guidance counselors, policemen, and surrogate parents as well as teachers.

All of this is exacerbated by the information explosion of the second half of the twentieth century: teachers are caught between the traditional institutional pressure to cover their subject matter and their own growing realization that such coverage, in the familiar sense, is now impossible (Sizer, 1985). Lacking reliable criteria for making curriculum choices, they run faster and faster to meet society's expectations, yet still they fall further and further behind. The resulting frustration affects morale and leaves teachers all too willing to leave curriculum decisions to someone else. The entrenched bureaucracy, of course, is happy to step in and provide standardized guidelines, prepackaged units, and "seven steps to effective teaching."

6. Behavioral, not structural, change is what is needed.

Americans seem inclined to believe that if an organization isn't functioning well, the problem can be solved by rearranging the structure of the organization. People are moved around, lines of authority are changed, a new organizational chart is proudly released. Perhaps the organization is even renamed. With these changes made, everyone settles down again—into routines just like the old ones. Employees can get cynical after enduring several such cycles of so-called change.

Seldom, in fact, is adequate attention given to institutionalizing the new *behaviors* which employees would have to use—consistently and permanently—if the desired organizational changes are to work. People are simply expected to fit into the newly reorganized structure and carry on as best they can. Or, in cases when some retraining is provided, it is short and superficial ("Attend this workshop on managing cooperative learning—"), and little or no follow-up coaching, to help "fix" the new behaviors, is given.

We believe we know that, for an educational innovation such as global education to truly become a permanent and living part of a classroom teacher's repertoire, significant attention must be given to *changing certain aspects of that teacher's existing behavior.* For example, teachers who are most comfortable using a frontal, direct teaching mode will find that global education actually works best if some alternative grouping strategies are occasionally used. The teacher then faces a dilemma: shall I try some new approaches, even though I'm not really comfortable with them; or shall I just forget about the new program and keep on doing things the way I've always done them? As was mentioned in chapter 8, one of the most important roles of the on-site change consultant (interventionist) is that of the *supportive coach.* This role involves sensing when and just how to push for behavioral change, and how best to support a teacher's efforts to try something new.

7. The principal's ability to provide real leadership is critical to the long-term success of a new program or change effort.

The key role of the principal in setting the tone for the school and in facilitating or retarding change has been well documented in the literature. In the study reported in this book, three critical elements of principal behavior seemed most important to the success of teachers' efforts to infuse global perspectives into their teaching. The first of these, goal focus, is an area for further exploration which will be discussed later in this chapter. The second was mastery *and utilization of* leadership skills.

We define leadership skills as those behaviors oriented toward change which have as their purpose the development of the school site as a healthy organism, characterized by high teacher morale and productivity and a cooperative, collegial adult work environment. In recent years there has been much talk among school administrators of providing "instructional leadership" and "vision." *Talking* about these, however, does not mean they then exist where they did not exist before. The reality of daily life for school site administrators, in fact, makes it unlikely that leadership behaviors will replace the more comfortable and familiar role of administrator-manager. Like teachers, principals daily must juggle dozens of competing demands. The superordinate system and the institutional structure of American education require that principals act as administrators, as guardians of the status quo. People expect it. And as a rule, the rewards tend to go to those who are good managers first and foremost. Finally, programs designed to train school site administrators emphasize management skills. Units on budgeting, scheduling, and school law are common in administrative credential programs, and even in many so-called leadership programs, while genuine leadership skills such as process facilitation, shared goal-setting, decision-making, problem-solving, and open communication are much less often taught.

The third crucial element of principal behavior which proved important to this project was *observable support for the new program.* For example, the schools which made the most real progress in introducing global perspectives tended to be those in which the principal *went through all or most of the staff development experiences* right along with his or her teaching staff. Such participation, when everyone knew the principal must have had dozens of other things to do, sent a clear message: "This project is important for our school."

These, then, are some of the things we believe we know about schools and about the change process. Such knowledge is grounded in the literature on educational change, on prior work done by the authors on this topic, and on what we have learned from the totality of our past and present professional experience. This study, in particular, with its in-depth exploration of the internal dynamics of the eleven project schools as they worked to adopt an innovation, reconfirmed the basic reliability of these seven general propositions.

We turn now to a number of propositions about which we feel much less certain but which we find extremely intriguing. Hypotheses, not proofs, properly emerge from descriptive research studies such as this one, and the next set of findings are offered in hypothetical terms, for possible further investigation by others.

What We Hypothesize: Recommendations for Further Exploration

1. People develop dynamic new meanings as they engage in activity. In turn, new meanings lead to higher levels of understanding and action. If this is true, it is probably unnecessary to spend much time and energy trying to define key concepts prior to beginning an innovative project. It would be better to become immediately involved in activity, and spend time along the way reflecting upon the emergent meanings.

In the CHI project, school people did not spend time at the beginning in defining global education. Rather, they engaged themselves in trying out lessons they thought might be "global." Through activity, those who participated moved from awareness of global education to more in-depth understanding of it to more comprehensive action on behalf of global concepts (Shiman and Conrad, 1977). This was evidenced in the increasingly sophisticated definitions of global education people in the schools gave as time passed and in the increasing sophistication of actual classroom and school-wide projects. As was stated in chapter 4, this paradigm seemed to closely parallel the learning curve model that Havelock (1971) developed regarding the adoption of educational innovations.

Many researchers have taken the position that definitions should precede action. Duggan and Thorpe (1986), for example, contend that definitions of global education are crucial to its integration into the K–12 curriculum and Fullan (1982) states that they determine purpose, content, and decisions made by policymakers. He further suggests that studies of educational change, in general, have shown that both advocates and recipients of any innovation must have a shared understanding of that innovation.

The fact is that most global education projects pay early attention to getting (or giving) a common definition of global education. Unfortunately, once this is done, few people seem to spend time in reflecting upon how activity alters meaning and how this altered meaning ultimately affects the movement from awareness to understanding to meaningful action in the school setting. What this leads to, we believe, is both a static definition and a corresponding set of static activities.

This may seem to some an argument over which comes first, the chicken or the egg: activity or definition. It is not. In fact, the tendency in schooling toward the use of static, linear change models may be the main reason that so many well-intentioned innovations never quite succeed. What is being proposed here is that people at a school identify a general area for improvement—global education—they immediately engage in action of some kind—classroom units, schoolwide international celebrations—and during this activity and immediately following it, they spend time individually and collectively reflecting upon what happened and what it meant for students, community, school, and themselves. From there, they plan new activity. It is this *moving back and forth between action and reflection* which is critical; which is so often neglected; which can lead to new meanings and deeper understandings; and which, finally, may result in significant school improvement. It is an idea which certainly should be tested further when people attempt to answer the question "What does it take to bring a global perspective to the curriculum of a school?"

2.   The success of the current restructuring movement, school-based decision-making, and school innovations such as global education will depend in large measure on the ethos of the local school district. Currently, the *interchangeable-parts* nature of districts, in reference to standardization of what is allowed to happen at local schools, is so strong that real innovation is not possible.

Currently there is a good deal of rhetoric about restructuring. There is discussion of school-based decision-making, empowerment, community involvement, and the like. However, there is almost no discussion of altering the behaviors of those who occupy positions of authority in superordinate systems: states, counties, districts. Underneath all of the rhetoric is the real message: "We (administrators, politcians) will allow you to be involved in some aspects of decision-making. However, we still hold all the power, the money, means of external evaluation, the reward systems. If you do not measure up to our expectations, we will take away your opportunity to be involved." The *system* must be maintained pretty much as it is, with its interchangeable parts. This is malefic generosity (Benham, 1978) and it is destructive of spirit and progress because it is not honest.

Unfortunately, the ethos which we have created in our school districts, borrowed from the theories of scientific management in business and industry and applied with a vengeance, really does mitigate against school improvement. Until this ethos itself is changed, efforts at restructuring will probably have as little impact as the other educational reforms of the 1980s and that is very little, indeed. Further, and as was suggested at the beginning of this book, global education probably has a better chance of being implemented if the school is viewed as the critical unit of change.

Seven specific components of *district ethos* emerged in this study. It is hypothesized that these components are what should be focused upon in restructuring efforts. They are:

I. *The management style of the superintendent.* Superintendents are expected to be in charge, to be autocratic. Until those expectations are replaced by ones which call for him or her to be democratic, to respond appropriately to situations, and to focus upon leadership acts rather than administrative ones, no real restructuring will take place.

II. *The practice of standardizing across schools* (e.g., moving principals around, judging achievement on the basis of district and/or state norms, aligning curricula). Since so many people (curriculum workers, textbook publishers, state and district consultants, central office administrators) have a vested interest in *causing things* to be standardized, this will be a difficult tendency to overcome.

III. *The directing orientation of school districts.* The development of a *service* instead of a *directing* orientation will be equally difficult because of the vested interests of those who have become used to directing (or thinking that they do). Teachers in the network schools had a very hard time believing that CHI personnel were in their schools to serve them. They just hadn't been used to such behavior. Restructuring will require such a service orientation from all of those in the superordinate system. Further, it will require that district personnel search for ways to help to link schools to knowledge they need and want rather than deciding for them what knowledge is good and who has that knowledge.

IV. *Communication in most school districts flows downward rather than both ways.* Until such a time as there is adequate communication and a multiple directionality to it, restructuring will not be successful.

V. *How a district is perceived as treating its workers is also important to the success of any restructuring effort.* This is not as simple a matter as it might seem. Certainly, being fair and trustworthy are critical. However, at a much more complex level our cultural view of the purposes of organizations is involved. Currently, schools are seen as units responsible for outputs, usually achievement. Thus, workers are dealt with so that output is maximized. If this means laying them off, reassigning them, whatever, it is justifiable. Perhaps such an attitude cannot change until we reconsider the very purpose of an organization such as a school. How, for example, would schools be different if we believed that their purpose was to create good work for people, including teachers and students, instead of merely increasing output?

VI. *The most commonly discussed component of restructuring is decision-making.* There is much said about decentralizing it. Decision-making about what and decentralizing to whom are not quite clear, however, and they need to be. Other issues need to be made clear, also. What if decision-making about an issue is delegated to the school level, but district administrators don't like the decisions being made? The rules need far sharper refinement.

VII. *The role of the principal as the leader in her or his school needs to be expanded and supported if restructuring is to work.* Further, principals probably are going to have to undergo retraining because, to date, success has been defined by administrative behavior and not by leadership. In the CHI study it was found that principals who had focused goal styles, who concentrated on the accomplishment of a few well-articulated goals, were seen by teachers as true leaders. Those principals who had a diffuse goal style (picked up on every new thing which came along) or a coping goal style (seemed only able to respond to demands placed upon him or her) were not seen as providing leadership. This typology of goal styles is offered as a hypothesis in need of further exploration.

3.   The current *accountability* movement has made it popular to blame teachers for the lack of success of innovative ideas. Somehow, teachers are labeled as "resistant" to ideas for change which are imposed from outside the school. As a result of CHI work with teachers in global education, it is hypothesized that the readiness of individual faculty members to participate in new activity (global education) can be predicted based upon a set of identifiable factors which relate to the meanings which they give to that activity rather than some generalized resistance factor. There are so many demands upon teacher time in today's schools that they have learned to engage in adaptive behaviors of many kinds. It is hypothesized that such adaptive behaviors, seen as defense mechanisms, have a direct relationship to the overall morale and resilience levels of the individual school.

It seems unfair to label teachers as "resistant" because they question or do not approve a given innovation. In the CHI project, it was quite clear that people responded on the basis of the meaning the concept had for them. Those faculty members most willing to engage with global education were ones who were open to the ideas of the movement right from the start. Many already perceived themselves as globalizing before CHI arrived. Another significant group engaged with the project because it was a new idea and they either saw it as having potential to change current practice or they simply were attracted to new ideas. A third group, substantial in size, readily participated because they were interested in doing something about the school's need to develop better cross-cultural understanding among the growing ethnic diversity of the student population. Interestingly, some people never did see the connection between global and multicultural education. Such a connection did not fit with their meanings of the two concepts.

There were teachers who waited some time before they joined the project. They were not sure at first what they were supposed to do and they wanted to see what it "looked like" in the classrooms of their colleagues. A number of these folks stated that they had seen too many other new programs come along and then quietly die out. Unfortunately, too many of our new ideas are not well thought out or lack classroom specificity. *Waiting to see* is not resistance, nor should it be labeled as such. Another group of people felt that global education was something for the social studies curriculum. They had to be shown that *all* subjects can be infused with a global perspective.

The largest group of teachers which was not immediately attracted to the project was made up of people who simply did not feel they had the time that it would take. Innovations such as global education *do* take time. It requires the learning of new content—global issues and systems; and it means adding new strategies to the teaching repertoire—cooperative learning, critical thinking.

There were a few faculty members in network schools who were concerned that global education was seen as somehow being un-American or as a form of secular humanism. Some of these people had seen attacks by right-wing extremists upon schools in the past and were understandably cautious.

The point is, it is inappropriate to label people as resistant to change simply because they question global education (or any other innovation). People often have legitimate concerns about new programs as they search for the meanings which are attached to them. It is incumbent upon leadership and so-called change agents to attempt to assist people to find those meanings which are appropriate both to the innovation and the individual.

Closely related to the idea of resistance to change is that of adaptive behavior, or building defense mechanisms, to fend off a consistent barrage of perceived demands which press on teachers from every direction. In the CHI project, six kinds of defense mechanisms were observed. They ranged from *burnout* to *selective participation*. *Burnout* is not really a defense mechanism. Rather it is a consequence of not having made use of other "buffer behaviors." *Refusal* is a fairly strong defense mechanism. Teachers simply say, "No, not one more thing. We won't do it." *Avoidance* was another behavior commonly observed. Here, teachers would not talk to CHI staff or, if they had to attend faculty meetings where global education was a topic, they simply did not become engaged. In this group, also, were a number of people who frequently told us of their intention to become involved, but who never did. *Withdrawal* was a necessary defensive move for some teachers. They got involved early in the project but, because of so many other demands, withdrew from it. There were not many teachers in this group and most of them continued to teach in a changed way. *Negotiation* was a healthy strategy utilized by some teachers. Sensing that the principal and/or district was supportive of global education, and knowing full well that they could not meet all demands placed upon them, they negotiated the loosening up of expectations in other areas. Finally, *selective participation* seemed to be the most functional of the defense mechanisms observed in this project. Teachers simply made realistic choices as to how to use their outside-the-classroom time.

Those who wish to involve teachers in new programs might be well advised to observe the defense mechanisms which are being used. There is no doubt that there are too many demands upon the time of teachers. It is hypothesized here that negotiation, selective participation, and even withdrawal are fairly healthy behaviors suggesting that there is not yet overload. However, evidence of avoidance, refusal, and burnout probably means that the system is in trouble. In any case, expectations of teacher participation should be accompanied by the provision of adequate time.

Finally, it is also hypothesized that *the defense mechanisms used by a critical mass of teachers at any given school has a direct relationship to the overall morale and resilience levels of that school.* Such mechanisms are a direct measure of the climate, or unique personality, of the school.

4.   We learned that a number of developments can be potentially

problematic to the success of an innovative project. Each of these needs to be studied further in order to be better understood:

I. *The culture of the school can defeat efforts to introduce a change.* The culture of the individual school is a complex concept which has engaged education researchers and theorists for many years and is still not fully understood. It comprises an interactive mix of school history and traditions, the characteristics of the community served by the school, the nature of the student body, and the dynamics of adult relationships within the school, including both those between teachers and the administration and those among teachers. Teacher morale is a major component of the school culture, we believe; and morale is directly affected by the press of competing demands (and, as mentioned above, the defense mechanisms used to cope with these), the nature of leadership provided by administrators, and the extent to which the staff feels capable of solving school problems.

    External change agents charged with the responsibility of helping a school to implement a new program need to pay particular attention to the school culture, or climate, early on in the project, and be on the lookout for a combination of characteristics which could be fatal to the effort. These might include: harrassed faculty who feel they cannot manage to take on one more thing, lukewarm support by the principal, seriously dysfunctional rifts within the faculty or between departments, and substantial community opposition to the new program.

II. *The project will never become an all-school effort if, in its early stages, it is "taken on" by a small subgroup of faculty.* Change facilitators find it tempting to work with those teachers who respond positively to the new idea or process, and may unintentionally help to create a situation in which other teachers feel either left out, if they are interested in the project, or justified in not participating: "Oh, that's just for the core team—the task group—the social studies department (or whichever group is viewed as having ownership)."

More work needs to be done to understand the dynamics of dissemination of a new program among a faculty composed of people who are differentially attracted to it in the first place, and for each one of whom it may have a different meaning. Strategies designed to involve whole faculties right from the beginning (instead of a slow winning over that begins with early adopters and spreads out to include those who held back at first) need to be tried and evaluated. It may be that gaining at least a "Let's give it a try" commitment from an entire faculty, and then deliberately building on that through the use of inclusive implementation activities, would yield greater success in the final analysis.

A related problem is that which can occur if the project, in its early stages, fails to attract the participation of the informal opinion leaders on the faculty and instead attracts the weaker or for other reasons less respected teachers. Part of every school's culture is its status hierarchy, whether we like it or not; and some teachers are more powerful and influential with their peers than others. The challenge for the external consultant is to *quickly* identify the formal and informal leaders on the faculty, and gain their support. A proposition in need of further study is that *once some key opinion-leaders are seen as involved, the involvement of more marginal or nonmainstream teachers will not hurt the project; but if the faculty leaders hold back while the nonmainstream adopters jump right in and take ownership, the project will not succeed.*

III. *Motivation and commitment are difficult for teachers to maintain when confronted with the daily realities of schoolkeeping.* One of the patterns noted time and again by CHI staff in the project schools involved frequent statements of interest and support by some teachers—and then a nearly total lack of follow-through. For some time, staff members experienced a feeling of being let down by these teachers, because hours of work spent in putting together packets of resource materials specially tailored to the teachers' stated interests seemed to have been wasted.

Before long, however, hypotheses about this phenomenon began to emerge in the weekly staff meetings, and subsequent theoretical sampling—formal and informal conversations with teachers, as described in chapter 2—yielded two possible explanations. First, we realized that despite verbal expressions of interest, some of these teachers simply were not yet personally ready to become involved with the project. (Timing, intersecting trajectories, and the fitting together of personal biographies were discussed fully in chapter 8.) Second, we began to more completely appreciate the impact on teachers of the steady, inescapable barrage of *competing demands* which they feel on a daily basis. This topic was explored in chapter 5, but it is complex and could lead other researchers in many interesting directions. Some questions which have occurred to us include, for example: "Are competing demands the institution's (or the society's) way of immobilizing teachers so that change will *not* occur and the status quo will be preserved?" "Why do some teachers juggle competing demands and all their other responsibilities more successfully than others?" "Does the principal who deliberately serves as a buffer for his or her staff maximize the chances that constructive change *will* occur?"

IV. *Some teachers need more structure than others, and will not respond to a project which is, in their view, too open-ended or nondirective.* The CHI philosophy was deliberately nondirective, and on the whole this seemed to make the project attractive to a great majority of the teachers who felt pleased that, for once, they were not being told what to do. There were a few, however, who held back from participation because they were uncomfortable with this degree of open-endedness.

While this was not a *major* problem, if the goal is to diffuse an innovation throughout an entire school, such a situation will hinder progress toward the goal. Each teacher must be approached and worked with during his or her moments of maximum receptivity (as discussed in chapter 8) and also in ways that are keyed to his or her personal style. The CHI staff came to feel, by the end of year 4, that perhaps some time should have been given to providing prepackaged "starter" units for teachers who didn't feel able to do their own curriculum development projects. This is a strategy which might be tested by others who are trying to diffuse a new program throughout a school—or a district. CHI's decision to focus on supporting teachers in projects which they themselves selected was the right one in this case, given the project's limited resources and nondirective philosophy.

V. *Personnel turnover is an ongoing challenge for change facilitators.* Processes by which existing staff will voluntarily initiate newcomers—long after the project is officially over—must be found. This is the only way to ensure that the change will be permanent and self-renewing. In this particular project, while teacher turnover was not dramatic, administrator turnover was. Principals were changed at six of the eleven project schools during the four years of the project, and an acting principal was in place at another for part of the time. CHI staff members met with each new principal almost as soon as he or she arrived, to explain the history and philosophy of the global education efforts at that school and to gain his or her support. Sometimes teachers were enlisted to help describe the kinds of things that were happening in global education at the school. This usually made the presentation more powerful, convincing the principal at an early stage that the teachers in his or her new school were behind the global perspectives effort there.

Toward the end of the project, a five-minute videotape was produced which explained the project and emphasized the importance of helping young people to develop an understanding of their world. Each school was given a copy of the video to use in introducing new teachers and administrators to global education. Such a product would have been helpful right from the beginning, but technical difficulties prevented its being developed then. Other innovative projects might try starting out with an audiovisual tool to use as part of the very first introduction of the project to teachers, and then to use in initiating newcomers to the project as time goes on.

Other ways of passing on the knowledge and the commitment and interest felt by teachers in the early years must be found as well, because otherwise the change will weaken bit by bit as teachers who were involved in it leave and others, who know little or nothing about it, take their place. This is an old story insofar as educational change or school improvement efforts are concerned. It explains why on any day, in any part of the country, one can walk into a school which used to house a model program—ten years ago—and find not a trace of that model program left in place. This is perhaps the single most critical problem of educational change, for unless and until it is solved schools will always regress toward the deep structure as the initial energy of the project is diluted by staff turnover.

VI. *More work needs to be done on the role of timing* in the success of an intervention, particularly on the impact of the natural cycle of the school year and on the larger cycles of rising and falling interest which can be charted over the course of several years. A good deal is known about how to recognize and work with *individuals* who are at different stages of adapting to a change (chapter 8), but better ways of identifying the best moments to make progress with *groups*, and to keep their interest and participation levels high, need to be developed. It seems that teachers are more receptive to new ideas or processes, and more likely to get involved with them, at certain times of the school year than at others. How can people who are responsible for implementation of an innovative project both capitalize on these times and, more importantly, find ways to sustain teacher interest through the more difficult times of year—the "winter slump," for example?

The CHI staff observed cycles of participation which rose and fell—and rose again, if the right incentives were in place—over longer periods of time, also. Change facilitators need to be aware of the "year three crisis" phenomenon, for example, and be ready with strategies for helping a new program to survive this difficult stage. There is a real need for research that will help practitioners to understand the role of timing and pacing in the life of a school, and the ways in which these can be utilized in support of change efforts.

VII. *Teachers do not respond to external change facilitators whom they perceive as lacking credibility.* CHI staff members had all been classroom teachers at some time in their lives, but discovered that this alone was not enough for them to be accepted by the teachers in the project schools. Without making a big deal about it, they had to slowly and quietly earn the respect and trust of the teachers. Above all, the teachers needed to feel that the CHI field consultants *truly understood* what they had to contend with on a daily basis. Some personal qualities and skills seemed better suited to achieving this than others, and our findings in this area were presented in chapter 8. More work could be done, however, to identify ways of matching the purposes and philosophy of an innovative program with the skills and characteristics of intervention staff. Especially for projects of relatively short duration—three to five years, say—it is important to have the right kinds of staff people in place from day one, insofar as this is possible.

5. In the CHI project, no particular intervention strategies seemed to do be better than others in terms of reaching the goal of globalizing the curriculum. It is hypothesized that the kinds of strategies one should use to reach such a goal is best determined by the kinds of meanings people are deriving from activity. Activity and the development of meaning are interactive.

At the beginning of the network project, most people were becoming aware of what global education was and what it might mean for them. At this point, awareness workshops, materials delivered to the school by CHI staff members, a newsletter with information about what others thought about global education and/or were doing about it were the kinds of things which seemed to appeal to the majority of teachers. On the other hand, a few people who were already knowledgeable and doing things in their classes needed help in finding specific materials or in shaping teaching and learning opportunities.

By working from a base of teacher interest and understanding, the project got maximum participation without requiring it. For example, early on, cross-cultural awareness was, by far, the most popular topic and network-wide and school site workshops were arranged in line with this interest. As more teachers gained some personal understanding of what global education was and what it might mean for them, various kinds of school- and classroom-centered programs were encouraged and/or emerged. As was indicated in chapter 4, four types of programs were developed in the schools. The first of these, infusion programs, were those in which teachers found ways to add a global perspective to what they were already doing. The facilitation of sharing of ideas about how to do this and assisting with the identification of materials of instruction which would assist them were the main tasks of CHI personnel.

The second kind of program included such things as international festivals, units on conflict resolution, the Walk in the Real World field trip to inner city Los Angeles by a middle school group, and the survey and report of racial attitudes at a high school. The point was that these were ideas that were outside of the regular curriculum, but which developed because teachers saw a need for them and understood their value. Again, the role of CHI staff was to facilitate the sharing of ideas and assist with the identification of appropriate instructional materials.

There were special programs initiated by CHI and this represented a third type of intervention strategy. Some of the projects, described in depth in chapters 1 and 4, were (1) "Orange County in the World" in which interested teachers planned and carried out classroom studies of various kinds of international connections which existed in the area, (2) telecommunications linkages between network schools and schools in other parts of the world, and (3) an international sports day for seventh grade students who played various games from around the world. Perhaps the most effective special program was that of small grants. Teachers designed their own classroom study proposals and submitted them for funding. A panel of teacher peers judged the proposals. Every school was touched by this program and in many cases two or more teachers submitted cooperative proposals.

Alternative programs were things such as Model United Nations, International Baccalaureate, and GEMNET telecommunications programs which stood on their own but which were related to the CHI global education project. In the case of such programs, CHI staff assisted with such things as connecting teachers to materials when asked. No attempt was made, however, to integrate or take over such efforts.

The CHI staff met very frequently (more or less weekly) to discuss the interaction of activity and meaning. Strategies and events were planned, carried out, and evaluated on the basis of these interactions. This is quite different than most so-called innovative programs of the 1980s, which tended to be much more linear in nature. That is, objectives and definitions are set forth initially, activity is related to these objectives and definitions, and evaluation is in terms of their attainment. Once objectives and definitions are "revealed," the concern for meaning is abandoned because it is assumed that it is clear. This linear way of thinking about educational change may be the main reason that so many basically good ideas never really get implemented in our schools and why so many seemingly sound innovations founder as they are tried. Those interested in globalizing the curriculum of schools might better look to more reflective strategies.

6.   Very little has been done to document, in any systematic way, what schools and the teachers in them go through when they decide to globalize the curriculum. There is a need to amass a significant amount of descriptive data about practice and then begin to examine these data for patterns, relationships, and exceptions. Through such a reflective research process, we will gain a better understanding of the complex phenomenon of schooling as well as those processes necessary for its improvement. More specifically, we will be able to generate hypotheses that create a grounded agenda for further study and action.

In chapter 2, an attempt was made to categorize the kinds of research efforts which have thus far been attempted vis-à-vis global education. Developmental studies, those which have to do with when and how children and youth are able to conceptualize attachments to entities beyond their own experience, constitute the strongest body of work so far. Some work has been done to evaluate the effectiveness of curriculum materials, but to date these studies have not been extremely strong and more could be done in this area. The need to promote "action research" projects involving teachers as primary investigators or as co-investigators with global educators from external agencies was called for and it was noted that little of this kind of research is currently being carried out.

The fourth kind of research which was called for in chapter 2 is research on the process of change, particularly as it relates to global education. It was pointed out that in any project there will be a history: participants will have stories to tell of what worked and what didn't. Unfortunately, those data are almost never captured. It is our position here that they should be and that they constitute a rich and deep description of what it is really like as people work to improve schooling, be that improvement the implementation of a global perspective or something else.

The amassing of descriptive data requires that the researcher spend a good deal of time in the school(s) observing and asking questions. It also requires that he or she share perceptions with the people at the site. Communication about things and events flows both ways: "This is how I see it; how do *you* see it? The choice of a qualitative methodology does not imply a general rejection of positivist experimental approaches. The point is, however, that before we experiment, we must know what the most significant questions are. An in-depth discussion of this qualitative paradigm of *research as reflection on practice* can be found in chapter 2.

Conclusion

The growing interdependence of the world is a fact. Our children and youth need to be prepared to live in such a world. Global education, which causes them to better understand the systems of the world and teaches them to see the perspectives of others, is a necessity. However, it is not clear how the curriculum of the school can be globalized while, at the same time, it must continue to do all of the other things which have come to be expected of it.

This book describes a four-year study of efforts to do just that: bring a global perspective to the curriculum of eleven schools in southern California. A nondirective strategy of support and encouragement was consciously chosen. What happened in the process was carefully documented. Much of what was learned was not generalizable, but has been reported in the form of hypotheses with the hope that others will test these ideas in other settings. In concluding our report, we are left with a handful of final, overarching thoughts which we hope will stimulate significant dialogue between educators and lay people concerned about the role of public schooling in a democratic and increasingly global society. These are:

1. Global education is an important social movement. The curriculum of every school should include global perspectives.

2. Schooling is a complex social system. The school site has got to become the focus for improvement and other levels of the system must play supportive and not directing roles. Trust, respect, open communication, the seeking of knowledge, and other professional behaviors must replace political notions of power, authority, and accountability.

3. We need to adopt more reflective modes of behavior in our institutions, including our schools. To date, our pragmatic spirit has caused us to focus almost solely upon "getting the job done." Now, in a more interdependent time, one with limited resources, we must be much more reflective about what we do. We need to develop forums for researchers, practitioners, and informed lay people to come together locally, regionally, nationally and internationally to reflect upon what it is we do in our schools and to consider how they might be improved. It is to such reflection that this book is dedicated.

References

Benham, B., "None So Holy as the Recently Converted: Malefic Generosity and Multicultural Education," *Educational Studies* (Summer 1978).

Duggan, S. J., and S. Thorpe, "Obstacles to Global Education," paper presented at AERA, April 1986.

Fullan, M., *The Meaning of Educational Change* (New York: Teachers College Press, 1982).

Havelock, R. G., *Planning for Innovation through Dissemination and Utilization of Knowledge* (Ann Arbor: Institute for Social Research, University of Michigan, 1971).

Sarason, S., *The Culture of the School and the Problem of Change* (Boston: Allyn & Bacon, 1982).

Shiman, D., and D. Conrad, "Awareness, Understanding, and Action: A Global Conscience in the Classroom," *The New Era* 58 (6) (December 1977).

Sizer, T., *Horace's Compromise* (Boston: Houghton Mifflin, 1984).

Tye, B., *Multiple Realities: A Study of 13 American High Schools* (Lanham, Md.: University Press of America, 1985).

APPENDIX A: END-OF-STUDY TEACHER SURVEY

Name of School _____

1. How much were you involved with CHI global education activities during the past four years? (check one)

   _____ I was never involved

   _____ I was involved once or twice

   _____ I was involved a few times

   _____ I was involved quite a bit

   _____ I was very active

2. If you were involved at all with CHI global education activities during the past four years, please give the reason(s) for that involvement by *rank ordering all of the following responses.* 1 = the most important reason for becoming involved, 2 = the second most important reason, etc. If you were never involved, go on to the next question.

   _____ I felt that I was part of an important educational movement

   _____ I saw it as a professional opportunity (e.g., the chance to learn and do something new)

   _____ I wanted to meet and share with other teachers

   _____ I sought validation or recognition of work in which I was already involved

   _____ I received monetary assistance to carry out educational projects other (explain):

3. Please check those items below which *get in the way* of your being involved with the CHI global education project

   _____ lack of time

   _____ lack of money

253

_____ CAP/CTBS testing

_____ large classes

_____ don't believe in global education

_____ don't understand global education

_____ lack of instructional materials

_____ lack of principal support

_____ lack of district support

_____ other (please list)

4. Please complete the following sentences by checking the appropriate response.

At this school, the number of...

	very large	large	about half	not very large	small	none
staff involved in global education is	—	—	—	—	—	—
staff opposed philosophically to global education is	—	—	—	—	—	—
staff who feel they are too busy with other things is	—	—	—	—	—	—

5. Please *rank order the four items* below which have the highest priority at this school.

_____ academic preparation (basics)

_____ anti-gang projects

_____ developing a global perspective

_____ developing a positive self-concept; self-esteem

_____ drug education

_____ good citizenship

_____ physical development

_____ sex education

_____ vocational preparation

_____ (other): _____

6. Please indicate to what extent you agree or disagree with each of the following statements about yourself or your school.

strongly agree — moderately agree — mildly agree — mildly disagree — moderately disagree — strongly disagree — I don't know

a. It is clear to me what global education is

b. I am more aware of global issues today than I was four years ago

c. If I am more aware of global issues, it is due, at least in part, to CHI's presence

d. Global education is important and all students should be exposed to it

IN THIS SCHOOL...

e. I usually look forward to each working day

f. The district is supportive of global education

g. Parents are supportive of global education

h. The Board of Education is supportive of global education

i. I do not feel free to experiment with my curriculum because of CAP/CTBS testing

j. Most people find their job rewarding in other than monetary ways

k. Information is shared between teachers from different departments, teams, or grade levels

l. Goals and priorities are clear

m. Administrator(s) and teachers collaborate in making the school run effectively *strongly agree* *moderately agree* *mildly agree* *mildly disagree* *moderately disagree* *strongly disagree* *I don't know*

n. Staff members are flexible; they can reconsider their positions on issues and are willing to change their minds ___ ___ ___ ___ ___ ___ ___

o. The staff is continually evaluating its programs and activities and attempting to change them for the better ___ ___ ___ ___ ___ ___ ___

p. Staff members are proud to be working here ___ ___ ___ ___ ___ ___ ___

7. Please indicate the effect you believe the following State mandates have on *your teaching*

very helpful *somewhat helpful* *neutral* *somewhat detrimental* *very detrimental* *I don't know*

Model Curriculum Standards ___ ___ ___ ___ ___ ___

State Curriculum Frameworks ___ ___ ___ ___ ___ ___

CAP/CTBS Testing ___ ___ ___ ___ ___ ___

8. Please indicate the effect you believe the following State mandates have on *global education at your school*

very helpful *somewhat helpful* *neutral* *somewhat detrimental* *very detrimental* *I don't know*

Model Curriculum Standards ___ ___ ___ ___ ___ ___

State Curriculum Frameworks ___ ___ ___ ___ ___ ___

CAP/CTBS Testing ___ ___ ___ ___ ___ ___

9. Please rate the following CHI activities.
   If you are not familiar with one, mark
   "I don't know."

   Rating scale: outstanding, very good, O.K., not very good, poor, I don't know

   Computer Hook-up with
   International School   ___ ___ ___ ___ ___ ___

   International Sports Day
   (Jr. Highs Only)   ___ ___ ___ ___ ___ ___

   Library Materials and Handouts ___ ___ ___ ___ ___ ___

   Mini-grants   ___ ___ ___ ___ ___ ___

   Newsletters   ___ ___ ___ ___ ___ ___

   Presentations at this school ___ ___ ___ ___ ___ ___

   Theme workshops   ___ ___ ___ ___ ___ ___

   Your Community and the
   world Project   ___ ___ ___ ___ ___ ___

10. Please check the appropriate response
    to each of the following statements.

    Involvement with CHI has affected:

    Rating scale: a lot for the better, somewhat for the better, somewhat fir the worse, a lot for the worse, not at all

    my teaching   ___ ___ ___ ___ ___

    my curriculum   ___ ___ ___ ___ ___

    my long term teaching goals ___ ___ ___ ___ ___

    my personal understanding of
    global issues   ___ ___ ___ ___ ___

    my personal awareness of global events ___ ___ ___ ___ ___

    the kinds of activities in which I
    participate outside of school ___ ___ ___ ___ ___

    the way the other teachers teach
    at this school   ___ ___ ___ ___ ___

    the way the other teachers teach
    at this school   ___ ___ ___ ___ ___

    the curriculum of the school ___ ___ ___ ___ ___

    students' understanding of global issues ___ ___ ___ ___ ___

    student attitudes towards others ___ ___ ___ ___ ___

    my relationships with my colleagues
    here at the school   ___ ___ ___ ___ ___

11. Please respond to *one* of the following statements about your personal plans vis-a-vis global education.

a. I started to introduce global lessons into my teaching

_____ In 1985–86

_____ In 1986–87

_____ In 1988–89

_____ I have always tried to include global awareness in my teaching

OR

b. I haven't yet started to introduce global lessons in my classes

_____ and I don't really plan to do so.

_____ but I have plans to do so before the end of this year.

_____ but I plan to do so in the future.

12. Please check the *one* statement below which most accurately describes your principals' level of support of the CHI program. (Note: the "second principal" column applies only if there has been a change of principal at your school since 1985.)

	first or only principal	second principal
actively supportive/participates		
Verbally supportive		
Willing to let us be involved, but unwilling to get involved himself/herself		
Lip service only —not really supportive		
Opposes global education		

13. Please respond to the personal questions below. Please remember that all of your responses are anonymous. These are important data for our study.

a. (Secondary) The major subject I teach is _____

OR

(Elementary) The grade level I teach is _____

b. The number of years I have taught at this school is _____

c. Sex: Male ____ Female ____

d. I have served overseas in the Armed Forces: Yes ____ No ____

e. I have lived overseas (other than in the service): Yes ____ No____

f. I have travelled in the following areas (Please check):

____ Africa
____ Australia and/or New Zealand
____ Canada
____ Central America/S. America/
      Caribbean
____ Eastern Europe and/or USSR
____ Hawaii
____ India/Pakistan

____ Japan
____ Middle EastMexico
____ Korea/Phillipines
      and/or Taiwan
____ Peoples
      Republic of China
____ Southeast Asia
____ Western Europe

g. I began following world news when I was (choose one):

____ a Child
____ a teenager
____ in college

____ a working adult
____ I dont' follow it

h. My parents discussed current events with me
   when I was growing up: Yes____ No____

14.   What does the term "global education" mean to you?

15.   What could CHI have done to have *more* of an impact at this
school?

APPENDIX B:
STRUCTURED END-OF-STUDY INTERVIEW AGENDA

Name _____

School _____

Subject _____

Date _____

INTERVIEW QUESTIONS

Introduction:

Thank you for giving us some of your valuable time to help us better understand our work with global education at this school. Please answer the questions I ask you as openly as you can. It does not matter whether you have been involved with CHI activities or not. Your perceptions are important. Please be assured that your responses will be kept confidential. We hope to present an aggregate report to you after the data are compiled.

1.   When did you first hear about CHI?

2.   What was your initial reaction to CHI?

3.   How do you feel about CHI now?

4. Have you been involved in any CHI activities? If yes, answer the following. If not, go to the next question:

Yes____ No____

   a. Why did you decide to get involved? Who or what influenced you? When did this occur?

   b. Did the extent of your involvement change over time? If so, how? For what reasons?

   c. Were there any satisfactions that you didn't expect when you first began?

OR

   a. Why did you decide not to get involved with CHI?

5. Have others encouraged you to become involved with CHI?

Yes _____ No _____

If yes, who? _____

In what ways?

6. Has anyone discouraged you from participating in CHI activities?

Yes _____ No _____

If yes, who? _____

In what ways?

7. What characteristics do you believe distinguish those teachers who have been involved with CHI?

8. Is global education at all a political issue at this school?

Yes _____ No _____

9. Are there teachers who are actually opposed to global education? What do you feel are their reasons?

10. How do you believe it was decided that this school should become involved with CHI?

11. Please describe how global education spread at this school.

12. If there was a turnover of principals during the time CHI has been involved here, do you think that turnover had an effect on CHI efforts at the school? In what way(s)?

13. What role has your present principal played in involving teachers with CHI activities? Your former principal (if appropriate)?

14. What role has your district played in supporting or involving teachers in CHI activities?

15. What goals are high on your present principal's agenda? Your former principal's agenda (if appropriate)?

16. Were you involved in any global activities *outside of school* before CHI came to your school? If so, which ones?

17. Has there been any change in your participation in outside global activities since CHI has been at your school? If so, please explain. Did CHI influence that change in any way?

18. What do you believe it would take to 1 the curriculum of this school?

19. Would it have made any difference if CHI had been more directive and structural in its approach?

APPENDIX C:
OBSERVATION SCHEDULE

Date_____ Teacher_____ School _____

Grade_____ Class/Subject _____ No. Students _____

Title/Theme of Lesson _____

- -

Classroom climate

    active learning/lecture/other
    student/student interaction
    student/teacher interaction

Pedagogy

    clear explanations, directions, objectives
    corrective feedback
    positive reinforcement
    variety of learning activities
    students actively involved

Materials

    check those used in *this* lesson:

_____ computer(s)	_____ workbook	_____ supplementary books
_____ music	_____ work sheet	_____ cultural artifacts
	_____ film strip or slides	_____ charts, graphs, tables
	_____ videotape	_____ guest speaker/performer

FOLLOW-UP INTERVIEW

Teacher   Date

What were your objectives for this lesson?

How well do you feel they were achieved?

What would you have changed today, if anything?

Where did you obtain the materials you used in today's lesson?

How often this year did you build global awareness into your lessons? (estimate)

Describe your students, please:

    Ability level(s):

    Global sophistication:

    Socioeconomic level(s):

    Attitudes towards other peoples:

    Changes this semester/this year:

Describe the formal training you have had in teaching global awareness (CHI or other):

Other comments/observations (use back side of this page if needed)

APPENDIX D: MINIGRANT APPLICATION

CENTER FOR HUMAN INTERDEPENDENCE
GLOBAL EDUCATION GRANTS

Application Form
1988-89

Up to 15 grants will be awarded to teachers in the ten Chi network schools. This year, mini-grants will be awarded primarily for the development of lessons, units, and/or teaching materials for classroom use. Proposals which involve collaboration between teachers in two or more subject areas will be given priority. *The major criterion, however, will be the degree to which the proposed project furthers the development of global awareness in teachers and/or students.* A panel of Network teachers and CHI staff members will screen the applications and winners will be announced by November 6, 1988 RETURN THIS COMPLETED APPLICATION FORM TO YOUR PRINCIPAL'S OFFICE BY OCTOBER 17 1988

Name(s) _____

School: _____ Amount Requested: _____

Purpose of Project:

Brief Description of Proposed Activity:

Expected Outcome (Product):

Expected Date of Completion: _____

INDEX

accountability, 11, 81, 113, 158, 239

Alger, Chadwick, 73, 83, 100, 106

Anderson, Lee F., xv-xxi, 28, 29, 52, 83

Argyris, Chris, 159, 161, 169, 190

Bales, R., 169, 190

Bass, Bernard and Stogdill, Robert, 158, 190

Benham, B. J., 32, 49, 79, 83, 237, 251

Bennett, M. J., 101, 106

Birmingham Middle School, 72, 96-97, 100-101

Blumer, Herbert, 27, 29, 35-36, 49, 85, 106

Boston, Jane, 131, 145, 155, 164, 176, 190

boundary maintenance, 122-123, 174, 183

Boyte, H. C., 67, 84

Buena Vista School, 65, 72, 96, 100, 170-176

Caldwell Elementary School, 72-74, 96, 145-150

Callahan, Raymond, 158, 190

Cannings, Terry, 148

Caporaso, J. A. and Mittelman, J. H., 63, 84

Carnegie Report on the Condition of Teaching 1990, 11, 29

Center for Human Interdependence: formation of, 14-17; goals of, 14; history of, 19-28; philosophy of, 17-18; staff of, 75; success of, 247-249

Center for Teaching International Relations (CTIR), 63

Central High School, 74, 97, 99, 101, 116

change: and bureaucratic structure, 162, 231-232; and deep structure of schooling, 8-9, 13, 131, 230-231

change process: assumptions about, 7-13; need to understand, 7, 13; never-ending, 227; research about, 33-34

change strategies: behavioral change needed, 233; different rates of adoption, 243; four basic types, 81-82; linear models may fail, 236

Clinton, Governor Bill, foreword, xi-xii

Columbus Intermediate School, 100, 150-154

competing demands: and principal goal focus, 167; and teachers' use of time, 215, 227; as a barrier to participation, 110-129; as an institution's way of resisting change, 128-129, 231; effect on principal behavior, 234; examples of, 112-113, 151; imposed by state, 113-115; imposed by school district, 115-122; labor disputes as, 152; personal choices and private lives, 123-125; principal expectations, 122; school projects and, 123; too little time, 110-113, 244

conflict resolution, 24

context: importance for change efforts, 210; pressure of, 213

controversy: contending world views model, 62–63; issue of balance, 64; teaching of, 61

Crandall, D., 216, 224

cross-cultural understanding: and interethnic tension, 24; connection to global education, 173; importance for teachers, 53–54, 101–102, 247

culture of a school. *See* school culture

culture studies: as a starting-place, 101–102

Cunningham, Greg, 63, 84

curriculum: balance, 64; expansion (history of), 1–3; increasing globalization of, 3, 6; infusion strategies, 14, 52, 59

data feedback, 38, 44, 75, 82, 196

data gathering: emerging themes, 45–46; process of, 41–45; verification of patterns, 44–45

deep structure of schooling: definition of, 8–9; 131, 230–231; relationship to change efforts, xvii, 8–9, 13, 52, 205–206; system overload and, 128–129

deprofessionalization of teachers, 78–79, 128–129, 232–233

district ethos: affected by economic conditions, 122; communication flow and, 119–120, 238; effect on principals, 169–170, 186–187, 189; 239; importance for success of restructuring, 236–239; locus of decision-making and, 121, 238–239; management style of superintendent and, 117–118, 237; service orientation of district and, 118–119, 238; standardized practices and, 118, 237; treatment of employees and, 120–121, 238

Doll, Ronald C., 216, 224

Duggan, S. J. and Thorpe, S., 86, 106, 235, 251

Eicholz, G. C., 81, 84, 105, 107

Eisner, Elliot, 132, 155, 203, 224

ESL project, 23, 74

external change agent: adaptive behavior needed by, 206–219; credibility of, 21, 247; delicate position of, 56; expectations of by teachers, 21–22, 214, 247; feelings of, 219–224; knowledge of how schools function, 202–203; necessary skills and abilities of, 201–205; personal qualities of, 199–201; roles and responsibilities of, 193–224; self-study by, 195–197; three major functions of, 193–196; value of, 12–13, 70; visible and available, 22, 216–219; work load of, 198–199

Fiedler, Fred, 160, 190

field notes: coding of, 42–44; emerging themes, 45–46; recording of, 27, 41–42; verification of patterns in, 44–45

findings: as emerging themes, 45–46; as recommendations for further exploration, 235–250

Fullan, Michael, 86, 107, 235–236, 251

Glaser, N. and Strauss, A., 27, 29, 40, 45, 49

global education: activities developed by teachers, 90–91, 96–101; as a social movement, xv–xix, 51–83, 251; charges of elitism, 60; definitions of, xvi–xvii, 6, 85–93, 235–236; funding for, 77; importance of, xi, 6, 53, 227; in Arkansas, xi; legitimization of, 7, 52, 67–70, 81; opposition to, 26, 63–67, 105, 229–230; rationale for, 52; research about, 31–33, 249–251; reasons for involvement of teachers in, 53–54, 59–61, 102–105; reasons for nonparticipation by teachers, 59, 105; support for, 7, 10, 234

global systems, 3-5, 6, 228
goal orientation: of school principals,
    163-169, 170, 175, 182, 189
Goodlad, John I.: A Study of Schooling,
    230
Goulet, Dennis, 18, 29
Grant, C. and Zeichner, K., 200, 224
grounded theory: steps in search for,
    40-49
Gusfield, Joseph, 51, 84

Hanvey, Robert, 52, 57, 84, 86-87, 107
Harvey, D. F. and Brown, D. R., 81, 84
Havelock, Ron, 40, 49, 94, 107, 207,
    209, 212, 225, 235, 251
Hersey, P. and Blanchard, K., 161-162,
    190
Hess, R. and Torney, J., 31, 49
Hursh, Heidi, 64, 84

infusion strategies, 14, 52, 59, 95-97
instructional materials, 70-71, 215
international festivals: as a starting-
    place, 101-102
international sports day, 23, 72
intervention: as evolutionary process,
    205-219
involvement of teachers: xx, 53-54,
    59-61, 193-195, 208-213; by gen-
    der, 60; cycles of high, low partici-
    pation, 211, 246; negotiation for
    time, 213-216

Johnson, D. and Johnson, F., 169, 190

Kniep, Willard, 52, 84
knowledge transfer. See also linkage;
    strategies for, 70-77
Kobus, Doni, 49

Lamy, Steven L., 61-64, 66, 84
La Puente Elementary School, 98, 100

leadership: and principal goal focus,
    168, 189; and vision, 176, 188-190;
    by key teachers, 243; key theories
    about, 157-162; measuring
    (LBDQ), 159; of school principals,
    157-162, 234
legitimization, 52, 67-70
Lessor, Roberta, 35, 41-42, 49, 194, 204
Lewin, K., Lippitt, R. and White, R.,
    159, 191
library, 75-76, 194-195
Likert, Rensis, 160, 191
linkage: to sources of new knowledge,
    12-13, 70-77
Lipham, James, 157, 191
Little, J. W., 225
Lofland, J., 42, 49
loosely-coupled systems, 12, 81

MacGregor, Douglas, 159, 191, 199, 225
Malinowski, B., 38, 50
Mann, F. C., 13, 29
Mayo, C., 158, 191
McDonald, J. P., 18, 29, 225
meaning: and behavioral change,
    36-37, 85-106; and success of
    efforts to globalize, 247-248;
    evolves through activity, 93-102,
    106, 175, 206-208, 235; fitting
    together of biographies, 209-210;
    of global education, 36-37, 85-93,
    235; related to turning-points,
    207-208
media coverage, 26, 69
Mesa Junior High, 40, 55-56, 78,
    95-96, 99, 118, 210
Miles, M. B. and Huberman, A. M.,
    38-39, 41, 43, 44, 45, 50
Miles, M. B., Saxl, E. R., and Lieber-
    man, A., 199, 225
mini-grants, 20-21, 76, 100, 180, 248

National Commission on Excellence in
    Education: A Nation At Risk, 178,
    191

National Governors' Association
Report: on the necessity for global
education, 7, 29, 30
neoscientific management, 158, 169,
179
networking, 25-26, 70
newsletter, 20, 71-72
North High School, 39-40, 72-74, 97,
101, 119, 176-187, 210
Novotney, J. and Tye, K., 158, 191

Orange County in the World, 23,
73-74, 98, 100-101
Otero, George, 94
ownership: by a clique, 78, 242; need
for widespread, 78, 231

Pacifica Middle School, 65, 66, 97, 210
Pareto, Vilfredo, 13, 30
participating schools: characteristics of,
17
Patterson, C. J., 221, 225
perspective-taking, 6, 173
Phillipsen, Joy, 215, 225
principals: and district ethos, 169-170,
189-190, 239; as administrator-
managers, 157, 234; goal orientation of, 163-169, 175; importance
of, 157-190, 122, 233-234;
turnover of, 25, 245; working with,
xx, 24-25

qualitative methodology: choice of,
37-38; relationship to other
methodologies, 38-39
quantitative data: end of project interview of teachers, 47-48; end of project questionnaire for teachers,
46-47, 52-53

readiness to participate: engagement/
resistance typology, 103; of individual teachers, 102-105; related to

meaning, 102-106, 239; turning
points, 207-210
Reich, Robert B., 3, 30
research component: about global education, 31-33; and reflection, 251;
and role of interventionist, 195; as
never-ending, 227; basic research
question, 27; brief description of,
26-28; complete description of,
31-49; grounded theory and,
40-41; non-linear, 249; self-study of
research by researchers, 195-196,
197; skills needed by interventionists, 204-205; symbolic interaction
theory, 35-40; teacher involvement
with, 32-33; three dimensions of,
41-42; underlying philosophy of, 34
resilience hypothesis, 127-128, 241
resistance to change: and school culture, 242; institutional resistance,
128-129, 162, 230-231; not necessarily bad, 81, 239-241
restructuring, 162, 231-232, 236-239
Rist, Ray, 41, 50

Sarason, Seymour B., 8, 30, 80, 84,
168, 230, 251
Schatzman, L. and Strauss, A., 38, 43, 50
Schlafly, Phyllis, 64, 84
Schein, E., 168, 191
school-based management, 79, 121,
162, 231-232, 236
school culture, xx, 80, 206, 210, 251
bureaucratic, 162, 236; principal
goal focus and, 168; resistance to
change and, 242-243
Sergiovanni, Thomas, 165, 191
Sherif, M. and Sherif, W. C., 61, 84
Shiman, D. and Conrad, D., 94, 107,
235, 251
single school as unit of change, xx,
10-11, 13, 162, 236-239, 251
Sizer, Ted, 232, 252
social movements: components of,
51-83; conditions which produce,
51-54, 67; definition of, 51; global

education as, 51–83, 251; in America, 51; membership in, 54–61, 66; sociopolitical context of, 61–67, 83; structural properties of, 67–79

South High School, 65, 66, 74, 99, 117, 137–145

special projects: initiated by CHI, 72–74, 248; initiated by teachers, 97–99, 247–248

standardized testing: as a barrier to participation, 114

Stogdill, R. and Coons, A., 159, 191

Study Commission on Global Education: national report, 7, 30

superordinate system: and competing demands, 113–122; appropriate role of, 11–12, 13, 231–232, 251; effect on principal leadership, 234

symbolic interaction theory: assumptions, 35–36; background of, 35; compatible with CHI philosophy, 38–40; grounded theory and, 40–41; methodology, 37–49

Tancredo, Thomas, 63

Tannenbaum, Robert and Schmidt, Warren, 160, 191

Taylor, F., 158, 191

teachers' defense mechanisms, 125–127; negotiation for time, 215–216; resilience of a school, 127–128; response to competing demands, 125, 240–241

teacher isolation, 11, 77–78, 128–129

telecommunications projects, 22, 72–73, 148

theme workshops and teacher interests, 19–20, 72

time, use of, 110–113; and lack of follow-through, 243–244; negotiating for time, 213–216

timing: of change efforts, 10, 13, 208–213, 244, 246; missed opportunities, 209; natural rhythm of the school year, 211, 246; "year 3 crisis," 211–212, 246

Torney-Purta, J., 31, 50

treatment of teachers: active respect, 18, 54; earning trust, 21–22, 57–58; empowerment, 79; inclusion of all, 18, 54, 78, 216, 243–245; no arm-twisting, 16; non-directive approach, 15, 18, 24, 54, 244–245; no-strings policy, 16; some need more structure, 244

Tucker, Jan, 12, 30

turning points: fitting together of biographies, 209–210, 243; related to adoption of an innovation by individuals, 207–208, 243

turnover: of principals, 25, 245; of teachers, 245–246

Tye, Barbara Benham, 8, 30, 31, 49, 50, 230, 252

Tye, Kenneth A., 6, 13, 30, 31, 32, 49, 50, 77, 84, 121, 129, 184, 191

unique personality of each school, 8–9, 79–80, 131–154, 206; resilience of, 127–128

University Elementary School, 98

voluntary membership in project, 16–17, 207, 214, 216

Weick, K. E., 11, 30, 81, 84

Western International Studies Consortium: member organizations, 25